THE ORIGINS AND DEVELOPMENT
OF LABOR ECONOMICS

THE ORIGINS AND DEVELOPMENT OF LABOR ECONOMICS

A Chapter in the History of Social Thought

Paul J. McNulty

The MIT Press
Cambridge, Massachusetts, and London, England

This book was set in VIP Baskerville by Achorn Graphic Services, Inc. and printed and bound by The Alpine Press Inc. in the United States of America.

Library of Congress Cataloging in Publication Data

McNulty, Paul J
   The origins and development of labor economics.

   Bibliography: p.
   Includes index.
   1. Labor economics—History. 2. Economics—History.
I. Title.
HD4901.M22   331'.09   80-15320
ISBN 0-262-13162-5

For Michael, Gregory, and Clare

CONTENTS

ACKNOWLEDGMENTS

In preparing this book, I have benefited from the counsel and encouragement of a number of colleagues. Some read parts of the manuscript and offered suggestions for its improvement; others helped by calling my attention to relevant materials; still others, by discussing the issues with which I was dealing, gave me the benefit of their knowledge and insight. For their assistance and support in these and other ways, I wish to thank Neil W. Chamberlain, Eli Ginzberg, Dale L. Hiestand, Raymond D. Horton, James W. Kuhn, David Lewin, Giulio Pontecorvo, B. J. Widick, and Maurice Wilkinson.

I owe a special debt of thanks to Ivar Berg of the University of Pennsylvania for his careful and thoughtful review of the entire manuscript and for the many suggestions which led to its improvement. The sustained interest he showed in the project from its inception was a major source of encouragement and is deeply appreciated.

Kay Preston has been of great help in typing large portions of the manuscript and in other ways as well. It is a pleasure to acknowledge her assistance.

I also want to express my appreciation to Dean Boris Yavitz of the Columbia University Graduate School of Business for the financial support provided through the School's Faculty Research Fund.

THE ORIGINS AND DEVELOPMENT
OF LABOR ECONOMICS

INTRODUCTION

John R. Commons once remarked that it was surprising how many and how varied were the theoretical economic systems erected on the single concept of labor: "From John Locke to Adam Smith, to Ricardo, Proudhon and Karl Marx, it is possible to build a whole system of political economy on the one foundation of labor. . . . The word Labor has as many meanings as you wish to read into it."[1] This book is a study of how labor has figured in the history of economic thought, not from the standpoint of the various meanings that have attached to the word but rather from that of how the study of labor within economics has shifted over time.

Like society, the subject of their analyses, the social sciences are always in the process of becoming; both are continually evolving and developing. For example, the approach economists take to a problem such as the impact of the labor union, the questions they raise in connection with it, and the ways in which their interest in the subject is distinguished from that of other professionals are all initially conditioned by the received body of economic analysis available to them or, to use Robinson's phrase, by the "box of tools" assembled by their predecessors in the analyses of similar problems.[2] But in the process of analysis, some of these tools may be found to be inadequate and may have to be discarded, and others may be newly forged. Thus the persistence of large-scale labor organizations in nineteenth-century England ultimately forced economists to go beyond the confining limits of pure or perfect competition and mathematically determinate economic models to the analysis of bilateral monopoly and indeterminate bargaining situations and to abandon as well the wages fund doctrine on which they had so long relied to explain the general level of wages. The interest of economists in the problem of labor unions was initially conditioned, however, by the traditional focus of their discipline: value and distribution theory as part of the larger problem of the relationship of resource allocation to economic welfare and individual freedom. Thus the emphasis of the classical and neoclassical economists on the labor union as a monopoly and their failure to analyze it as an operating institution from a standpoint similar to that of later, specialized, labor studies must be seen as due largely to their overriding concern with price theory and allocative efficiency. On the other hand, the fact that economists whose principal interests have been in the progress and problems of labor have often been (or have tried to be) reformers of economic analysis no less than of economic society is no coincidence; it is, rather, of a piece with the ongoing interaction between the identification of economic problems and the formulation of analytical methods of economic science.

"Much more than in, say, physics," Schumpeter once wrote, "it is true in economics that modern problems, methods, and results cannot

2   INTRODUCTION

be fully understood without some knowledge of how economists have come to reason as they do."[3] The study of labor is a particularly significant vantage point from which to view the changing content and methods of economics, for the problems of men and women at work constitute the core problems of an industrial economy. Surely no other influence has broader implications for people's lives in modern society than their employment. It determines generally where and how they live and the kind of education their children receive, and it intimately affects most of their relations with the community and the larger society. Our most pressing economic problems—poverty and unemployment, inflation and the balance of international payments, the impact of technological change, the quality and direction of our educational programs, the problems of energy, environmental pollution, and resource conservation—are or are directly related to the problems of men and women at work. The worker interest is also becoming a more general social interest. One of the most significant historical aspects of the economic development of the United States has been the persistent decline of independent proprietors as recipients of national income and a concomitant rise in the number and the importance of wage earners. The percentage of hired employees among total American income earners has risen from less than 15 percent a century and a half ago to more than 90 percent today. Truly the problems of labor are those of modern society.

For the discipline of economics, too, labor occupies a position of critical importance. Ever since economics emerged as a distinct field of inquiry, apart from the broader realm of moral and social philosophy, no other single factor has occupied so central an analytical role. "Labour," Adam Smith asserted, "was the first price, the original purchase money that was paid for all things. It was not by gold or by silver but by labour that all the wealth of the world was originally purchased."[4] The primacy of labor, thus established, dominated classical economics for the next century. It is not Karl Marx but John Stuart Mill who wrote that "labour alone is the primary means of production. . . . Tools and materials, like other things, have originally cost nothing but labour."[5] The mercantilist writers of the sixteenth and seventeenth centuries had also stressed the primacy of labor as a factor of production, believing that "in numbers of people at work lay the chief source of economic power," while even earlier, in the medieval period, the scholastic doctors justified entrepreneurial profits in terms of the labor involved in transport, storage, and the other activities of businessmen.[6] In our own time, emphasis has shifted from the accumulation of physical capital or improvements in its physical form due to technological change to an increased awareness of the importance of human capital as a source of national economic growth and individual economic welfare. It is hardly an exaggeration to say that "the development of political economy has gone hand in hand with a recognition of the importance of labor."[7]

Although labor has long figured importantly in economic analysis, the way the subject has been approached by economists reflects significant differences over time, which are often slighted in statements concerning the origins of labor economics and industrial relations. The result is a bevy of what seem at first to be contradictory statements. J. Douglas Brown, for example, after noting that "the study of the problems of men at work is as old as the study of any aspect of political economy," and that since Adam Smith opened the *Wealth of Nations* by entitling book 1 "Of the Causes of Improvement in the Productive Powers of Labour and of the Order According to Which Its Produce Is Naturally Distributed Among the Different Ranks of the People," concluded that the members of "the Industrial Relations Research Association can therefore claim Adam Smith as the first discoverer of the importance of our special field."[8] Edwin Witte adopted a similar point of view on the origins of the academic study of labor:

Labor figured in every part of the political economy of free enterprise which Adam Smith developed in his *Wealth of Nations*. Many of his observations on labor problems are still very pertinent. . . . Every subsequent writer of general treatises on economics has assigned labor a prominent role in his discussion and in every part of the subject. Labor received attention in the universities from the day political economy was first recognized as a subject of instruction, and even earlier when it was still a part of philosophy.[9]

Philip Taft, on the other hand, placed the date of emergence of labor economics a century later: "The study of labor, or labor economics . . . may be said to have begun with [Richard T.] Ely's book [*The Labor Movement in America*] in 1886."[10] Joseph Dorfman has moved the date up even further, to the years following World War I: "In the field of labor, the period from 1918 to 1929 presented a paradox: While organized labor was declining in both strength and numbers, a new specialty, labor economics, achieved acceptance and began to produce a distinct body of theoretical and empirical literature."[11] The reconciliation of these views lies in the fact that the study of labor, or labor economics, meant something different in 1776 in England from what it meant in 1886 in the United States, and it meant something different still in the 1920s and in the 1970s. One fundamental difference between these periods is the extent to which the study of labor problems and institutions has been integrated with the mainstream of economic theory.

Labor problems of a modern character emerged as a matter of serious social concern during the sixteenth, seventeenth, and eighteenth centuries, when the combined forces of agricultural reorganization, the decline of certain medieval institutions, and the rising elements of incipient industrialism led to the emergence and compelling presence of a poor and landless laboring class. The primacy of labor as a factor of production in the mercantilists' intellectual schema, together with the pervasive problem of pauperism throughout England and much of Europe, produced a body of policy-oriented economic literature that because of its dual emphasis on the problems of poverty and unemployment can reasonably be considered the beginning of modern labor economics. The work of Adam Smith thus reflected a long-standing concern, especially of English social theorists, with labor problems, and his analysis of these problems is generally very much at one with his economic theory in *The Wealth of Nations*. In contrast, the beginnings of a separation between the mainstream of economic theory and the practical problems of labor are discernible early in the nineteenth century, when, due in no small part to the influence of David Ricardo, the determination of long-run price under postulated conditions of pure competition became the overriding concern of economic inquiry. Although many nineteenth-century economists devoted their attention to labor problems—Nassau Senior is an outstanding example—their work in this field was seldom integrated with their economic theory. During the nineteenth century, it was the historians, especially the Hammonds and the Webbs, who did much of the best work in the analysis of labor institutions and labor conditions.

Among the many differences reflected in the economist's approach to the study of labor over the years, one of the most fundamental and significant is the extent to which analysis is built on purely economic or market forces, compared with the extent to which analysis extends to the operation of nonmarket institutions. This difference manifests itself in the kinds of topics chosen for analysis and in the analytical approach used. Both the medieval and the mercantilist economic writers, for example, were concerned with questions of income distribution, but neither stressed the influence of competitive market forces. Although their approaches to labor problems were different in some fundamental respects, they were similar in that they produced no theory of wage determination but a voluminous literature on wage administration; they were concerned not with what wages would be under postulated conditions but with what wages should be in order to realize certain socially desirable goals. To take another example, the difference between the Smithian and the Ricardian analyses of labor problems is largely the difference between a not-too-rigorous adherence to a framework of competitive markets and an appreciation of sociological and political complexities, on the one hand, and, on the other hand, an analysis specifically limited to cases where prices and wages are determined by competition alone. The contrast between the approach to the study of labor in Marshall's *Principles* and that of the Webbs's *Industrial Democracy,* both products of the same age and social setting, is largely the difference between market reasoning and analysis based on nonmarket customs and influences. Clearly the belief that the competitive market was no longer the effective economic force that it had been in an earlier era was one of the principal influences in the emergence of an essentially institutionalist labor economics during the late nineteenth and early twentieth centuries in the United States.

The history of labor economics reflects a shifting pattern of relations between labor students and economic theorists that is only partially the result of the not-infrequent expressions of dissatisfaction with traditional market analysis by labor economists. Also of significance is the rather more normative criticism of the market process by many early labor economists whose attitudes and outlooks were often directed to finding institutionalized means of improving labor's position. Nonmarket controls such as labor unions, unemployment insurance compensation, minimum wage laws, and the like were thus not simply focuses of analysis but also items of advocacy on the agenda of many labor economists. Rejecting the market and competition as, at best, incapable of doing as much for the workers as these other institutions, and as, at worst, actually leading to a deterioration of their position, labor economists frequently became defenders of institutions generally considered by economic theorists to be monopolistic and harmful. An ideological cleavage between theorists and labor students was a natural consequence of these divergent viewpoints.

The present period is a particularly appropriate time for an analysis of the development of labor economics, for the field has undergone a major transformation during the past few decades. A generation ago, Lloyd Reynolds noted two tendencies among labor economists. One was for the economist working in the field of labor to try "to grasp the phenomena of his field *in toto* by turning himself into a multiple-social-scientist," by acquiring the rudiments of the several relevant disciplines. The other approach was for this economist "to remain within the confines of economic analysis" by confining his studies to the limitations of his method.[12] When Reynolds wrote, the first of these was the more general tendency. For several decades, institutional labor economists had been rejecting economic theory as traditionally constituted and had been trying to turn themselves into the multiple-social-scientists referred to by Reynolds. Since the 1950s, the tendency has been generally in the other direction. Modern labor

economists are more likely than their predecessors to eschew any
significant reliance on the methods or the findings of psychology,
sociology, or political science, or at least to avoid any serious effort to
integrate these diciplines with economics in the manner of the institutionalists of a generation or two ago. Instead they try to integrate
economic theory and market analysis more fully with their specialized
field of interest.

The growing integration of labor economics with economic theory,
however, does not fully or uniformly characterize the field. In the
1960s and 1970s, the interdisciplinary approach has received continuing emphasis on the part of those who hold that if economic
analysis is to make a significant contribution to the field of labor, "it
must extend its frontiers . . . [since] reliance on market tests and the
traditional market analysis will fail to supply satisfactory answers" to
many questions of pressing social importance.[13] Discussions of methodology have often been prominent in the annual conferences of the
Industrial Relations Research Association.[14] There have been efforts
"to bring a more international perspective to American labor economics."[15] Some labor economists believe that their field is failing to
attract "a proportionate share of the more promising and talented
graduate students who pursue advanced degrees in the social sciences."[16] Indeed the Industrial Relations Research Association was
told in the 1960s that "labor economics was an exciting field in the
immediate pre-and-post-war period . . . [but that] since then labor
economics has lost its appeal [and] . . . has been generally stagnant."[17]
That this was not an altogether isolated view is suggested by the title
of a symposium conducted at about the same time by a major professional journal, in which a number of leading labor economists were
asked to address themselves to the question, "Are Labor Courses Obsolete?"[18] The extent to which the basic directions and approaches of
the field have thus been brought into question within the past generation suggests the timeliness of an inquiry into the evolution and development of labor study and of its changing position within the
broader field of economics.

The literature of labor economics is voluminous, and any historical
treatment must be selective. Detailed consideration of particular
topics commonly included in labor economics, such as the theory of
wages, labor union theory and history, collective bargaining, specific
labor market analysis, the trend of real earnings, and other particular
subjects is accordingly specifically disclaimed here. Most of these
topics have been the subjects of special studies by others, and the attempt to deal at all adequately with them in connection with the present effort would produce a volume of unmanageable proportions. On
the other hand, since "economics is what economists do," these and

other such items cannot escape attention.[19] But they will figure here only to the extent that they serve the central purpose of this inquiry: to discern the changing contours and quality of the economist's study of labor and to identify and interpret the forces that seem relevant in explaining them.

THE HERITAGE AND THE BACKGROUND

1

Economists' concern with labor is shaped by their special focus of interest. Their treatment of the subject is conditioned by their particular skills, both the theoretical tools of economic analysis and their detailed knowledge of the institutions that are a part of or border on their special area of interest.[1] Economists have not always been in agreement, however, on the relative importance of the possession and mastery of each of these types of skills. One need only note the difference in approach between, say, John R. Hicks and John R. Commons in the study of unions and wages during the 1920s and 1930s in order to appreciate the significance of the analyst's conception of the best way to examine a subject. Although controversies over methodology are perhaps less common in economics today than at several times in its past, it is nonetheless true that the relative use an economist makes of, say, the legal, political, or historical aspects of the question to which he is directing his attention is a function of his view of the nature of the discipline.

A historical illustration is useful to clarify this point. In his analysis of mercantilism, Furniss has highlighted the significance of the point of view of the typical economic writer of the day: uncritical acceptance of the necessity for state action governing wages. And "so long as wages were the object of consistent regulation and before there was any thought that competition could operate as an impartially just distributive force, the principles appealed to in the discussion of wages would be principles of social justice and national expedience, not those of economic theory."[2] By the nineteenth century, the common view among English social theorists was that of economic activity "as dependent upon impersonal and almost automatic forces," and economic analysis was often presented as a positive science modeled on the analytical precision of the physical sciences.[3] Nassau Senior, whose *Political Economy* (1836) conceived of the function of the economist as purely positive and theoretical, could thus reasonably avoid discussing questions of wage policy and distributive justice.[4] This does not mean that Senior was unconcerned either with public policy or with the question of justice and morality in social dealings; it simply means that his conception of science was not inclusive of these matters.

These observations point to the necessity of examining some of the issues that have arisen concerning the nature of economics as a discipline and that of scientific method, for many of the issues associated with the economist's study of labor have hinged on just such considerations. Such an approach will be advantageous in permitting us to view in their historical context those issues in economic thought that are pertinent to this study and to examine the extent to which their influence has shaped further developments. It is, in fact, only with reference to particular historical settings that many devel-

opments in the maturation of the discipline are explicable. As Frank
Knight once observed, "The evolution of economics must be seen as
integral with that of economic life."[5]

THE MARKET AND ITS SIGNIFICANCE

The emergence of economics during the eighteenth and nineteenth
centuries as a distinct discipline, apart from the broader realm of
moral or social philosophy, of which it had long been a part, was a development in the history of ideas that was intimately related to the
growing importance of impersonal market forces over custom, tradition, or authority in economic decision making. Since that time, there
has probably been no analytical concept more fundamental to economic reasoning than that of the market—the institution through
which transactions are effected and, in a free enterprise economy, resources are allocated. "I should venture to assume," wrote even the institutionalist Robert F. Hoxie of economics, "that this science deals
with human activity and the social process from the standpoint of
market choice or market valuation."[6] In economic theory, buying and
selling are isolated as the critical elements in the social process, and
the economy is viewed not as a complex set of varied and changing institutions but simply as "a system of interrelated markets."[7] Business
firms in economic theory differ only with respect to the markets in
which they buy factors of production or sell goods and services. As
Allyn Young once so aptly put it, for purposes of economic analysis,
"The whole material equipment of human living is recast in molds
fashioned after the notions of catallactics."[8]

Its position of primacy in economic theory would alone make the
market centrally important to this inquiry, but its significance is
heightened by the fact that labor as an economic concept is defined by
the market. In modern economic thought, labor is one of two human
factors of production and is distinguished from the other, entrepreneurship, on the basis of its availability in the market. The laborer
contracts to undertake more or less rigorously specified assignments
in return for a wage payment. The entrepreneur—the one factor of
production who cannot be hired in the marketplace—combines labor
and the other factors in order to produce and sell a product or service
for which he receives a noncontractual payment, either as profit or as
loss.

That it is the labor market, and not the possession or lack of managerial or other abilities, that fundamentally distinguishes between
labor and entrepreneurship is illustrated by the impossibility of applying to entrepreneurship the theory of factor and income distribution. Although there are various explanations of profit, there is none

that is quite of a piece with those of other factor returns such as rent, wages, and interest, for there is no consistent explanation in economic theory of how the scarce resource for which profit is paid—entrepreneurship—is allocated by means of a pricing system. In terms of partial equilibrium analysis, "the marginal product of the entrepreneur to the firm has no meaning,"[9] since entrepreneurship as a factor of production is traditionally conceived of as one and indivisible,[10] while in general equilibrium under perfect competition, entrepreneurs "as such would have no functions and receive no income."[11] The theoretical explanation of profit in a price-directed economy thus usually runs in terms either of imperfect competition or of business behavior under disequilibrium conditions, and it is generally conceived of as the payment for the assumption by the businessman of certain noninsurable risks,[12] as a temporary and constantly threatened return to the innovator,[13] or as windfall or monopoly gains. The one activity of the businessman for which profit is not a functional return in economic theory is labor of the type that might be sold for a price in the market.

This distinction between labor and entrepreneurship on the basis of the employment contract is much more modern than economic discussion of either of these concepts, and it reflects essentially the social structure of the developing European economies of the eighteenth and nineteenth centuries. "The industrial community," wrote John Stuart Mill—following the example of Adam Smith, David Ricardo, and, more fundamentally, the French physiocrats—"may be considered as divided into landowners, capitalists, and productive labourers. Each of these classes, as such, obtains a share of the produce. . . . These three classes are considered in political economy as making up the whole community."[14] While it may be true that "if distribution is a phenomenon of competitive valuation, classes have nothing to do with it," they nonetheless had a very great deal to do with the way economists came to view the economic process as an interaction of land, labor, and capital.[15] The addition of the entrepreneur as a fourth factor of production toward the end of the nineteenth century was but part of a larger effort to clarify the conceptual differences between interest and profit and did not disturb the basis of the older tripartite division of factors as far as labor was concerned. It would henceforth simply be the entrepreneur, and not the capitalist, who hired labor and set it to work.

Among the criteria for distinguishing between labor and the business skills of either the capitalist or the entrepreneur, the most fundamental, as earlier noted, is its availability in the market. As a pervasive social institution in which the greater part of the people must find the principal source of their income, the labor market is a modern development. Although markets of various types seem to have characterized social relations since mankind's earliest days—a phenomenon that so impressed Adam Smith that he described as a "propensity in human nature" the desire "to truck, barter, and exchange one thing for another"[16]—the free exchange of labor services has not been a characteristic feature of human history. On the contrary, slavery or bondage appears to have been fairly common at an early date and is not very far removed from recent memory in many parts of the world. The economies of both ancient Greece and imperial Rome were based to no small extent on slave labor, and during the Middle Ages, the free contracting of labor services was of extremely limited significance throughout Europe. Indeed although the emergence of the modern Western world from the medieval involved the gradual transformation of a vast complex of social institutions, no single change was more fundamental than the rise of the labor market. Conversely while he would find much of the social pattern of medieval Europe difficult to comprehend, "strangest of all to the modern student, suddenly set down in the midst of a typical medieval society, would be the labor system."[17]

THE MEDIEVAL SETTING

Mobility is a central feature of modern life and an important prerequisite of a market system. The medieval system, in contrast, was one in which the principle of tenure was fundamental to social organization, with the result that throughout all of Western civilization, for several centuries, "the personal equation was largely merged in the territorial. One and all, master and man, lord and tenant, were 'tied to the soil.' "[18]

The emergence and development of the feudal and manorial organization through which those ties were institutionalized is best viewed as a response to the compelling need of the time: the restoration of the security that Roman legal, military, and economic organization had earlier provided. The system that gradually emerged—if one can use the word *system* to describe a social structure with so many variations—generally combined features of earlier Roman and Germanic life with modifications developed according to the needs of the times. An outstanding feature of that system was the extent to which social life was organized on the basis of personal, rather than purely economic or financial, relationships. The feudal lord's army, for example, consisted not of hired soldiers but of vassals who owed him personal service. These vassals, in turn, were lesser lords in that they held fiefs, lands granted to them by the lord in order to enable them to maintain the necessary fighting establishments. The land was organized so as to support the military establishment and was occupied by agricultural workers possessing varying degrees of freedom—with none fully free in the modern sense—and owing various dues, both in labor and in kind, to the lord. Like the vassals who held the fiefs on grant from the higher lord, the working peasants were paid by their tenancy of land. One's position in this system of tenure and interpersonal obligations was determined largely by birth.

In the towns, too, personal relationships predominated. The high degree of self-sufficiency that characterized manorial life, the handicraft technology of the age, and the difficulty and costliness of transportation, especially over land, meant both limited markets and limited production possibilities, with a resulting widespread prevalence of local monopoly. The essence of a competitive transaction, in the economic sense, is its impersonal character, which, in turn, is the result of the very large numbers of buyers and sellers who are transacting in the purchase and sale of goods and services, which are generally indistinguishable from those of their competitors. But in terms of demand and supply, the medieval economic setting lacked the necessary conditions for such impersonality. On the contrary, the highly personal character of economic activity facilitated the merger of the economic with other facets of life. The guild, for example, an institution that illustrates not only the monopolistic and personalized aspects of medieval industry and trade but also the difficulty of drawing sharp distinctions, for that period, between laborer and entrepreneur, was not merely an economic institution but also a social and religious grouping. The apprentice could expect from his master not only vocational training but education and discipline in other aspects of social living. The master did not merely hire an apprentice but rather assumed responsibility for his personal and vocational development, taking him into his home, in many cases, quite like a member of the family. Other masters could not hire the apprentice away. The association with the guild ensured the urban craftsman a tenure not unlike that of the agricultural worker on the land. It was a lifelong association, in most cases, extending from the day the young lad entered apprenticeship to the day his guild brethren attended his funeral mass and, sometimes, going beyond that to the guild's continuing support of his wife and children.

The personal character of economic relationships in medieval Europe and the intermingling of the economic with other aspects of life was reflected and reinforced in the social thought of the period. "Anyone," writes Alexander Gray, "who would essay to present in a few pages what purports to be a statement of the economic doctrines current in the Middle Ages must be conscious, if he has a conscience, that he is postulating a simplicity that does not exist."[19] Conditions in

Europe during the many centuries between the fall of Rome and the Renaissance, even during the Dark Ages, are now recognized to have been far less static and unchanged than was often supposed in the past, and economic doctrines also varied over time and among writers. Yet during much of this time, there was sufficient consistency in economic thinking to have constituted what can reasonably be called "the medieval point of view."[20] That point of view, importantly shaped by the Church as the dominant institution of the age, was one in which economic activity was generally regarded as but "one among other kinds of moral conduct," and in which economic analysis proceeded according to a set of principles that together constituted "a body of laws, not in the sense of scientific laws, but in that of moral precepts designed to ensure the good administration of economic activity."[21] This body of thought, of which the central underlying principle was the necessity for commutative justice, reached its apogee in the twelfth and thirteenth centuries, most notably with Saint Thomas Aquinas. It is in his writings that we best see the interaction of the two great molding forces of medieval social thought: the philosophy of Aristotle and the teachings of Christ and the apostles.

The combination of Greek and Christian thinking gave to labor a position of primacy in medieval economic doctrine that it had lacked with the Greeks. Although the principle of division of labor formed the basis of the social class structure for the ancient Greeks, it was a division based on supposed innate differences among people and was never developed as an economic principle of increasing returns.[22] On the contrary, the whole question of productive efficiency was of minimal significance to the ancient Greeks. Although the etymological roots of the word *economics* derive from classical Greece, the term as then used referred to household management. The economic interest of the Greeks was strongest, perhaps, in the areas of monetary theory and the theory of value. It was particularly weak in labor economics. Throughout much of the ancient world, labor was often the subject of despotic control, and where this is the case, special concern for or with labor is not likely to be found.[23] Although recent scholarship has modified somewhat the traditional view of the Greek contempt for work, it is still true that the Greek societal setting was one in which labor as such lacked any peculiar dignity and worth.[24] The citizen, not the laborer, was the key figure in Greek social thought, and citizenship and labor had little in common.

In this respect, medieval thought represents a sharp break from that of the Greeks, for the Church, "from the beginning . . . never ceased to proclaim the obligation to work as a divine law."[25] Labor was no longer despised; the insistence was rather on the nobility and dig-

nity of work.[26] Owing, no doubt, in large part to the example of Christ
the carpenter, and the workman background of the apostles, "a life of
idleness was considered something to be avoided instead of something
to be desired, as it had been in the ancient civilizations."[27] Labor in
medieval Europe was the rightful source from which to earn one's
sustenance. "If any would not work," Saint Paul had said, "neither
should he eat."[28]

Yet the debt to the Greeks was not insignificant. There was a
wholehearted acceptance of the Aristotelian dictum that man by nature is a political animal: "He who is without a community is either
above humanity, or below it; he is the tribeless, lawless, heartless one,
whom Homer denounces—the outcast who is a lover of war; he may
be compared to an unprotected piece in the game of droughts."[29]
The Hebraic heritage, too, was one in which the concept of community was important. It was thus natural that Christianity, with intellectual roots in both the Hebrew and the Greek traditions, should
have stressed from the beginning that man is a social being. The
Pauline doctrine of the Church as the Mystical Body, with Christ as
the Head, to whom all were joined as members infused by one Spirit,
enhanced the idea that one's individuality was ultimately realized in
communion with others. The strong consciousness of community in
the medieval mind was reflected in the allocation of a relatively large
proportion of the economic product to public purposes, such as the
erection of the great cathedrals. That these were a manifestation of a
strong religious spirit is not to be denied, but they were also a reflection of community spirit and of the collective life of the time. The
medieval cathedrals belonged "in a real sense to all the local inhabitants, in an age in which everyone was at least nominally a communi-
cant."[30] The relative anonymity of the individuals who designed and
decorated these buildings, in contrast to the individual fame accorded
the great Renaissance artists, is but another illustration of the primacy
of the concept of community in the earlier period.

The basis and nature of the community in medieval thought also
drew heavily on Aristotelian thinking. The community was conceived
of not simply as a collectivity of individuals or social groups possessing
essentially similar rights and obligations but rather as a hierarchically
organized body made up of groups whose rights, duties, and responsibilities differed according to their station in life. The Christian ideal
of the equality of all people before God was conceived of in terms of
their souls and their eternal destinies and not their transitory human
condition on earth. From this point of view, a condition like slavery
could be accepted (although some doctors of the Church condemned
it) as a manifestation of man's state of imperfection; what was more

important, however, was the possibility of salvation for the slave. The inclusivity of Christianity in this sense is indicative of the all-embracing nature of the community in medieval thought.

Although the doctors of the Church rejected the extreme difference between the free and the unfree, inequality in terms of ability, wealth, and freedom was accepted as inevitable and, indeed, as part of the divine plan.[31] "Riches," wrote Saint Antonino of Florence, "are not equally distributed. But this comes not by man's intention, for we often see that the most industrious are the least successful and the most idle abound in good things; nor is it due to the domination of some evil spirit acting without the Divine permission. But from the Lord God, either by direct ordinance or at least by his allowing it, comes this unequal distribution of wealth."[32] The variety apparent in nature was used by the medieval writers to argue against any common level of human existence, and the variety in human nature was presented as corresponding to the variety of the parts and organs composing the human body.[33] Society was seen as a functioning organism in which each individual and group, like the various parts and organs of the human body, had its own function to perform. "In political matters," according to Aquinas, "all belonging to one community are reckoned to be like one body, and the whole community like one person."[34] That some were meant to rule and others to be ruled was as natural as the rule of the human brain over that of the tongue, the hands, and the feet. But it was not so much a matter of rule as of system, of cooperation, of order according to a preordained divine plan.

It is commonly said that the principal economic doctrines of the Middle Ages were the prohibition of usury and the idea of the just price. Certainly discussion of these topics tended to dominate medieval economic literature. Yet as Alexander Gray has pointed out, "these two principles are neither independent nor are they fundamental. They are but two aspects of a deeper and more comprehensive conception," the necessity for justice in all social dealings.[35] It was a fundamental principle of Aristotelian thought that "justice is the bond of men in states, and the administration of justice, which is the determination of what is just, is the principle of order in political society."[36] This notion, coupled with the Christian ideal of neighborliness and brotherhood best expressed, perhaps, in the Golden Rule of the New Testament, formed the primary theme of medieval economic doctrine.[37] In the development of that theme, the concept of labor played a central role.

All of the characteristics of the medieval age—the primacy of the community and its organic nature, the highly personal character of economic relationships, the prevalence of local monopoly, the view of economic activity as but one aspect of moral behavior, and the general approval with which work and labor were viewed—contributed to the medieval conception of justice as the maintenance of the individual's rightful and proper position in society. The chief threat to this justice was not business or economic activity but economic advancement sought for its own sake or at the expense of someone else.

The well-known medieval concern over the justness and propriety of interest and profits to some extent reflected Aristotelian thought both in terms of the supposed sterility of money—a commodity that ought not to multiply—and of the less than fully respectable status of business and trade, but it was also a reflection of the concern of the doctors of the Church with an emerging pattern of market exchange, the advantages and disadvantages of which were not immediately obvious. That concern did not extend to a condemnation of business per se as an illegitimate field of human endeavor but was manifested in a condemnation of unjustified business gain. What justified business profits was the labor of the businessman, for clearly the laborer, if not the merchant, was "worthy of his hire." Business in the medieval period was, of course, primarily in the form of trade, and "trade profits, so far as they were justified, were regarded as quasi-wages *(quasi-stipendium)*—as reward for the labour of transport. The profits of the exchanger, so far as they were justified, were the reward for the labour of carrying the money from place to place . . . the same idea was applied to the analysis of every economic phenomenon."[38] Aquinas's younger contemporary, John Duns Scotus, drew the distinction between legitimate and illegitimate business on precisely this basis:

Beyond the rules . . . as to what is just and what is not, I add two. The first is that such an exchange be useful to the community, and the second, that such a person shall receive in the exchange recompense according to his diligence, prudence, trouble, and risk. . . . This second rule follows because every man who serves the community in an honest function ought to live by his work. But such a one as transports or stores goods is of honest and useful service to the community, and should, therefore, live by his work. And, moreover, one can sell his effort and care for a just price. But great industry is required of one who transports goods from one country to another inasmuch as he must investigate the resources and needs of the country. Therefore, may he take a price corresponding to his labor beyond the necessary support for himself and those of his establishment employed according to his requirements, and thirdly, something beyond this corresponding to his risk.[39]

Scotus was emphatic on the necessity for some labor or effort on the part of the businessman—of transport, storage, or other useful activity—if business was to be justified:

It is evident from these two conditions requisite in just business how some are called business men in a vituperative sense, those to wit who neither transport, nor store, nor by their own industry better a salable article, nor guarantee the worth of some object for sale to one who lacks the necessary knowledge of it. These people who buy only to sell immediately, under none of the above conditions, ought to be crushed by the community and exiled. Such persons are called by the French *regratiers* because they prevent the unhampered exchange of those who wish to buy or make an economic exchange, and as a result, they render a salable and usable article dearer to the buyer than it should be, and dearer to the seller. Thus the contract is defective on both sides.[40]

That the labor theory of value, which played so important a role in nineteenth-century economics, had roots extending back to medieval thought is apparent. But it would be incorrect to suggest that the medieval writers held strictly to a cost of production theory of value in, say, the Ricardian or Marxian sense. In the first place, the common estimate of what constituted a just price is not without some resemblance to the modern concept of demand. More importantly, the medieval thinkers did not purport to explain value in general on the basis of the expenditure of human labor.[41] Indeed in view of their conception of economics as a branch of morals and ethics, we can hardly ascribe to the efforts of the medieval writers the character of a search for an objective, scientific theory of value, based on a principle of economic rationality. They simply employed the concept of labor—for them, the application of human effort, whether hired or self-employed—as the principal element in legitimate business activity and, ultimately, as the justification for what we would today call interest and profit. Like Adam Smith and his immediate successors, the medieval theorists did not distinguish between these two functional returns, but in their efforts to determine whether these payments were morally defensible, they were forced to ask the question that is central to any theoretical formulation of income distribution: what is it, exactly, that these payments are made for? With respect to profit and interest, they had to consider the positive question of what is, as well as the normative question of what should be. Their delineation of the functional activities of the businessman is, to that extent, at one with the spirit of modern economic analysis, and they produced positive theoretical results in this area. As Schumpeter has pointed out, the "risk-effort theory of business profit is undoubtedly due to them, [and] . . . no less certain is it that they launched the theory of interest."[42]

In contrast to their analytical contributions in the realm of interest and profit and despite the position of centrality of the concept of labor in their system of thought, the medieval theorists produced no theory of wages. Since they did not raise the theoretical question of what it is that wages are paid for, their discussion in this area was limited to moral considerations of justice as a guide to policy. They were concerned not with what wages were, as functional payments, but only with what wages should be in order to ensure justice in social dealings. Perhaps Schumpeter has explained the lack of analytical treatment of wages in the only way possible: "Presumably they felt that nobody needs to be told what it is that wages are paid for."[43] Reduction to wages was a usual practice in explaining profit or interest, which, evidently, did need to be justified in some sense. Clearly the moral problems of avarice and greed, and gain for its own sake, with which they were primarily concerned, were perceived to be greater for those receiving business profits, or interest on loans, than for those getting wages. Finally the failure of the medieval theorists to consider the wage question analytically reflects the absence, in their time, of a significant wage-earning group and the undeveloped character of the contemporary labor market.

Although avarice and prodigality were moral evils and gain for its own sake a serious sin, the medieval writers did not look with disfavor on temporal riches or regard poverty as a private or social virtue. "The occasions of sin are to be avoided," wrote Aquinas, "but poverty is an occasion of evil, because theft, perjury, and flattery are frequently brought about by it. Therefore poverty should not be voluntarily undertaken but rather avoided."[44] Although the medieval Church admitted the merits of self-imposed poverty when specifically undertaken as a source of spiritual enrichment, such as by those entering the mendicant religious orders, the amelioration of general poverty through charity was central to its social teachings. It was not simply that poverty was a source of evil and ought to be alleviated; rather the act of giving was itself a moral good. The primacy of the idea of charity in Christian theology, together with the doctrine of the Mystical Body, combined to make the relief of the suffering poor perhaps the greatest of Christian values; indeed, according to Saint Matthew charity is the essential basis for salvation.[45]

In his *Wealth of Nations,* Adam Smith pointed out that, in terms of a standard of living defined by the possession of material goods, the European peasant of the eighteenth century was much better off than "many an African king, the absolute master of the lives and liberties of ten thousand naked savages."[46] Yet the African might well have felt richer than the European peasant, for poverty is best viewed as a relative condition, perceived in terms of one's comparative position within his own social setting. By today's standards, most of medieval society was badly impoverished. Yet poverty then was not the pressing social problem that it later became with the advent of enclosures, for the system of tenure, both on the land and in the trade and craft guilds, assured most people a comparatively decent subsistence. If we speak of medieval poverty in terms of a high death rate, low life expectancy, and a subsistence level of living—all indexes by which poverty is today measured—we are speaking of general technological limits and social conditions, and not of those special circumstances that defined poverty for the people of the time. Given the social organization and technological limits of the age, medieval poverty was largely a matter of individual misfortune. There were not large numbers of able-bodied poor whose poverty was the result of involuntary unemployment caused by economic forces over which they had no control and of which they had no understanding—rather, for most it resulted from a crippling accident, or a long illness, or old age. Or the father may have died, "leaving a widow with a family of small children. The average expectation of life in thirteenth-century England was only a little more than thirty years, and the canonists were always particularly concerned about the protection of widows and orphans."[47]

The personal character of medieval poverty invalidates much of the criticism made by later historians of medieval social policy. The historian of early English poor relief, E. M. Leonard, wrote, for example, concerning the monasteries as relief centers, that since "monks were not primarily intended to be relieving officers, and were not placed where they would be most useful to that purpose; and since there might be many in one neighborhood and few in another, the charity distributed by the monks therefore was to a great extent unorganized and indiscriminate and did nearly as much to increase beggars as to relieve them."[48] Sir William Ashley also criticized "the haphazard charity which current religious notions encouraged" and spoke of "the mischief of indiscriminate charity." "The reckless distribution of doles," he maintained, "cannot have failed to exercise a pauperizing influence." He held that the monasteries were "centres of pauperization" and that "the crying need was to put an end to the old pauperizing system of indiscriminate charity."[49] But the strictures of Ashley, Leonard, and other nineteenth-century English writers concerning medieval poor relief must be considered in the light of the assumptions current during their own times—assumptions, as Tierney points out, that underlay the English Poor Law Act of 1834 and that were widely accepted in English society throughout most of the nineteenth century: "It was assumed that if a man was destitute he was probably an idle lout who deserved punishment. It was further assumed, apparently, that all working people were idle louts at heart who would not work if public or private relief for the destitute could be had without the most bitter humiliations and hardships. To men influenced by such principles there seemed a kind of outrageous perversity in the naive medieval view that the kindest way of dealing with a hungry man was to feed him. This they called 'pauperization.' "[50] The nineteenth-century attitude toward the poor, which owed a great intellectual debt to the theories of T. R. Malthus, was also conditioned by the implicit belief in Say's law, the doctrine that general unemployment was impossible under conditions of flexible prices. It followed that work was available to all who wanted it and that therefore poverty was a self-imposed state associated with sloth. The nineteenth-century attitude was also affected by the existence of a restless urban proletariat, possessing the capacity to produce great social unrest.

Medieval poverty, however, was of a wholly different character. The medieval mind was no more tolerant of voluntary idleness than was the nineteenth-century one, and there were undoubtedly men in that age, as in any other, who would abuse charity. But during the high Middle Ages, the provision of charity was not likely to have had the pauperizing effect it might later have had because of the security provided most members of society by the manor, the guild, and the other institutions. Whether a particular system of administering poor relief will have a corrupting social effect ultimately depends, as Tierney has rightly stressed, "at least as much on the structure and mores of the society as on the precise organization of the charity. Above all it depends on the social and economic stability of the lowest-paid laboring classes who are most likely to fall into destitution."[51] As long as the medieval system of tenure obtained, the lowest-paid laboring classes were assured such security and stability. It was the dissolution of that system, a process effected earliest and most completely in England, which was the crux of the problem of the instability of the laboring classes during the early modern period which, in turn, formed the backdrop against which English social policy would be formulated for centuries to come.

THE LABORER IN THE EARLY MODERN ERA

The position of the laborer in the social thought of the early modern period—between the Protestant Reformation and the industrial revolution—was conditioned by two outstanding characteristics of that age: the growth of pauperism and the rise of nationalism. The twin problems of dealing with poverty of a type and on a scale far different from anything that had been experienced in medieval Europe, and of enhancing the power and prestige of the national state resulted in the production of a substantial body of policy-oriented literature in which labor figured prominently.

This era is often called the age of mercantilism. That term, however, is usually rather narrowly associated with policies aimed at strengthening the international balance-of-payments positions of the emerging national economies and fails to suggest the full extent and nature of the social changes taking place. In this age, a number of new worlds were being created: the overseas expansion; the price revolution associated with the inflow of specie from the New World to the Old and resulting in a pattern of inflation that helped to disrupt many of the old established relationships between social and economic groups; and the agricultural revolution, which involved both technological innovations and other technical and scientific improvements. The last made possible a greatly expanded output, and, of perhaps even greater significance as far as the laborer was concerned, changed the property relationships that went with the enclosure of formerly open fields. Both new and formerly underdeveloped industries were growing, and new methods were emerging in some of the older industries as well.

In England, the civil wars of the seventeenth century were having a profound effect in transferring political power to those possessing economic power: the improvement-minded landlords, who were bent on putting agriculture on an individual and market-oriented basis, and the merchant manufacturers, who had replaced the medieval marketing of raw wool with the rapidly developing cloth trades as the essential basis for national prosperity. Not only in terms of the political revolutions but, in fact, in most of these developments, England led the way, and, in the process, changed its international position from that of an outpost to that of the world's leading industrial power. The modern laborer, and the problems posed by his position in industrial society, emerged first in England.

A money economy did not spring upon England suddenly. Throughout the thirteenth century, some serfs had sought, sometimes successfully, to commute their labor services for monetary payments, and some lords had found it expedient to lease their lands to an enterprising farmer and thereby become dependent upon a rental income rather than on the income from the direct operation of the estate.[52] In the fourteenth century, this process was considerably accelerated by the effects of the Black Death, which reduced population by between 25 and 33 percent. The plague "remained endemic for two generations, producing an abnormally high death rate and a dwindling population. By 1400 the population of England was little more than half the preplague figure; it continued to decline until the second decade of the fifteenth century, and then only very slowly began to recover."[53]

The immediate effect of this demographic revolution was a great shortage of labor. Those workers who were already free and receiving wage payments demanded higher wages. Those still in the position of serfs and obligated to perform customary service for their lords increasingly clamored to be free in order to take advantage of the buoyant conditions in the labor market. Largely in response to the complaints of the landholding class concerning the difficulty of securing laborers, the Ordinance of Labourers was proclaimed in 1349, and, two years later, this was followed by the Statute of Labourers, important landmarks in the evolution of British labor policy. Although they were designed to keep wages from rising and to restrict the mobility of workers, they are not properly viewed, as is sometimes suggested, as being "entirely consistent with medieval economic practice" or as being merely an effort to maintain the status quo.[54]

In the first place, the laws were national in scope. They mark the beginnings of a transition from an economy in which labor policy was based largely on local custom or the law of the manor—that is, law on a personal and decentralized basis—to one in which an effort was being made to gain effective national control over the economy. The method of enforcement used for several centuries, employing justices of the peace and other local officials whose personal interests were often in conflict with the policies of the crown, in fact prevented the implementation of a uniform national labor policy, but the conception and formulation of a scheme national in scope is suggestive of the changes taking place and of the extent of the weakening of the medieval order. In the second place, the employers, whose interests were clearly paramount with Parliament, were often not the old feudal lords of the manor but rather the emerging smaller gentry and tenant farmers representative of a new agricultural middle class. It is true that the great landlords were in support of their tenants, recognizing the potential threat that rising wages would mean to their rent receipts, but the direct quarrel is not incorrectly viewed as lying "between two classes of peasants, the small farmer and the landless labourer whom he hired."[55] As early as the fourteenth century, then, English labor law was reflecting the central division around which social argument and policy would revolve for centuries to come: that between those owning property and hiring labor, and those possessing no property and dependent for their security on the ability to market their labor. The nineteenth century worker, would, indeed, raise precisely the question raised five hundred years earlier, during the Peasants' Revolt, by John Ball:

When Adam delved and Eve span
Who was then the gentleman?

The fourteenth-century statutes anticipated yet another characteristic feature of later English labor policy in their underlying conception of the problems of wage levels, unemployment, and poverty as integrally related. The medieval concern with just prices and wages had been largely distinct from the problem of the relief of poverty, which was not generally considered a pervasive social problem. But the Statute of Labourers merged the problems of poverty and wages by requiring that all ablebodied men and women under the age of sixty and without visible means of support accept employment, if offered, at wages prevailing in 1347 and forbidding the giving of alms to the ablebodied unemployed.[56] The later laws of settlement were also foreshadowed in the requirement of the Statute of 1351 that workers remain during the summer in the same locality in which they had lived during the winter. This combination of the problems of poverty and wages is the beginning of the tendency to identify the concept of the laborer with that of the pauper, a feature of social analysis that Malthus incorporated into the first edition of his *Essay* and that would not be fully reversed until the Poor Law Reform Act of 1834.[57]

Although English attitudes and policies toward labor reflected fundamental differences from the outlook characteristic of the medieval period, there was one important respect in which continuity in social thought was maintained. Throughout the early modern period, from the time of the Statute of Labourers to that of the immediate forerunners of Adam Smith, social theorists essentially agreed with their medieval predecessors on the necessity of avoiding competitive pricing of labor. Throughout the sixteenth, seventeenth, and even, to a large extent, the eighteenth centuries, when the medieval regulatory principle of the just price had been generally abandoned in favor of the free interaction of market supply and demand, the desirability of wage regulation nonetheless remained a widely accepted postulate of social analysis. In his classic study of mercantilist labor policy, Edgar Furniss noted the dichotomy between wages and other prices: "the doctrine that values should be determined by the unrestricted operation of competitive forces had won the consent of the best minds" and "increasing liberalism was the tendency; the old order of strict governmental regulation of England's domestic economy was changing. . . . The rise of the trading classes to a position of dominance in the social and political structure gave the widest possible diffusion to the spirit of capitalism which had been generated within this group and that spirit proved then, as always, inimicable to the policies of restriction and regulation which had flourished in an earlier day." But the preference for the free market was decidedly limited, for with respect to wages "no champion of the laissez-faire policy appeared; the interest of the dominant classes remained on the side of regulation and the writers of the time continued to exhibit the habit of mind formed when the rating of wages was a matter of course."[58]

Although many of the economic commentators during the age of mercantilism were themselves tradesmen, pleading their own causes, it would be cynical and shortsighted to dismiss the general approval of the idea of wage regulation, so prevalent in the economic literature of the period, as merely a self-serving effort to advance the interests of the trading and employing class. The mercantilist writers, no less than Adam Smith and the classical economists, were concerned with the wealth of nations and they generally were "deeply conscious of a possible antithesis between the national interest and the trader's well-being."[59] Where they differed most fundamentally from Smith and the other classical economists was in their conception of national wealth. Not only the general preference for wage regulation, which remained a characteristic feature of social analysis throughout the early modern period, but, in fact, the whole approach taken to the labor problem is ultimately explicable only in terms of the wider conceptions of mercantilist thought.

The mercantilist departed from the medieval theorist in his implicit belief in the possibility of progress. As J. B. Bury has stressed, the idea of progress is a recent phenomenon in intellectual history. The ancient Greeks and Romans lacked the historical knowledge of mankind's previous efforts and accomplishments that might have given them the raw materials for a theory of progress, and, in any event, their essentially pessimistic conception of the relationship between mankind and time led them to articulate no very hopeful statements in this respect.[60] In the medieval period, with the crumbling reminders of past Roman grandeur all around them, men often looked back to the days of classical antiquity as having been the apogee of human accomplishment. As Bury points out, "So long as men believed that the Greeks and Romans had attained, in the best days of their civilisation, to an intellectual plane which posterity could never hope to reach, so long as the authority of their thinkers was set up as unimpeachable, a theory of degeneration held the field, which excluded a theory of progress."[61] But the speculative and empirical work of the early modern period—reflected in the achievements of men like Bacon and Descartes—was in the direction of undermining the authority of ancient thought and of reinforcing the opening of the several new worlds then emerging. The belief in the possibility of progress that that work fostered would ultimately be reflected in economic literature in the liberal and optimistic thought of Adam Smith and other Enlightenment figures, but it was first, albeit partially and imperfectly, reflected in the literature of the mercantilists, whom Smith so despised.

The mercantilist writers took as an axiom the possibility of national economic growth, and the literature they produced was directed primarily toward showing how this growth might be achieved. The mercantilist scheme of thought was dynamic, however, only with respect to the domestic economy and did not include the modern notion that economic growth can be enjoyed by all. For the mercantilist, one nation's economic growth was at the expense of another; the static conception of a fixed world supply of economic resources led, in turn, to the endless series of commercial wars. This, as Heckscher has pointed out, was "the tragedy of mercantilism." [62] Nor did the mercantilist use the modern index of growth, per-capita income, for he did not agree with Adam Smith that individual "consumption is the sole end and purpose of all production." [63] Mercantilism was above all a system of economic nationalism and in such a system, "national wealth is composed of only that part of the economic goods which is serviceable . . . in prosecuting group aims and purposes." [64] It is precisely this difference in the conception of national wealth that weakens Adam Smith's criticism of the earlier writers. According to Smith, "the interest of the producer ought to be attended to only so far as it may be necessary for promoting that of the consumer. The maxim is so perfectly self-evident, that it would be absurd to attempt to prove it. But in the mercantile system, the interest of the consumer is almost constantly sacrificed to that of the producer; and it seems to consider production, and not consumption, as the ultimate end and object of all industry and commerce." [65] The mercantilist, however, was interested in maximizing not individual consumption but that portion of the national wealth that could be devoted to national purposes. He could argue, therefore, that consumption should be minimized, for he "did not perceive that the poverty of the majority was incompatible with the wealth of the whole." [66] On the contrary, "he came to believe that the majority must be kept in poverty that the whole might be rich." [67]

Economic literature during the early modern period was conditioned by two compelling forces: (1) the desire to enhance the wealth, power, and prestige of the national state, and, in the process, to weaken the positions of other states, which were viewed generally as competitors in this respect, and (2) the necessity of dealing with the growing body of landless poor resulting from the breakdown of the medieval social order and the enclosure movement. This duality of conditioning forces explains what Schumpeter noted as a paradox in the economic literature of the age: "That governments and writers who were enthusiastically populationist never ceased to worry about how 'to set the poor to work' or how to combat 'idleness.'" [68] This duality of conditioning forces lies behind the combination of increasingly liberal attitudes and policies toward industry and trade with the maintenance of a generally repressive and restrictionist outlook toward labor.

The economic aim of mercantilism was to maximize national wealth by importing goods of low value and exporting goods of high value—that is, to make as high as possible the value added of exports. For England, this meant exporting finished or semifinished goods, like cloth, rather than raw materials, such as the unfinished wool, which it had exported in an earlier age.

The characteristic feature of mercantilism is its emphasis on trade. Classical economics was also to stress the benefits of trade but with some considerable difference. The classical case for trade was built on the basis of the principle of comparative advantage. The source of the surplus—the difference between the larger total product available after specialization and exchange and that which would be available without such cooperation—was found in the productive efficiency associated with the minimization of opportunity costs that occurred with specialization based on comparative advantage. With mercantilism it was otherwise: "The only surplus the mercantilists knew arose if a profit was made in selling."[69] With the mercantilists, the act of exchange itself seemed to be the source of the increase in economic wealth.

The emphasis on growth through improvement in the terms of trade led to the advocacy of policies of domestic cost reduction, which, taken alone, are not inconsistent with the goals later advanced by Adam Smith ("cheapness of consumption and the encouragement given to production, precisely the two effects which it is the great business of political oeconomy to promote") and to the espousal of programs of full employment that were eminently compatible with the policy implications of modern macroeconomic theory.[70] The environment in which the mercantilist literature was produced was not unlike that found in many underdeveloped economies today; capital was in extremely short supply and productive techniques were relatively simple, labor-intensive ones, with agriculture still the principal occupation. In such a setting, land and labor were seen as the two principal forces in the economic process, and the literature of the period reflected some concern over the question of "whether land or labor was the more important of the two factors of production."[71] Most of the English mercantilists gave primacy to labor. Whereas the French physiocrats would hold, with Quesnay, that the land is the ultimate source of wealth, the English economists of the early modern period were generally of a mind, with Hume, that "in the stock of labor consists all real riches and power." "Work," Petty asserted, "is the father and active principle of wealth, as lands are the mother."[72]

The primacy of labor as a factor of production was closely related to a larger conception: the contemporary view of people as the real wealth of nations. The intellectual roots of the modern concept of human capital are easily discernible in the literature of English mer-

cantilism. It is not correct to suppose, Petty wrote, "that the Greatness
and Glory of a Prince lyeth rather in the extent of his Territory, than
in the number and industry of his people, well united and governed."
On the contrary, "Fewness of People is real poverty." People, argued
Davenant, are "the most Important Strength of any Nation." And
Defoe said, "I cannot but Note how . . . the Glory, the Strength, the
Riches, the Trade, and all that's valuable in a Nation, as to its Figure in
the World, depends upon the Number of its People, be they never so
mean or poor."[73] The emphasis on the benefits of a large population
led to a flood of proposals for its increase, ranging from family subsidies based on number of children, to taxes on bachelors and programs aimed at attracting immigrants from foreign shores, and to
much discussion among economists over the question of whether col-
onizing tended to depopulate the mother country.

The basis for the advocacy of a large population rested partly on
demand considerations, associated with the "fear of goods" which
Heckscher found so characteristic of the age.[74] "It is a strange blind-
ness," wrote Roger North, "to esteem Numbers of People a Burthen,
when so much Good comes from them; their very eating and drinking
is a profitable Consumption of our Country's product." And, along
lines similar to those Mandeville would later use in his *Fable of the Bees,*
Defoe argued that "the people support one another by their Extrava-
gence and Luxury, their Gaiety and Pride; Gluttony and Drunken-
ness assist to maintain the Nation."[75] But the mercantilists' peculiar
conception of real economic gain as taking place at the expense of
other countries in the international market led them to regard home
consumption as ultimately less beneficial than production for sale
abroad. Population came consequently to be "looked upon mainly as a
factor of production [and] only incidentally as a factor in consumption," and the emphasis was on increasing the number of gainfully
employed workers within the population, especially in those industries considered likely to enhance the nation's trade balance on international account.[76]

Among the topics considered in connection with proposals for
increasing the labor supply of the country, probably none received
more attention than that of the poor law. The codification of English
poor law in 1601 had incorporated some features of earlier laws—
both medieval canon law and certain provisions of the Statute of
Labourers—and had left the country with a policy toward the poor
that would stand essentially unchanged until the nineteenth century.
Begging was prohibited; pauper children were to be apprenticed; the
aged and the impotent were to be aided by the organized collection
and distribution of alms; and the ablebodied were to be identified in
two separate categories, "those willing to work, for whom work was to

be provided, and those unwilling to work, on whom punishment was to be inflicted." The overseers of the poor for each parish were directed by the statute of 1601 to provide "a convenient stock of flax, hemp, wool, thread, iron and other stuff to set the poor to work," and, according to Lipson, "the reign of Charles I . . . [was] conspicuous for the attempts made to enforce this provision." But after the civil war, the increase in parish autonomy resulted in a decline in this activity in favor of increased reliance on outdoor relief, in the form of a weekly pension at home. "In all England," wrote Sir Matthew Hale about 1659, "it is rare to see any provision of a stock in any parish for the relief of the poor."[77]

This complaint was echoed by other writers. "Who," asked Roger North, "by these laws, are supplied with work?" "What country parishes have raised stocks of hemp, flax, etc., and kept the same going as the law requires, whereby the poor may have a constant employment?" His reply was that very few indeed had been so supplied, and he concluded that the poor law had reduced neither begging nor unemployment to any significant extent.[78] The trouble, as another writer put it, was that the provision of work for the unemployed, "although the law of the land, is not the practice of the land."[79] It was the consensus of the economic writers of the age that the Elizabethan poor law was, in fact, reducing the available supply of labor. The author of the *Grand Concern of England Explained* expressed a point of view typical of the period when he wrote that the law "makes a world of poor, more than otherwise would be, prevents industry and laboriousness: men and women growing so idle and proud, that they will not work, but lie upon the parish wherein they dwell for maintenance."[80] Davenant held that "the act for maintenance of the poor is the true bane and destruction of all the English manufacturers in general. For it apparently encourages sloth and beggary; whereas if the legislative power would make some good provision, that workhouses might in every parish be erected, and the poor, such as are able, compelled to work, so many new hands might thereby be brought in, as would indeed make the English manufacturers flourish."[81]

The belief in the efficacy of workhouses for the unemployed poor was widely shared by the economists of the day. Roger Coke's was only one of many such proposals: "That in every Village a Work-House be erected, . . . to instruct the Youth of both Sexes in such Arts or Mysteries as are more proper in them, whereby the nation may reap the benefit of their Imployments, and the poorer sort of People not forced to flee out of their Country, or become a burden to it."[82] The employment of the poor in this fashion not only would add to the productive output of the nation by assuring full employment of otherwise unemployed and underemployed people; it would also help to obtain that output on the cheapest possible terms. The need for cost minimization runs like a leitmotif through the mercantilist literature. In 1673, the author of the *Grand Concern,* noting the loss of certain English markets abroad, gave voice to a commonly held view: "No other reason can be given, but that Foreigners are able to make their work cheaper than we do, and thereby are able to undersell us wherever we come; . . . the more reason there is then . . . to endeavour the reducing the wages of our Manufacturers, and themselves to a more sober and less expensive way of living."[83] In this process of wage reduction, the unemployed poor could be used to good advantage, since by setting the parish poor to work, they would

help to manufacture the staple commodities of the Kingdom at cheap rates and thereby bring down the wages of handicraftsmen, which now are grown so high, that we have lost the trade of foreign consumption. . . . this mischief of high wages to handicraftsmen is occasioned by reason of the idleness of so vast a number of people in England as these are: so that those that are industrious and will work make men pay what they please for their wages: but set the poor at work and then these men will be forced to lower their rates: whereby we shall quickly come to sell as cheap as foreigners do and consequently ingross the trade to ourselves.[84]

The association of large numbers with low wage levels was not uncommon. Child observed that "much want of people would procure greater wages," and the author of *Brittania Languens* asserted that "the odds in Populacy must also produce the like odds in Manufacture; plenty of people must also cause cheapnesse of wages: which will cause the cheapnesse of the Manufacture."[85]

Although these authors suggest a supply and demand theory of wages, such an interpretation runs counter to another widely shared viewpoint of the time, that expressed by Cary that "wages must bear a rate in all Nations according to the prices of Provisions."[86] "If the yearly subsistence of . . . [laboring] persons in France is purchased by two-thirds of the Price that is given for the Subsistence of like Persons in England," another commentator wrote, "this will very well account for their receiving no more than the two-thirds of the English wages. And from hence it appears that the French refugees, when they came first to settle here, perpetually undersold the English; till they raised themselves by degrees to our Country Diet."[87] This view, however, was challenged. Defoe, for example, "conceive[d] it to be a mistake in those People . . . who say Labour is cheap . . . because Provisions are cheap, . . . [for] 'tis plain Provisions are cheap because Labour is cheap."[88] While agreeing that wages and subsistence costs were positively correlated, he concluded that the price of labor affected the price of food but was itself freely determined in the market. Petty, on the other hand, denied the positive correlation between wages and food prices: "It is observed by Clothiers and others, who employ great numbers of people that when Corn is extremely plentiful that the Labour of the poor is proportionately dear: and scarce to be had at all (so licentious are they who labour only to eat or rather to drink)."[89]

The diversity of views on the relationship of labor supply, wage rates, and the cost of subsistence partly reflects the imperfect and underdeveloped nature of economic theorizing at this time. But the persistent attention given to the question of wages indicates a widespread recognition of the importance of labor in a growing economy. It is necessary, in this respect, to keep in mind the essential character of the mercantilist literature. The goal of these writers was not so much a rigorous and consistent theoretical treatment of wage determination as it was the enunciation of a practical guide to action in matters of wage policy. They were not trying so much to explain what is as they were advocating what they thought ought to be, in a manner undisguisedly normative or prescriptive. It was not, indeed, until well into the eighteenth century, and not consistently then, that Englishmen thought of economics as a science.

This wedding of the economics with the politics of mercantilism underlies an apparent paradox in the labor theory of the time. That theory encompassed the doctrine of the social priority of the laborer (the notion that in the value-adding activities of the domestic artisan lay the ultimate source of national wealth) and (quite in contrast to the diversity of views concerning the relationship between wages and labor supply) considerable agreement on the social utility of low wages. Thus Petty, who argued that working people constitute the real wealth of the nation, also held that the law appointing wages "should allow the labourer but just wherewithal to live."[90] As Furniss has noted,

The question naturally arises . . . why, if the most useful, should the laboring class have been the poorest of all social classes? How account for the fact that while the social observers of the period united in elevating the theoretical importance of the workingman, the cumulative effect of their policies was to reduce his share in the social income? . . . The laborer's unique social importance was attributed to his service to the nation in making possible a favorable balance-of-trade, and . . . the belief [was] that this service could be rendered effectively only by a laboring class kept in poverty. For a highly paid, and therefore prosperous, laboring body would, it was thought, fail to produce the favorable balance-of-trade. The laborer, then, must be kept poor that the nation might be rich.[91]

The mercantilist would thus dissent most strongly from Adam Smith's dictum that "the liberal reward of labour" is the "necessary effect and cause of the greatest public prosperity."[92] On the contrary, public prosperity necessitated "a multitude of labourious poor."[93] The difference here is not one of economic analysis but rather one of goals or ends—in this case, a difference in the conception or meaning of national well-being.

At one with the ideas of the mercantilists on the merits of low wage levels, and their view of the national interest as necessitating a large number of laboring poor, was an image of the worker as inherently lazy and prodigal, for whom want and hunger were necessary stimuli to effort. In this connection, the influence of Puritan thought is clearly apparent in the emphasis placed on the evil of idleness. The English laborer was considered especially profligate and was frequently compared unfavorably with the Dutch worker, whose thrift and industriousness were held up as principal reasons for the commercial success of that nation. Even Thomas Mun, who was in fact more sympathetic toward the English worker than were many of the mercantilist authors, wrote that "this great plenty which we enjoy, makes us a people not only *vicious* and *excessive,* wasteful of the means we have, but also improvident & careless."[94] Of the English worker, Defoe wrote:

In English ale their dear enjoyment lies,
For which they'll starve themselves and families.
An Englishman will fairly drink as much
As will maintain two families of Dutch.[95]

Actually attitudes toward the laborer were not consistent throughout the many generations of mercantilist writers. Under the Tudors, for example, there appears to have been "a genuine solicitude for the lower classes," a feeling that "perhaps came of the knowledge that disaffection with an absolute monarch can have disastrous results."[96] Beer has noted that, in general, those writing in the century prior to the civil war were friendlier to the workman than those writing after the weakening of the monarchy and the ascendancy of the middle class. Thomas Mun, writing about 1630, allowed that "for as much as the people which live by the arts are far more in number than they who are the masters of the fruits, we ought the more carefully to maintain those endeavors of the multitude in whom doth consist the greatest strength and riches both of King and Kingdom."[97] By contrast, during the century that began with the Puritan revolution of 1640, when "the masters of the fruits" had demonstrated the power of capital over king, few voices were raised in favor of the worker.[98]

Recent scholarship has detected another shift in attitudes among economic writers during the third quarter of the eighteenth century. A. W. Coats has noted that, anticipating Adam Smith, a more sympathetic view of the workman emerged in economic literature after 1750: "Apart from a few isolated advocates of a 'high wage economy,' most British economists before 1750 regarded low wages as an essential precondition of the maintenance of a high volume of exports." By contrast, there emerged during the third quarter of the eighteenth century "growing support for the view that high wages and rising living standards were not merely compatible with, but were even a necessary concomitant of the prosperity of . . . [British] domestic and exported manufacturers."[99] Behind this transition in social thought lay certain refinements in economic reasoning; an increased awareness of the possibilities of technological progress, which, in turn, stimulated reconsideration of the position of the worker in the economic order; and a growing sympathy for the individual in society as part of the general spirit of the eighteenth-century Enlightenment.

Eighteenth-century writers on the whole were more sensitive to the impact of income distribution on aggregate spending and employment than their predecessors had been. Davenant, Postlethwayt, and Berkeley, among others, all favored a more equal distribution of income and wealth, but Defoe was perhaps the most explicit on the macroeconomic benefits to be obtained in this way:

The consumption of provisions encreases the rent and value of the lands, and this raises the Gentlemen's estates, and that again encreases the employment of people, and consequently the numbers of them. . . .

As the people get greater wages, so they, I mean the same poorer part of the people, clothe better, and furnish better, and this encreases the consumption of the very manufactures they make; then that consumption encreases the quantity made, and this creates what we call the Inland trade, by which innumerable families are employ'd, and the encrease of the people maintain'd; and by which encrease of trade and people the present growing prosperity of this nation is produced.[100]

The opinion that high wages would mean high spending had to contend with the common view of the worker as inherently lazy, but the literature of the eighteenth century reflects an emerging belief that high wages might stimulate an increase in the worker's effort. Jacob Vanderlint suggested increasing real wages (by reducing money wages by 25 percent and the price of necessities by 50 percent) and argued that "the working People can and will do a great deal more Work than they do, if they were sufficiently encouraged."[101]

Another factor that helps to account for the increasingly liberal attitude toward high wages during the eighteenth century was the growing tendency to distinguish between labor costs and money wages, manifested in the increased attention paid to the question of labor productivity. D. C. Coleman has argued that the economy of seventeenth-century England offered but limited possibilities for increasing output by means of improved techniques: "Low productivity, static techniques, and labour as the main factor of production meant long hours of arduous toil to produce a small amount." Not only was capital in extremely short supply, but "the scope for its application was slight. The labour-saving or productivity-increasing devices which were in use at the time were often centuries old."[102] Surely these conditions help to account for the widespread emphasis placed on quantitative increases in the labor force. By the middle of the eighteenth century, a greater variety of mechanical devices was available, and increasing emphasis was placed on the skill, dexterity, and quality of the art with which labor was applied. In an important sense, art was coming to be recognized as an explicit factor of production. As an example of its economic significance, Cary cited the clockmaker, who "hath improved his Art so high that Labour and Materials are the least part the Buyer pays for."[103] Mechanical help in manufacturing was also being stressed. "If by the help of new inventions," wrote George Blewitt, "any piece of work that now requires two men can be done in the same time by one man, all that labor so sav'd would be so much real gain to the public."[104] Although some writers feared that unemployment might result from the introduction of machinery, Coats has concluded that the "majority view . . . was optimistic" and that the emphasis was on the importance of labor-saving innovations "as a means of reducing production costs in both agriculture and manufacturing, and thereby increasing employment and sales, both at home and abroad." To be sure, the arguments of those advocating cost reduction in this way were not directly based on the possibility of thereby raising wages. But "the growing awareness of the efficacy of mechanical aids undoubtedly reinforced the arguments of those who feared that falling real wages would have harmful effects on the labour force, while the increasing importance of capital outlays may have tended to reduce the former emphasis on wage reductions as the principal method of reducing total costs."[105]

The increasingly sympathetic attitude toward the worker is but one element in the general optimism of the eighteenth-century Enlightenment. In that system of thought, man came to be viewed as innately perfectible, and as capable, in turn, of perfecting his social order, the essential purpose of which was neither the preparation of the soul for eternal life nor the enlargement of the wealth and power of the state, even at the expense of the individuals who composed it. The purpose of the social order was, rather, simply to ensure the happiness and liberty of the individuals composing it, during their own lifetimes on earth. The common purpose of Montesquieu, Rousseau, and Turgot in France, Locke and Hume in England, and Jefferson and Franklin in America was the perfection of the earthly life of man. It was under the influence and in the spirit of this system of thought that political economy emerged as a separate field of inquiry, at the hands of one whose views were eminently at one with the temper of the Enlightenment and more openly sympathetic toward the laborer than most of his contemporaries. The nineteenth century would see, following Malthus, a limited return to the spirit of harshness toward the laboring poor that had characterized the earlier age of mercantilism, but it would be difficult to dislodge the laborer from the position of primacy that he would first come to occupy in the economic system of Adam Smith.

THE LABOR ECONOMICS OF ADAM SMITH

Adam Smith is often spoken of as the father of political economy, a reputation due less to his original theoretical contributions than to the remarkable integrative ability with which he fashioned into a more or less systematic whole the several emerging strands of the doctrine of free enterprise. Although many of the ideas contained in the *Wealth of Nations* had been expressed earlier—by Cantillon, Quesnay, and Turgot in France and by Locke, Petty, Hume, Steuart, and others in England—no one before Smith so masterfully combined the theory of competitive markets with as many perceptive insights into the historical and institutional foundations of the economic process.

The breadth of the *Wealth of Nations* reflected not only the ten years Smith spent in writing it and the long years of studying and teaching that led up to it (Smith was fifty-three when it was published) but also its author's wide interests as a professor of moral philosophy. So diverse, indeed, were Smith's interests, and so catholic was his approach to the subject of political economy that almost any specialty in economics can today claim Smith's major work as being in its province. Morris Copeland, one of the principal architects of modern national income accounting, has suggested that Smith's major contribution was that "he crystallized economic thinking in terms of the national income and product account, i.e., in terms of a two-sector economic circuit," and George Unwin has stressed Smith's role as "the first great economic historian. . . . There is scarcely a page of the *Wealth of Nations* where history and theory are sundered from each other."[1] Ultimately, of course, the fact that any specialty within economics can claim the work of Adam Smith as being in its tradition rests on the lack of special fields within economics—even, indeed, of economics as a special field apart from the broader realm of moral or social philosophy—at the time he wrote. Be that as it may, Adam Smith can nonetheless, with considerable justification, be called the first labor economist.

There are several reasons for emphasizing Smith's role as a labor economist. He opened the *Wealth of Nations* with a chapter entitled "Of the Causes of Improvement in the productive Powers of Labour, and of the Order according to which its Produce is naturally distributed among the different Ranks of the People." He associated the principle of increased returns attendant upon division of labor with the source of the greatest increase in productivity. His openly sympathetic attitude toward the laboring classes, a characteristic not uncommon among labor economists, especially in an earlier era, stands in sharp contrast with the rather harsh attitudes toward the workers previously expressed by most of the mercantilist writers. His conception of political economy as a part of public administration fits well with the policy orientation that has always marked labor economics.[2]

Much of the type of analysis he engaged in has remained a prominent part of labor economics, and many of his observations on labor problems are relevant even today. As Schumpeter has rightly noted, Smith's "performance in the field of labor economics is highly characteristic and in fact a fair sample of his work as a whole. Moreover it acquires additional importance by virtue of its having been the first fully systematic treatment of the subject."[3]

CONDITIONING FACTORS AND FORCES

The role and position of labor in Adam Smith's intellectual schema was the product of several influencing forces. There was, first, the conception of man's relations with his fellow men derived from the so-called sentimental school of moral philosophers and communicated from the founder of that school, Lord Shaftesbury, by Francis Hutcheson to Smith who was his pupil, disciple, and successor as professor of natural religion, ethics, and civil policy in the University of Glasgow. The term *sentimental* is not to be construed in any opprobrious sense but rather in that employed by Smith in his first well-known work, *A Theory of the Moral Sentiments* (1759). It refers to a conception of human morality based not alone on reason but also on sentiments, human feelings or emotions that stand somewhat apart from strict rationality. In an early and often-quoted passage in the *Wealth of Nations,* Adam Smith posited self-interest as the basis of economic relationships: "It is not from the benevolence of the butcher, the brewer or the baker, that we expect our dinner, but from their regard to their own interest. We address ourselves, not to their humanity but to their self-love, and never talk to them of our own necessities but of their advantages. Nobody but a beggar chuses to depend chiefly upon the benevolence of his fellow citizens."[4] The significance of this quotation must not be exaggerated, for only in the narrowly economic sense did Smith see self-interest as the ruling principle of human action. His larger conception was of man as basically sympathetic toward his fellow human beings and as ultimately realizing his humanity in a common concern for others.

It is possible to construe Adam Smith's emphasis on self-interest in the *Wealth of Nations* as actuating only the price system, and sympathy, or feeling for one's fellow man, so prominently featured in the *Moral Sentiments*, as an antecedent principle and overall conditioner of the moral, legal, and social environment in which the price system operates. But the considerable institutional material contained in the *Wealth of Nations* shows much evidence also of the influence of the sentimental philosophers. For example, Smith's sympathetic attitude toward the laboring classes, at one with the main themes and spirit of the Enlightenment, is clearly more closely related to the teachings of Shaftesbury and Hutcheson than to those of the English mercantilists.

Yet despite his trenchant attacks on what he called the mercantile system and despite his quite different conception of national well-being, based generally on consumption of goods and services by individuals rather than on the influence of the producers of the nation in international markets, the *Wealth of Nations* manifests the influence of the mercantilist literature on Smith's own thinking. This influence is not limited to the strong sense of nationalism that permeates Smith's work, his belief that defense was more important than "opulence," and his defense of the acts of navigation and trade. He continued to maintain the mercantilist emphasis on labor rather than land as the primary factor of production and showed traces of the populationist attitude so common to earlier thought: "The most decisive mark of the prosperity of any country is the increase of the number of its inhabitants."[5] More fundamentally, perhaps, Smith inherited from mercantilist thought an overriding concern with national economic growth and of the importance of the operation of the price system in its realization. The mercantilist writers typically found in the act of exchange itself the ultimate source of economic surplus. For them, improvements in the organization or technique of production were less important as a means of increasing wealth than were such opportunities as might arise to manipulate the terms of trade to one's own advantage. That point of view is, of course, readily understandable in terms of the shortage of capital and the limits of technology with which they were faced. It is fair to say that the organization and techniques of production, although by no means entirely static, were changing less rapidly during the sixteenth, seventeenth, and eighteenth centuries than trade and markets were being expanded.

Adam Smith, however, was a contemporary of Matthew Boulton, James Watt, and John Wilkinson, and other great inventors, and he was thus a witness to the profound changes being wrought by the technological and entrepreneurial dynamism of his age. Nor was Smith unaware of the character of these changes, for by "the division of labour," with which he associated the greatest economic progress of mankind, he meant precisely the productive and organizational relationships within the business enterprise. But having opened the *Wealth of Nations* with an unprecedented tribute to the efficiency to be found within the contemporary business firm, Smith proceeded thereafter to lay the same stress on market relationships outside the firm as had long characterized mercantilist literature. His early emphasis on division of labor could have led him toward a theory of management or, perhaps, of technological change. Instead he followed the mercantilist tradition in emphasizing market exchange. In that tradition, the core of his economics—and the whole of that of some of his successors—would be the theory of price. So far did the idea of market exchange dominate Adam Smith's thinking that labor itself was subsumed under its rubric. "Labour," he wrote, "was the first price, the original purchase-money, that was paid for all things. It was not by gold or by silver, but by labour, that all the wealth of the world was originally purchased."[6]

A third force that helped to shape Adam Smith's economic scheme was the thought of the French physiocrats, although the extent to which the latter were truly influential in shaping his thinking has been a matter of some controversy.[7] There is some suggestion of physiocratic influence in Smith's agrarian bias that appears throughout the *Wealth of Nations*, illustrated, for example, in his remark that in agriculture "nature labours along with man," with this in turn accounting, evidently, for some special agricultural productivity or surplus. Such an interpretation is reinforced by his assertion that "it is the surplus produce of the country only, or what is over and above the maintenance of the cultivators, that constitutes the subsistence of the town, which can therefore increase only with the increase of this surplus produce."[8] Although it has been pointed out that Smith's "most favorable reference to any social 'class' was that to 'the country gentlemen of Great Britain,' the class of men least affected with the wretched spirit of greed and monopoly," a preference for agriculture was, after all, a common theme in eighteenth-century thought.[9] Indeed the idea has roots that go back to the natural law philosophy of the Middle Ages and beyond that to the social thought of classical antiquity.

A rather more direct relationship between physiocratic economics and the work of Adam Smith, and one of greater significance in terms of the subsequent development of labor economics, seems to inhere in the physiocratic emphasis on distribution. The English mercantilist literature had given little or no attention to the question of distribution, except incidentally in connection with the policy of minimizing wages in order to keep costs down. The mercantilist's interest in the laborer has been called "a product of his interest in the form of the nation's wealth; and the labor doctrines he evolved were projected as means toward increasing the aggregate of nationally serviceable wealth, irrespective of its distribution within the country."[10] Physiocracy, on the other hand, has been described as "essentially the search for a scheme of economic partition."[11] And, according to Edwin Cannan, Adam Smith "acquired the idea of the necessity of a scheme of distribution from the physiocrats and . . . he tacked his own scheme (very different from theirs) on to his already existing theory of price."[12] The idea of a society divided into three classes, composed of

laborers, landlords, and capitalists, which was to occupy so prominent
a place in nineteenth-century economics, has itself been attributed to
the French economists.

It is rather more the physiocrats, then, than the mercantilists to
whom we must look for the beginnings of the theory of wages. The
mercantilist not only accepted the prevalence of wage regulation; he
advocated it. The physiocrat, on the other hand, postulated a system
of competition. No less than Adam Smith, he was concerned to lay
bare the faults of detailed state regulation. The mercantilist was concerned with what wages should be, given certain national goals. The
physiocrat was interested in what wages would be under the postulated conditions of laissez-faire and provided a good part of the
theoretical underpinnings of what later developed as classical wage
theory.[13] In connection with the relationship between the physiocrats
and Adam Smith, it is interesting to note that the latter's *Lectures on
Justice, Police, Revenue and Arms* constituted in essence "an early draft
of what subsequently developed into the *Wealth of Nations*." The fact
that these lectures contained no trace of the theory of distribution
lends considerable support to Cannan's view that the incorporation of
such a theory into the *Wealth of Nations* was "due to the acquaintance
with the French *Economistes* which Adam Smith made during his visit
to France with the Duke of Buccleugh in 1764–6."[14]

LABOR AS A PRODUCTIVE FACTOR

In the introduction to the *Wealth of Nations*, Adam Smith established
the primacy of labor as the ultimate source of economic wealth: "The
annual labour of every nation is the fund which originally supplies it
with all the necessaries and conveniencies of life." A country's wealth
therefore would be determined both by "the skill, dexterity and
judgment with which its labour is generally applied" and "by the
proportion between the number of those who are employed in useful
labour, and that of those who are not so employed." The number of
useful and productive laborers, Smith asserted, was "everywhere in
proportion to the quantity of capital stock which is employed in setting them to work, and to the particular way in which it is so employed," but, in any event, it was the quality rather than the quantity
of labor employed that was the real key to a country's well-being.
"Among the savage nations of hunters and fishers," Smith noted,
"every individual who is able to work is more or less employed in useful labour," yet such nations were generally miserably poor. "Among
civilized and thriving nations, on the contrary, though a great number
of people do not labour at all, many of whom consume the produce of
ten times, frequently of a hundred times more labour than the greater

part of those who work; yet the produce of the whole labour of the society is so great, that all are often abundantly supplied, and a workman, even of the lowest and poorest order, if he is frugal and industrious, may enjoy a greater share of the necessaries and conveniences of life than it is possible for any savage to acquire."[15]

The importance of labor as a factor of production was a commonly stressed theme of English mercantilist literature, but the emphasis had traditionally been on the quantity of labor supplied, with public policy being generally oriented toward securing the largest amount of labor at the lowest price. And although the post-1750 literature reflected a growing emphasis on the efficiency with which labor was employed, no economic writer before him gave to labor quite the significance it acquired at the hands of Adam Smith. Despite the increased attention paid by the later English mercantilists to art and to the quality of the labor force, the notion of the primacy of trade as the source of wealth was never fully overcome. The French physiocrats, on the other hand, generally held, with Quesnay, that the land was the only source of wealth.[16] Thus Smith's strong emphasis on labor as the ultimate source of economic wealth and the substantial basis of economic activity stands as a major innovation in the history of economic thought.

Smith's next task was to seek out the causes of the improvement of labor. These he found principally in the phenomenon of economic specialization and division of labor: "The greatest improvement in the productive powers of labour, and the greater part of the skill, dexterity, and judgment with which it is any where directed, or applied, seem to have been the effects of the division of labour."[17] The recognition of the importance of this division within society was not original with Adam Smith; his contribution was the association of it with a principle of increasing returns and the identification therein of the principal source of economic progress. In a work as early as Plato's *Republic*, we find division of labor identified as economically significant. "There are diversities of natures among us which are adapted to different occupations," said Plato. "Thus then all things are produced more plentifully and easily and of a better quality when one man does one thing which is natural to him . . . and leaves other things."[18] The medieval writers also stressed the differences among men and the necessity for some division of labor, which characterizes even primitive societies, is probably so obvious and ubiquitous as to justify the designation given it by Schumpeter, "this eternal commonplace of economics."[19] Neither the ancient nor the medieval writers, however, employed the concept of division of labor to explain increased productivity or efficiency, except insofar as different men possessed different talents and abilities. This latter aspect was eliminated from economics at a later date (although subsequently it was partially reintroduced by Cairnes in the concept of noncompeting groups). Adam Smith, for example, reflecting the psychology of environmental determinism so characteristic of the Enlightenment, confidently asserted that "the difference between the most dissimilar characters . . . seems to arise not so much from nature as from habit, custom, and education."[20] Smith's employment of the principle of division of labor was fundamentally different from that of both the Greeks and the medieval writers. In his famous illustration of the pin factory, labor is a homogeneous factor. There is no comparative advantage associated with the possession of particular skills on the part of the pin makers. But decreasing costs (increasing productivity) follow upon one man's concentrating on one small aspect of the job, apart altogether from whatever comparative advantages (special abilities) he may possess for pin making as against possible alternative employments. No such construction is to be found in the economics of Plato, Aristotle, or Aquinas. Division of labor proceeds simply from differences in ability, with the result that its significance for economics was not fully exploited. Again we are reminded that in earlier social thought, economics was intermingled with ethics and politics, with the latter two overshadowing the former. Whereas Adam Smith separated the economic from the sociological effects of the division of labor, for the Greek and medieval writers division of labor was only part of the total scheme of class or occupational stratification.

Although labor as a general category was the primary factor of production for Adam Smith, he did not consider all labor to be of equal economic significance: "There is one sort of labour which adds to the value of the subject upon which it is bestowed: there is another which has no such effect. The former, as it produces a value, may be called productive; the latter, unproductive labour."[21] This distinction was, according to Alexander Gray, "an evil legacy of the Physiocrats," but, in fact, although no economic writers before them quite so narrowed the field of productive economic activity as did the physiocrats, the general distinction between these two types of labor was common among British writers during the mercantilist period.[22] According to E. A. J. Johnson, "Lawyers, doctors, clergymen, retailers, stock jobbers, and men of letters were generally regarded as unproductive, while farmers, manufacturers and merchants were esteemed as most productive."[23] For the physiocrats, on the other hand, farmers alone constituted the productive class. Turgot, in his *Reflections on the Formation and the Distribution of Riches*, stated:

The Husbandman is the only person whose labour produces something over and above the wages of the labour. He is therefore the sole source of all wealth. . . . It is the physical result of the fertility of the soil, and of the wisdom far more than of the laboriousness, of the means which he has employed to render it fertile. As soon as the labour of the Husbandman produces more than his wants, he can, with this superfluity that nature accords him as a pure gift, over and above the wages of his toil, buy the labour of the other members of the society. . . . He is, therefore, the sole source of the riches, which, by their circulation, animate all the labours of the society; because he is the only one whose labour produces over and above the wages of the labour.[24]

But even in agriculture, "it is not [the farmer's] labor but the land which is conceived to be the source of the surplus. The surplus is a free gift of nature."[25] In fact, by *husbandman,* the physiocrats evidently meant not the agricultural laborer but his employer, the agricultural entrepreneur. In sum, the physiocrats negated the very concept of labor productivity. As James Bonar has remarked, "Physiocracy as an economical theory is a glorification not of the labourer, but of the capitalist, though only in one field of action."[26]

Adam Smith was never able fully to overcome a certain agricultural bias, but he extended the concept of productive labor well beyond its physiocratic limits. "The capital error of this system," he wrote of physiocracy, "seems to lie in its representing the class of artificers, manufacturers and merchants as altogether barren and unproductive."[27] For Smith, any labor was productive that "realizes itself in some particular subject or vendible commodity, which lasts for some time at least after that labour is past. It is, as it were, a certain quantity of labour stocked and stored up to be employed, if necessary, upon some other occasion."[28] Thus the labor of the artisan or the manufacturer was productive, while that of the menial servant, the sovereign, the military, and the civil service was unproductive, as was that of "churchmen, lawyers, physicians, men of letters of all kinds; players, buffoons, musicians, opera-singers, opera dancers &c," all of whose work, said Smith, "perishes in the very instant of production."[29] Thus Smith was closer to the traditional distinction of English mercantilist literature than to that of the physiocrats, yet he believed that "the labour of farmers and country labourers is certainly more productive than that of merchants, artificers and manufacturers." His qualification was that the "superior produce of the one class, however, does not render the others barren or unproductive."[30] Moreover the superiority of agriculture in this respect was not quite the same as that espoused by the physiocrats, for it was intimately at one with Smith's emphasis on the primacy of labor, rather than land, as the ultimate source of wealth. So secure was labor, in this sense, in Adam Smith's thought that it extended to all elements in nature, including cattle and horses—even, indeed, to nature itself.[31]

But although labor in agriculture was fundamentally more pro-

ductive than in industry, it was not as amenable to specific improvement over time because it was not as easily identified with the greatest
source of such improvement, the division of labor:

The improvement in the productive powers of useful labour depends, first,
upon the improvement in the ability of the workman; and, secondly, upon
that of the machinery with which he works. But the labour of artificers and
manufacturers, as it is capable of being more subdivided, and the labour
of each workman reduced to a greater simplicity of operation, than that
of farmers and country labourers, so it is likewise capable of both these
sorts of improvement in a much higher degree. In this respect, therefore, the
class of cultivators can have no sort of advantage over that of artificers and
manufacturers.[32]

Modern economics, of course, eschews any such distinction between
productive and unproductive labor and considers all value-adding
activities as production, either of goods or of services, both of which
enter into the computation of national product. There is clearly a
certain materialist bias in Smith's conception of national wealth, limited, as it is, essentially to tangible, physical goods. But there is
another aspect to the distinction between productive and unproductive labor. Ultimately labor is productive for Adam Smith if it is expended in such a way as to permit its storage—that is, if it is incorporated into a product that can be employed or consumed at some
future date. The output of productive labor is thus a store of value in
essentially the same way that money is a store of value in modern
economic thought. Smith's employment of the concept of productive
labor owes less perhaps to physiocratic thought than to his views on
labor as a source of value. In any event, his association of labor with
value was of critical significance not only for his own analytical schema
but for the subsequent development of economic thought.

LABOR AS A MEASURE AND SOURCE OF VALUE

If Adam Smith gave primacy to labor among the several factors of
production, he gave no less a primacy to the idea of exchange among
social relations generally. The division of labor, he wrote, "from
which so many advantages are derived, is not originally the effect of
any human wisdom, which foresees and intends that general opulence
to which it gives occasion. It is the necessary, though very slow and
gradual, consequence of a certain propensity in human nature which
has in view no such extensive utility; the propensity to truck, barter,
and exchange one thing for another.[33]

This propensity was, according to Smith, common to all men and
appears to have been for him one of the distinguishing features that
set men apart from other animals. "Nobody," Smith remarked, "ever

saw a dog make a fair and deliberate exchange of one bone for another with another dog. Nobody ever saw one animal by its gestures and natural cries signify to another, this is mine, that yours: I am willing to give this for that."[34] Smith noted that "in almost every other race of animals each individual, when it is grown up to maturity, is entirely independent, and in its natural state has occasion for the assistance of no other living creature. But man has almost constant occasion for the help of his brethren, and it is in vain for him to expect it from their benevolence only. He will be more likely to prevail if he can interest their self-love in his favour, and shew them that it is for their own advantage to do for him what he requires of them. Whoever offers to another a bargain of any kind, proposes to do this."[35] The propensity to exchange is thus encouraged by the principle of self-interest and encourages both the division of labor and the perfection of individual skills associated with it.

Since exchange is so dominant a feature of human life, Smith's interest not surprisingly turns to a determination of "the rules which men naturally observe in exchanging [goods and services] either for money or for one another." These rules "determine what may be called the relative or exchangeable value of goods," and an analysis of the principles that regulate the exchange values of goods takes him to an analysis of, first, "the real measure of this exchangeable value; or, wherein consists the real price of all commodities," second, "the different parts of which this real price is composed or made up," and, finally, "the different circumstances which sometimes raise some or all of these different parts of price above, and sometimes sink them below their natural or ordinary rate."[36]

Smith finds the real measure of value in labor. Once the division of labor has proceeded very far, as is the case in all but the most primitive and underdeveloped societies, it is only a very small part of one's total wants that one's own labor can supply. People must depend on the labor of others for the satisfaction of most of their wants, and therefore they are rich or poor according to the quantity of labor that they can command or afford.[37] Wealth, then, is reckoned in terms of the power to purchase the labor of others. Labor, however, is difficult to measure. "There may," as Smith says, "be more labour in an hour's hard work than in two hours easy business; or in an hour's application to a trade which it cost ten years labour to learn, than in a month's industry at an ordinary and obvious employment.[38] Moreover commodities are more commonly exchanged for other commodities than for labor, and, in an advanced society, this commodity is money. It is therefore common to estimate exchange value by the quantity of money rather than by the quantity of labor that can be exchanged for it.

The value of money itself changes over time, however, depending upon its own demand and supply. Clearly a good such as money, which varies in terms of its own value, cannot be an accurate measure of the value of other goods. The one thing that never varies in terms of its own value, Smith finds, is labor. Although the value of one's labor to another might vary over time, depending on conditions both in product markets and in labor markets, its value to the laborer is unchanging.[39]

The concept of labor as the real measure of value was reinforced by Smith's view that labor was the ultimate source of value in that it was "the first price, the original purchase money that was paid for all things. It was not by gold or by silver, but by labour, that all the wealth of the world was originally purchased."[40] For this view of the economic process, Smith drew directly on Hume, whose work he cited, but indirectly he was drawing on the earlier contribution of John Locke. In the *Second Treatise of Civil Government,* Locke had posited a state of nature in which man, by nature a free being and thus free to employ his faculties as he chose, was able to mix his labor with the abundant natural resources that God had given to all men in common and thereby create for himself a property that was exclusively his own. Locke wrote, "Every man has a property in his own person. This nobody has any right to but himself. The labour of his body and the work of his hands, we may say, are properly his. Whatsoever then he removes out of the state that nature hath provided and left it in, he hath mixed his labour with, and joined to it something that is his own, and thereby makes it his property."[41]

Locke's influence is clearly evident in Adam Smith's views on the labor origins of property. "The property which every man has in his own labour," Smith wrote, "as it is the original foundation of all other property, so it is the most sacred and inviolable. The patrimony of a poor man lies in the strength and dexterity of his hands; and to hinder him from employing this strength and dexterity in what manner he thinks proper without injury to his neighbour, is a plain violation of this most sacred property." Elsewhere Smith spoke of "the sacred rights of private property."[42]

The Lockeian conception of the state of nature also influenced the way in which Smith approached the question of the component parts of price. Adam Smith did not, like some of his successors, posit a labor theory of value for the England of his time. He recognized the role of property, both in the form of land and capital, as well as that of labor, as positive agents of production, and he spoke of rent, wages, and profit or interest all as being necessary factor payments. Like Locke, however, he commenced his discussion of the question of distribution by referring to a state of nature in which labor alone was the source of wealth. However, this state of affairs "could not last beyond the first introduction of the appropriation of land and the accumulation of stock," and as "soon as land becomes private property, the landlord demands a share of almost all the produce which the labourer can either raise or collect from it."[43]

The emergence and development of the concept of private property, both in land and in other forms, undoubtedly deserved more rigorous analysis than that accorded it by Smith. Locke, of course, had as no part of his purpose the analysis of the function of property in economic life but was concerned only to explain its origins as other than in the divine right of kings. Locke's primary aim in *Civil Government* had been to refute the patriarchal theory of government advanced by Robert Filmer. Attacking Filmer's thesis that God had conferred upon kings both the right to govern and to dispose of property, Locke advanced the idea that resources had originally been given by God to all men in common, with the origins of property rights thus depending in the first instance upon labor. But for Adam Smith, whose principal purpose was to explain how labor and property combine to produce and share in the wealth of nations, the reliance upon the analogy with the state of nature was to have unfortunate consequences, for it was to lead to a view where rent, profits, and interest, even if necessary components of price, are nonetheless "deductions" from the "share" of the product going to labor. "As soon as stock [capital in the form of private property] has accumulated in the hands of particular persons," wrote Smith, "some of them will naturally employ it in setting to work industrious people, whom they will supply with materials and subsistence, in order to make a profit by the sale of their work, or by what their labour adds to the value of the materials." Thus in a society in which private property exists in the form of capital, "the whole produce of labour does not always belong to the labourer. He must in most cases share it with the owner of the stock which employs him."[44] Smith also failed to explain and analyze the role of the capitalist or entrepreneur. The resulting picture is of the capitalist as one whose finger is in the social pie, with the pie itself being the creation of the laborer.

The holder of private property in land was the cause of yet another deduction from the produce of labor, for

as soon as the land of any country has all become private property, the land-lords, like all other men, love to reap where they never sowed, and demand a rent even for its natural produce. The wood of the forest, the grass of the field, and all the natural fruits of the earth, which, when land was in common, cost the labourer only the trouble of gathering them, come, even to him, to have an additional price fixed upon them. He must give up to the landlord a portion of what his labour either collects or produces.[45]

The result is that "rent makes the first deduction from the produce of the labour which is employed upon land" and "profit makes a second deduction." Moreover "the produce of almost all other labour is liable to the like deduction of profit."[46] Thus although Adam Smith did not hold to a labor theory of value other than for a primitive economy and although he explicitly recognized the necessary interaction of land, labor, and capital in an advanced economic state, his view of rent, interest, and profit as being deductions from the output of labor could hardly have offered a better foundation both for the labor theory of value and for the theory of capitalist exploitation, which would subsequently be articulated by Karl Marx.

LABOR AS A RECIPIENT OF INCOME

The explanation and analysis of labor's share of the national income constitutes one of the most important tasks of modern economics, and one not yet altogether satisfactorily accomplished. Despite the fact that the "theory of the determination of wages in a free market is simply a special case of the general theory of value," the development of wage theory has lagged in relation to that of price theory generally.[47] This is probably due, at least in part, to the fact that the price of labor was still being regulated in England and on the Continent during the early modern period, well after the determination of prices of many other goods and services had been relegated to the free play of market forces.[48] Partly, no doubt, it reflects also the greater difficulties of conceptualizing the role and function of a human agent whose motivations and responses are complex and not so easily reduced to market terms as is true of other factors. As Lloyd Reynolds has rightly noted, "Economists have always been somewhat diffident about integrating labor into the market schema. Marshall, Pigou, Taussig, and other leading theorists were troubled by the 'peculiarities' of the labor market—the fact that the worker sells himself with his services, that his immediate financial need may place him at a disadvantage in negotiating with employers, that he is influenced by non-pecuniary motives, that he has limited knowledge of alternative opportunities, and that there are objective barriers to free movement of labor."[49]

The difficulties presented for economic theory by the purchase and sale of labor are well illustrated in Adam Smith's analysis of wages, which shifts from short run to long run, from influences narrowly economic to those more broadly social, and from market to nonmarket institutional forces. In the history of wage theory, Smith's role is that of synthesizer. To the extent that he spoke with ease of what should be—of what constituted desirable public policy toward labor—his approach was in the tradition of British mercantilist literature. To the extent that his was an analysis of what would be, under postulated conditions of perfect liberty or of laissez-faire, it was rather more in harmony with the work of the physiocrats. Reflecting both of these schools of thought and drawing on the earlier contributions of Locke, Petty, Steuart, Turgot, and others, Smith fashioned the most systematic theory of wages presented up to that time. Nevertheless a great many ambiguities and obscurities remained. One historian of economic thought has suggested that Smith's arguments lead to "no definite conclusions with regard to a tenable theory of wages; on the other hand, he suggests many trains of thought, and there are indeed few subsequent theories of wages which cannot appeal for support to some passage" in the *Wealth of Nations*.[50] For example, Smith's statements that "the produce of labour constitutes the natural recompense of wages of labour" and that wages stem ultimately from "the value which the workmen add to the materials" seem to suggest a productivity (albeit not a marginal productivity) theory of wages.[51] On the other hand, his treatment of rent and profit as deductions from the produce of labor foreshadowed "all the exploitation and bargaining-power theories of wages that the nineteenth century was to produce, and also suggested the idea that labor is the 'residual claimant.' "[52]

Although he was not as specific as he might have been concerning a time dimension, Adam Smith's several trains of thought on wages are best subsumed in the general distinction between the long run and the short run. By making that distinction, much of the eclecticism and apparent inconsistency in chapters eight and ten of the *Wealth of Nations* is eliminated, or, at least, reduced. Smith's long-run theory gave primacy to the supply of labor and led to the notion of a subsistence wage. His short-run theory emphasized the importance of demand and bargaining power and suggested the possibility of rising wages and improving economic conditions. In any actual situation, of course, the interaction of the two forces determined the wage rate. In book 5 of the *Wealth of Nations,* where Smith summarized his position on wages, he made it clear that his was a theory of supply and demand. Wages, he wrote,

are everywhere necessarily regulated by two different circumstances; the demand for labour, and the ordinary or average price of provisions. The demand for labour, according as it happens to be either increasing, stationary, or declining; or to require an increasing, stationary or declining population, regulates the subsistence of the labourer, and determines in what degree it shall be, either liberal, moderate, or scanty. The ordinary or average price of provisions determines the quantity of money which must be paid to the workman in order to enable him, one year with another, to purchase this liberal, moderate, or scanty subsistence.[53]

The idea that the minimal means of subsistence forms a standard or norm to which the wage rate will tend had been advanced by Child, Locke, and others and was a familiar theme in English mercantilist literature. It also formed the basis of physiocratic wage theory. Quesnay wrote on several occasions of the necessary connection between the wage rate and the price of food, but it was Turgot who best stated the physiocratic doctrine on wages, a doctrine containing many of the themes later enunciated by Smith and the English classical economists. For the physiocrats, the first step in the formulation of the theory was the establishment of the primacy of the agricultural worker, who furnished others their food and other necessities. Turgot said of the farmer, "What his labor causes the land to produce beyond his personal wants is the only fund for the wages which all the other members of the society receive in exchange for their labor."[54] And he then articulated more fully the economic position of the nonagricultural laborer:

The mere workman, who has only his arms and his industry, has nothing except in so far as he succeeds in selling his toil to others. He sells it more or less dear; but this price, more or less high as it may be, does not depend upon himself alone: it results from the agreement which he makes with him who pays his labor. The latter pays him as little as he can; as he has the choice among a great number of Workmen, he prefers the one who works cheapest. The Workmen are therefore obliged to lower the price, in competition with one another. In every kind of work it cannot fail to happen, and as a matter of fact it does happen, that the wages of the workman are limited to what is necessary to procure him his subsistence.[55]

Adam Smith incorporated these views into his wage theory, but with important qualifications. For him, the idea of the subsistence wage was rather more a long-run potentiality than an actual or a probable reality and was not the result of labor market competition among workers so much as of the character of the long-run labor supply function. The nature of that function was defined by two postulates. The first of these was the idea that there was a minimum level of subsistence below which wages could not go. The second was that of a naturally increasing population: "If the demand [for labor] is continually increasing, the reward of labour must necessarily encourage in such a manner the marriage and multiplication of labourers. . .

If the reward should at any time be less than what was requisite for this purpose, the deficiency of hands would soon raise it; and if it should at any time be more, their excessive multiplication would soon lower it to this necessary rate."[56] In modern terms, the long-run supply of labor is perfectly elastic at a level defined as subsistence. But since actual wages depend on the interaction between labor supply and demand, the actual quantity of labor offered and sold at any moment in time, and hence the wage rate, depends upon the demand for labor. Demand, in turn, depends on the funds used to pay wages: "the revenue which is over and above what is necessary for the maintenance; and . . . the stock which is over and above what is necessary for the employment of their masters."[57]

This concept of a fund from which the demand for labor was derived was closely related to the advances that Quesnay had made both the starting impulse and the continuing drive of the process of economic circulation described in the *Tableau économique*. But it was undoubtedly strengthened by empirical observations of the actual economic setting, in an age characterized by widespread individual proprietorships and, perhaps of greater direct significance, the putting-out system. When a man had more money than he needed for his subsistence, he would use that money to employ others and make more of a profit. Thus the demand for labor was a function of the wealth of the nation and would increase as economic growth took place.[58]

Smith thus arrived at a position quite different from that of the physiocrats: so long as an economy is growing, so too will be the demand for labor, and wages may be well above the subsistence level. It was not, Smith stressed, the actual wealth of a country but rather the rate at which that wealth was increasing that kept up wage rates. The essential dynamism of Smith's economics is clear. Economic growth, not merely great national wealth, was the key to high wages.[59]

Thus, even in a rich country, unless it were also growing, the competition of laborers for jobs would tend to bring the wage rate toward the subsistence level. Adam Smith denied that wages were close to the subsistence level in England at his time, asserting that there were "many plain symptoms that the wages of labour are no-where in this country regulated by the lowest rate which is consistent with common humanity." But, he noted, because North America was growing more rapidly than England, wages were higher there. "England," he observed, "is certainly in the present time, a much richer country than any part of North America. The wages of labour, however, are much higher in North America than in any part of England."[60]

The dynamic character of Adam Smith's economics, with its strong emphasis on economic growth and improving material conditions of life, thus led to a departure from the pessimistic conclusions of both mercantilistic and physiocratic wage theory. A return to those conclusions and the final formulation of the iron law of subsistence wages would make of economics in the nineteenth century the "dismal science," but this would be only after his successors had forsaken Adam Smith's interest in economic growth in favor of an almost exclusive concern with allocating a given quantity of resources.

Smith's concern with economic dynamics was complemented by his very strong attachment to empirical realism. Few other economists, before or since, have matched his ability as an observer of social and economic institutions. As Stigler has noted, "Smith did not set his task as simply the grinding out of a set of deductions from one basic principle—the contrivance of a sort of logical utopia. His strong sense of realism led him to give for every main argument, sometimes a homely and apt, sometimes a learned and penetrating historical, documentation. Nor could he be accused of neglecting or underrating the importance of non-economic factors such as the social and political structure."[61] It is, for example, Smith the labor market institutionalist rather than Smith the economic theorist who notes that "a man is of all sorts of luggage the most difficult to be transported."[62] These aspects of Smithian economics are worth noting, for a later generation of English economists was to build on the logic of Smith's price theory while eliminating the empiricism, history, and social philosophy that permeated the *Wealth of Nations*.

The institutional realism of Smith's economics is well illustrated in his treatment of short-run labor market conditions. "What are the common wages of labour," he observed, "depends everywhere upon the contract usually made between those two parties, whose interests are by no means the same. The workmen desire to get as much, the masters to give, as little as possible."

It is not, however, difficult to foresee which of the two parties must, upon all ordinary occasions, have the advantage in the dispute, and force the other into a compliance with their terms. The masters, being fewer in number, can combine much more easily; and the law, besides, authorises, or at least does not prohibit their combinations, while it prohibits those of the workmen. We have no acts of parliament against combining to lower the price of work; but many against combining to raise it. In all such disputes the masters can hold out much longer. A landlord, a farmer, a master manufacturer, or merchant, though they did not employ a single workman, could generally live a year or two upon the stocks which they have already acquired. Many workmen could not subsist a week, few could subsist a month, and scarce any a year without employment. In the long-run the workman may be as necessary to his master as his master is to him, but the necessity is not so immediate.[63]

Far from positing purely competitive conditions for his labor market analysis, Smith noted the ubiquity of combinations not among workers but among masters, who tacitly agree not to raise wages. According to Smith, "We seldom, indeed, hear of this combination, because it is the usual, and one may say, the natural state of things."[64]

Smith's factual realism is also well illustrated in his treatment of wage differentials. First, he anticipated the argument directed by many later labor economists to the conception of a single, or general, wage rate, by noting that the price of labor "cannot be ascertained very accurately any where, different prices being often paid at the same place and for the same sort of labour, not only according to the different abilities of the workmen, but according to the easiness or hardness of the masters" and he emphasized that all "we can pretend to determine is what are the most usual."[65] Thus when we speak of the wage rate, or of wages in general, we are admittedly simplifying what is in fact a highly complex and diversified wage structure and one recognized as such by Adam Smith. Nor did Smith suggest any tendency toward equality of wages. What Jevons later termed the law of indifference—the notion that only one price can obtain in one market at one time—had earlier been suggested by David Hume in connection with labor. "There cannot be two prices for the same species of Labour," wrote Hume in a letter to Turgot in 1766, "for the high price would tempt so many hands to go into that Species of Industry as must immediately bring down the price."[66] Smith's position was different and more analytically complete: any tendency toward equality was not of wages but of net advantages associated with the job:

The whole of the advantages and disadvantages of the different employments of labour and stock must, in the same neighborhood, be either perfectly equal or continually tending to inequality. If . . . there was any employment evidently either more or less advantageous than the rest, so many people would crowd into it in the one case, and so many would desert it in the other, that its advantages would soon return to the level of other employments.[67]

Adam Smith's treatment of wage differentials, one of the best analyses of that topic ever undertaken, offers an outstanding illustration of his factual completeness and insightfulness into contemporary economic institutions. Noting that wage differentials arise "partly from certain circumstances in the employments themselves, which, either really, or at least in the imaginations of men, make up for a small pecuniary gain in some, and counterbalance a great one in others; and partly from the policy of Europe, which no-where leaves things at perfect liberty," he concluded that the principal conditions accounting for different remunerations were "first, the agreeableness or disagreeableness of the employments themselves; secondly, the easiness and cheapness, or the difficulty and expense of learning them; thirdly, the constancy or inconstancy of employment in them; fourthly, the small or great trust which must be reposed in those who exercise them; and fifthly, the probability or improbability of success in them."

These five circumstances, Smith stressed, although they "occasion considerable inequalities in the wages of labour and profits of stock, occasion none in the whole of the advantages and disadvantages, real or imaginary, of the different employments of either. The nature of those circumstances is such, that they make up for a small pecuniary gain in some, and counter-balance a great one in others." However, he added, for equality of advantages and disadvantages to take place, three things were necessary in addition to perfect freedom. The employments had to be long established and well known, since where all other things were equal, wages tended to be higher in new trades than in old ones; the employments must be in an ordinary or natural state, with demand for labor being neither unusually buoyant nor unusually slack; and the employments must be the principal occupations of those so engaged since "when a person derives his subsistence from one employment, which does not occupy the greater part of his time; in the intervals of his leisure he is often willing to work at another for less wages than would otherwise suit the nature of the employment." [68]

Such were the circumstances underlying wage differentials even under conditions of perfect liberty. "But the policy of Europe," Smith added, "by not leaving things at perfect liberty, occasions other inequalities of much greater importance." It does so in three ways: "First, by restraining the competition in some employments to a smaller number than would otherwise be disposed to enter into them; secondly, by increasing it in others beyond what it naturally would be; and, thirdly, by obstructing the free circulation of labour and stock, both from employment to employment and from place to place." [69]

Adam Smith was a vigorous defender of high wages, both on economic and ethical grounds. "Our merchants," he noted, "frequently complain of the high wages of British labour as the cause of their manufactures being undersold in foreign markets; but they are silent about the high profits of stock. . . . The high profits of British stock, however, may contribute towards raising the price of British manufactures in many cases as much, and in some perhaps more, than the high wages of British labour." Moreover, "the liberal reward of labour . . . as it is the effect of increasing wealth, so it is the cause of increasing population. To complain of it is to lament over the necessary effect and cause of the greatest public prosperity." [70]

From an economic point of view, Smith argued that higher wages encouraged worker productivity, thus presenting an early version of the economy of high wages argument and refuting Petty's contention that higher wages would mean a smaller quantity of labor forthcoming. He reasoned: "A plentiful subsistence increases the bodily strength of the labourer, and the comfortable hope of bettering his condition, and of ending his days perhaps in ease and plenty, animates him to exert that strength to the utmost. Where wages are high, accordingly, we shall always find the workmen more active, diligent, and expeditious, than where they are low." [71]

Smith's argument in favor of high wages was not limited to economic considerations. It was also ethically grounded in the belief that society ought to provide well for its laboring class. Laborers, he stressed, constituted a majority of the population, and their efforts were at the base of English prosperity. It was, therefore, only right and proper that they should be entitled to a decent standard of living. [72]

Smith's extension of wage analysis from positive to normative considerations, and the facility with which he spoke of what ought to be, was at one with his conception of political economy as but one aspect of moral philosophy. His prescriptive pronouncements on wages and his strong interest in short-run economic problems of the labor market stem from a deep concern for the worker, which extended well beyond narrow economic boundaries.

LABOR AS A HUMAN CONDITION

There is perhaps no better illustration of the catholicity of Adam Smith's thought and of his special interest in the worker and the quality of his life than the reservations that he attached to the idea of economic specialization and division of labor in connection with its effects on the human condition. In his *Lectures* of 1763, he had already stressed that "when the mind is employed about a variety of objects, it is somehow expanded and enlarged, and on this account, a country artist is generally acknowledged to have a range of thoughts more above a city one. . . . It is remarkable that in every commercial nation the low people are exceedingly stupid. . . . The rule is general; in towns they are not so intelligent as in the country, nor in a rich country as in a poor one." Other disadvantages of the commercial spirit in general, and division of labor in particular, were "that education is greatly neglected" and that "the martial spirit and military courage diminishes. By having their minds constantly employed on the arts . . . [men] grow effeminate and dastardly." [73]

In Book V of the *Wealth of Nations*, Smith crystallized these views into a devastating attack on the basic principle of division of labor. The results of specializing—performing only one or a few simple operations—was that the laborer

has no occasion to exert his understanding, or to exercise his invention in finding out expedients for removing the difficulties which never occur. He naturally loses, therefore, the habit of such exertion, and generally becomes as stupid and ignorant as it is possible for a human creature to become. The torpor of his mind renders him, not only incapable of relishing or bearing a part in any rational conversation, but of conceiving any generous, noble, or tender sentiment, and consequently of forming any just judgment concerning many even of the ordinary duties of private life. . . . His dexterity at his own particular trade seems, in this manner, to be acquired at the expence of his intellectual, social, and martial virtues.[74]

The vigor and sharpness of this criticism of division of labor would not, perhaps, be so compelling were it not for the great significance that Smith attached to the principle in Book I, where the division of labor was posited as the source of the "greatest improvement in the productive powers of labour, and the greater part of the skill, dexterity, and judgment with which it is any where directed, or applied."[75] In turn it accounted "for the superior affluence and abundance commonly possessed even by the lowest and most despised member of civilized society, compared with what the most respected and active savage can attain to in spite of so much oppressive inequality."[76] Smith's emphasis on the economic division of labor was unique. Although the idea itself was by no means original with him, "nobody," as Schumpeter observed, "either before or after A. Smith ever thought of putting such a burden upon division of labor. With A. Smith it is practically the only factor in economic progress."[77]

The economic consequences of division of labor were the result of three circumstances: it led to an improvement in the dexterity of the workman; it helped to save time since workmen did not waste time changing tools or losing a train of thought; and it encouraged mechanization and invention because "men are much more likely to discover easier and readier methods of attaining any object, when the whole attention of their minds is directed towards that single object, than when it is dissipated among a great variety of things."[78]

As E. G. West has pointed out, Smith's argument of Book I "clearly suggests that the division of labour enhances man's mental stature" as well as his physical productivity, which, in turn, increases the quantity of goods produced. This view contrasts sharply with "Adam Smith's other views on the division of labour, . . . where, perplexingly, he seems to condemn the division of labour, in an unusual tone of outrage, for being the cause of moral degeneration." There clearly appears to be an element of contradiction here, for, as West notes, "while the argument in Book I is that workers become 'slothful and lazy' *without* the division of labour, Book V maintains that workers become 'stupid and ignorant' *with* it." West's own reconciliation of these apparently conflicting viewpoints runs in terms of the general distinction, not recognized by Adam Smith, that has since developed between economic theory and what might be called sociological evolutionism. According to Dugald Stewart, Smith's colleague and biographer, the *Wealth of Nations* was an essay in conjectural history. This "meant the systematic study of the effect of legal, institutional and general environmental conditions upon human progress." We have at several points noted the institutional realism and the sociological and historical richness of Smith's analysis. For West, it is precisely this wholeness of Smith's social science that explains his two views on division of labor. Having developed the economic principles in book 1, he proceeded in Book 5 to pursue the study of labor beyond economics into what later became industrial psychology or sociology.

It is possible that in Book V he worked back [from his general preference for rural over urban life and for agricultural workers in particular] . . . to make his social diagnosis. By contrast, however, his analysis of the productive advantages of the division of labour in Book I carried him forward buoyantly to reach conclusions about the incidental social effects which were positively favourable and optimistic. Proceeding from two different starting points, the sociological and economic methods thus yield different results.[79]

It is possible to exaggerate the contradiction in Smith's analysis. Nathan Rosenberg has suggested that "to concentrate solely on the impact of the division of labour upon the working class leads to the adoption of a very partial and misleading view of the economic and social consequences of division of labour," since Smith himself looked upon the process as one of broad social significance.[80] "In a civilized state," Smith noted,

though there is little variety in the occupations of the greater part of individuals, there is an almost infinite variety in those of the whole society. These varied occupations present an almost infinite variety of objects to the contemplation of those few, who, being attached to no particular occupation themselves, have leisure and inclination to examine the occupations of other people. The contemplation of so great a variety of objects necessarily exercises their minds in endless comparisons and combinations, and renders their understandings, in an extraordinary degree, both acute and comprehensive.[81]

Rosenberg's reconciliation of Smith's views on division of labor rests not on the distinction between its economic and sociological aspects but rather on that between the situation of the individual worker and the general character of the social system. For him, Smith's analysis suggests that although the intellectual attainment of most of the workers is quite low,

the sum total of the occupations in society presents extraordinary opportunities for the detached and contemplative philosophers. Although then the *modal* level of understanding is very low, the *highest* levels of scientific attainment permitted by the extensive specialization in the production of knowledge are quite remarkable. The *collective* intelligence of the civilized society,

THE LABOR ECONOMICS OF ADAM SMITH

then, is very great and presents unique and unprecedented opportunities for further technical progress.[82]

Smith's criticisms of the effects of the division of labor on the worker came in his chapter on the education of youth. His purpose was to point out that the deleterious effects of division of labor could be overcome or eliminated by governmental programs supporting educational or cultural programs in which the laboring poor could participate. No doctrinaire advocate of laissez-faire, Smith emphasized that "the education of the common people requires . . . in a civilized and commercial society, the attention of the public more than that of people of some rank and fortune."[83] More important, surely, than the question of the consistency or inconsistency of Smith's thought on the question of division of labor is the broad social concern he showed for the total development of the worker as a person.

This concern was further manifested in a variety of criticisms of and proposals for public policies toward workers. For example, Smith's objection to the laws of apprenticeship was based not only on the allocative inefficiencies associated with the immobility of labor and other market rigidities resulting from those laws, but was also grounded in the belief that they had a deleterious effect upon the worker as an individual member of society. Not the structure of the labor market but rather the character of the individual worker was at issue. Smith wrote that journeymen who work by the piece were likely to be industrious because they saw direct benefits from their exertions. But apprentices were likely to be idle because they received no direct benefits:

In the inferior employments, the sweets of labour consist altogether in the recompense of labour. They who are soonest in a condition to enjoy the sweets of it, are likely soonest to conceive a relish for it, and to acquire the early habit of industry. A young man naturally conceives an aversion to labour, when for a long time he receives no benefit from it. . . . But a young man would practice with much more diligence and attention, if from the beginning he wrought as a journeyman, being paid in proportion to the little work which he could execute, and paying in his turn for the materials which he might sometimes spoil through awkwardness and inexperience.[84]

Smith was also critical of the laws of settlement, through which the relief of the poor was administered on a parish basis. These laws, he believed, by preventing the free flow of labor from one parish to another, accounted for "the very unequal price of labour which we frequently find in England in places at no great distance from one another" and thus made it impossible for the impersonal system of market prices to reconcile public and private interests. The essential feature of Smith's attack on the laws of settlement was that they represented an infringement on the natural liberty of citizens generally and of workers in particular. "To remove a man who has committed no misdemeanor from the parish where he chuses to reside," he wrote, "is an evident violation of natural liberty and justice."[85] By natural liberty, Smith evidently had in mind the freedom of the worker to seek employment without governmental restrictions. His plea was to repeal existing laws so that workers who were laid off could travel anywhere in Great Britain or Ireland to find employment.

Despite his objections to legislative and other restrictions on the free play of market forces, Smith's sympathy with the position of the laborer is evident in his general tolerance of combinations of workmen, which he described as "defensive combinations" offsetting the earlier combinations of employers, and in his explicit remark about wage regulation that "when the regulation . . . is in favour of the workmen, it is always just and equitable; but it is sometimes otherwise when in favour of the masters." On the whole, Smith believed that the interest of wage earners was "strictly connected with the interest of the society."[86]

Adam Smith's criticisms of the laws of apprenticeship and settlement were not based on any nihilist attitude toward government generally, in favor of an undiluted program of laissez-faire, but were grounded in his conviction that those laws and others prevented the dominant force of self-interest from working itself out in socially desirable ways. As Nathan Rosenberg has rightly emphasized, the *Wealth of Nations* was not simply a defense of laissez-faire but was "a search for an institutional scheme which will establish and enforce an identity of interests between the public and private spheres," and much of its analysis was directed toward finding "the ways in which appropriate institutions contribute to the productivity of the human agent. . . . Appropriate institutions increase both the *motivation* and the *capacity* of the human agent whereas inappropriate institutions detract from these things."[87]

The pertinence of Rosenberg's remarks is also illustrated in Smith's treatment of slavery. His analysis was directed toward showing the inefficiency and unprofitability of that institution and represented, according to David Brion Davis, a "significant contribution to the antislavery cause." As Davis has pointed out, the Enlightenment "disseminated ideas that could serve the defender of slavery as well as the abolitionist. If the main current of secular thought ran against any institution that arbitrarily deprived men of liberty and happiness, discussions of servitude, prior to the 1760's tended to be cautiously abstract and hedged with qualifications."[88] Not so, however, the work of Adam Smith. In his *Theory of the Moral Sentiments,* published in 1759, he asserted without qualification: "There is not a negro from the coast of Africa who does not . . . possess a degree of magnanimity which the soul of his sordid master is too often scarce capable of conceiving."[89]

In the *Wealth of Nations*, Smith continued his attack upon slavery. It was, he said, an inefficient system from an economic point of view, because by destroying the possibility of property ownership, it interfered with the incentive to work: "A person who can acquire no property, can have no other interest but to eat as much, and to labour as little as possible."[90]

Smith undoubtedly abhorred slavery on moral grounds, but it was his conviction that, because of basic imperfections in human nature, an end to slavery would have to be based on an appeal to self-interest. Magnanimity alone could not be expected to put an end to slavery: "The late resolution of the Quakers in Pennsylvania to set at liberty all their negro slaves, may satisfy us that their number cannot be very great. Had they made any considerable part of their property, such a resolution could never have been agreed to."[91] Smith believed that economic causes explained the decline of serfdom in Europe. The great landlords came to understand that their own interests would be advanced by giving the worker the incentive associated with possession and ownership. "Those laws and customs so favourable to yeomanry," he concluded, "have perhaps contributed more to the present grandeur of England, than all their boasted regulations of commerce taken together."[92]

For Smith, the ownership of property, because of its connection with the incentive to work, was a principal basis of economic efficiency. He criticized corporations not only because of their interference with free trade but also because the separation of management from ownership led to internal inefficiencies within the company. Managers, he believed, would not be as careful as owners were with their own money.[93] On the other hand, because of the close connection between property ownership and the quality of the human effort expended in the economic process, the small proprietorship was the ideal unit of business organization. Smith was referring specifically to agriculture, but his message must have extended, in his mind, to the entire economic sphere: "A small proprietor . . . who knows every part of his little territory, who views it all with the affection which property, especially small property, naturally inspires, and who upon that account takes pleasure not only in cultivating but in adorning it, is generally of all improvers the most industrious, the most intelligent, and the most successful."[94]

Adam Smith's work in the field of labor constitutes a rich body of theoretical, historical, and institutional literature—one aimed not only at enhancing understanding of the natural laws of the economic process but also full of policy recommendations designed to produce an institutional structure that would best reconcile public and private interests. The problems he dealt with ranged over the whole field of labor and industrial relations. His occasional inconsistencies of thought are easily explainable in terms of the wide range of his interests. "Traces of every conceivable sort of doctrine are to be found in that most catholic book," Jacob Viner once remarked, "and an economist must have peculiar theories indeed who cannot quote from the *Wealth of Nations* to support his special purposes."[95] His successors would have less difficulty in this respect, for they would considerably narrow their range of interests, and the economist's approach to the study of labor in the nineteenth century would be of a fundamentally different character from that of Adam Smith.[96]

THE CLASSICAL APPROACH

"The classical economists," as John Maynard Keynes pointed out, was a term coined by Marx "to cover Ricardo and James Mill and their *predecessors*, that is to say for the founders of the theory which culminated in the Ricardian economics." But Keynes himself used the term to include "the *followers* of Ricardo, those, that is to say, who adopted and perfected the theory of the Ricardian economics, including (for example) J. S. Mill, Marshall, Edgeworth and Professor Pigou."[1] From the standpoint of this study, the Keynesian definition is the more germane. Indeed in terms of the study of labor, Ricardian economics represents the beginnings of the classical system. Both the general approach taken to the subject and the specific methodology Ricardo employed were distinctly different from those of Adam Smith; moreover the Ricardian system set the tone for much of the subsequent work in economics throughout the nineteenth and early twentieth centuries. It was the thesis of Joseph A. Schumpeter that Ricardian economics represented a detour in the history of economic thought. If that is so, it was a detour of magnificent proportions, and one from which the main road was found only many years later.[2] In view of his influence on the subsequent development of economics, it might be more accurate to say that "Adam Smith was not the father but only the grandfather of the classical theory of economics and political economy; its father was Ricardo."[3]

THE RICARDIAN INFLUENCE

Born in England in 1772 to a family of Dutch-Jewish background, David Ricardo followed in his father's footsteps and became a stockbroker at an early age. While still in his twenties, he acquired a sizable fortune on the London Stock Exchange and subsequently bought a country estate in Gloucestershire and became a member of Parliament. From about 1810 until his death in 1823, his professional interests and energies were largely focused on the study of economics, both in terms of formal abstract analysis and specific policy proposals in a number of fields, including that for which he is perhaps best known: the effort to repeal the protective tariffs known as the English Corn Laws, in connection with which he developed the theory of international comparative advantage. He was and is generally regarded as the outstanding English economist of his time.

Ricardo's influence on the study of labor was fourfold. First, he made distribution the central question in economics. "To determine the laws which regulate . . . distribution," he wrote, "is the principal problem in Political Economy."[4] It is difficult to exaggerate the difference between Smith and Ricardo on this point. Smith's primary concern was to determine the causes of the annual wealth of the nation—that is, the size of the national income and the forces contributing to its growth. Distribution was thus a decidedly secondary consideration. Ricardo, on the other hand, although he devoted some attention to the problems of economic growth, took the size of the national income for granted in his analysis of its distribution:

Political Economy [he wrote to Malthus] you think is an enquiry into the nature and causes of wealth—I think it should rather be called an enquiry into the laws which determine the division of the produce of industry amongst the classes who concur in its formation. No law can be laid down respecting quantity, but a tolerably correct one can be laid down respecting proportions. Every day I am more satisfied that the former enquiry is vain and delusive, and the latter only the true object of the science.[5]

Second, Ricardo importantly influenced economic methodology. He produced in his *Principles* a highly abstract treatise that was largely devoid of explicit references to institutions, history, and social change—devoid of the social philosophy that so permeates *Wealth of Nations*. And although John Stuart Mill was later to include "applications to social philosophy" as a subtitle to his major treatise in an apparent effort to recapture some of the spirit, and perhaps the appeal, of Smith, classical economics after Ricardo became increasingly abstract and rigorously logical. Nineteenth-century economics was to be Ricardian economics in this respect, and Ricardo's economics was altogether economic theory. Moreover his economic framework was much narrower than that of Adam Smith and was essentially limited to conditions that today we would call purely competitive. Ricardo was the first to use the word *laws* in connection with economic activity, and he sought to strengthen the character of economics as a science.[6] One way he did this was to abstract, as Adam Smith had not done, from the influence of all monopolistic, customary, or other noncompetitive forces. "In speaking, then," he specified, "of commodities, of their exchangeable value, and of the laws which regulate their relative prices, we mean always such commodities only as can be increased in quantity by the exertion of human industry, and on the production of which competition operates without restraint."[7]

Third, Ricardo solidified the identification of labor as a factor of production with labor as a social class. To some extent, of course, the idea of social classes underlay Adam Smith's analysis, but Ricardo's employment of the class concept was much more explicit: "The produce of the earth—all that is derived from its surface by the united application of labour, machinery, and capital, is divided among three classes of the community, namely, the proprietor of the land, the owner of the stock or capital necessary for its cultivation, and the labourers by whose industry it is cultivated."[8] This concept of the community had some permanence in economic theory throughout the classical period.

The primacy of distribution in classical economics, especially in the Ricardian system, probably had much to do with the prominence of social classes in economic theory. In any event, the class concept as employed was deficient from an analytical standpoint in that there seems to have been a confusion between groups of people interacting socially and manifesting common modes of thought and behavior (sociological classes) and economic agents whose contributions to the process of production are of a common type (factor classification in economic theory). For purposes of economic analysis, an agent who is hired to apply human effort to the productive process is categorized as labor—irrespective of his degree of education, skill, or social class. But as Frank Knight has observed, "If distribution is a phenomenon of competitive valuation, classes have nothing to do with it." [9]

It seems reasonable to suppose that attachment to the three-class system was partially the reason why classical economics failed to make a clear distinction between interest and profits, which, in the classical analysis, were usually lumped together as one return to one class, the capitalists. Moreover just when general economic theory eliminated the class concept and returned to a socially undifferentiated concept of labor—which happened with the development of marginal productivity analysis—early specialists in labor problems took it up. A leading labor text in 1905 held, for example, that "for the masses, indeed, it is true and increasingly true, that once a wage earner always a wage earner. This permanency of status makes the labor problem in one respect a class struggle." [10] As a result, for many years the term *labor* as used in the field of labor problems or labor economics had a narrower connotation than the term *labor* as employed in general economic theory.

A fourth way in which Ricardo influenced the economist's study of labor was in his emphasis on tendencies in the economic process, with primacy being given to what might be called the long run. It would not be correct to say that Ricardo was disinterested in the short-run economic problems and policies of the England of his time. On the contrary, it was precisely such policy-oriented problems as the Corn Laws, taxation, and monetary issues that first stimulated his interest in economics and led him to serious study of Smith's *Wealth of Nations*. Nor did Ricardo fail to maintain his interest in economic policy throughout the *Principles*, as, for example, when he addressed himself to such topics as the poor laws or the short-run effects on labor of the introduction of machinery. But his attention to such topics was, compared to Adam Smith's, cursory and underdeveloped, and his treatment of them lacked the institutional and the empirical realism of the

Wealth of Nations. Indeed Schumpeter labeled Ricardo's tendency to pronounce upon policy questions on the basis of conclusions that emerged from analysis almost as tautologies—by taking so much as given—as "the Ricardian Vice."[11] Much more than Adam Smith, Ricardo was interested in the long-term effects of economic policies and the long-term workings out of economic principles under assumed competitive conditions.

This preference for the long run had important consequences for the economist's study of labor, for it meant that the phenomena of actual markets could often be ignored in favor of a reliance upon tendencies. A good example of this is Ricardo's treatment of wages. The fundamental postulate of the Ricardian wage analysis was the proposition that labor was similar to commodities from the economic point of view. "Labour," Ricardo wrote, "like all other things produced and sold, has its natural and its market price":

The natural price of labour is the price which is necessary to enable the labourers, one with another, to subsist and to perpetuate their race, without either increase or diminution.

The market price of labour is the price which is really paid for it, from the natural operation of the proportion of the supply to the demand; labour is dear when it is scarce and cheap when it is plentiful. However much the market price of labour may deviate from its natural price, it has, like commodities, a tendency to conform to it.[12]

Since the tendency was for the market price to approach the natural price, the market price lost significance. As one student of the subject has remarked, "The center of attention for the investigating theorist became precisely this natural price of labor, a focal point around which market prices fluctuated."[13] The fluctuations themselves, it was widely felt, could be dismissed. For several generations of English economists, the facts of the labor market ceased to be of interest. "Political economy is not greedy of facts," Nassau Senior is said to have claimed. "Political economy is independent of facts." This was so because, as Wesley Mitchell later remarked, "to demonstrate that the conclusions of political economy were at variance with notorious facts did not discredit the conclusions. The tendencies it dealt with really existed though they might not be obvious; those tendencies would stand out clearly if real life answered to the economists' hypothesis; the conclusions were consistent with the postulates however the facts might stand."[14]

All of these characteristics of Ricardian economics—the emphasis on distribution, competitive conditions, the long run, and labor as a social class as well as a factor of production—are reflected in the approach taken by most other economists to the study of labor throughout the greater part of the nineteenth century. The core of that approach was the analysis of long-term wages under assumed competitive conditions.

Although he had little interest in what might today be called the institutionalist problems of labor and industrial relations and did not share Adam Smith's great interest in and sympathy for the worker in the emerging industrial society, labor was nonetheless central to Ricardo's economics. It was, first of all, the basis of his value theory. Quoting with approval Adam Smith's teachings that "labour was the first price—the original purchase-money that was paid for all things" and that "it is natural that what is usually the product of two days' or two hours' labour should be worth double of what is usually the produce of one day's or one hour's labour," Ricardo emphasized that "this is really the foundation of the exchangeable value of all things, excepting those which cannot be increased by human industry," and "a doctrine of the utmost importance in political economy."[15]

But Ricardo was not altogether satisfied with Smith's formulation of the theory of value and labor's role in it. Smith, he believed, had confused the labor bestowed on or embodied in a product with what that labor could command in the marketplace:

Sometimes he speaks of corn, at other times of labour, as a standard measure; not the quantity of labour bestowed on the production of any object, but the quantity which it can command in the market: as if these were two equivalent expressions, and as if, because a man's labour had become doubly efficient, and he could therefore produce twice the quantity of a commodity he would necessarily receive twice the former quantity in exchange for it.[16]

If that were true, Ricardo argued, the quantity of labor embodied in a commodity and the quantity of labor that commodity would purchase would be equal. But, he held,

they are not equal; the first is under many circumstances an invariable standard, indicating correctly the variations of other things; the latter is subject to as many fluctuations as the commodities compared with it. Adam Smith, after most ably showing the insufficiency of a variable medium, such as gold and silver, for the purpose of determining the varying value of other things, has himself, by fixing on corn or labour, chosen a medium no less variable.[17]

Agreeing with Smith that the values of gold and silver are subject to variation from many sources, Ricardo nonetheless insisted that the values of corn and labor were hardly less variable and concluded that "it is correct to say, as Adam Smith had previously said, 'that the proportion between the quantities of labour necessary for acquiring different objects seems to be the only circumstance which can afford any rule for exchanging them for one another.' "[18]

Another difficulty Ricardo had with Smith's value theory was in the distinction Smith drew between the primitive state and the English economy of his own day, in which not only labor but also land and capital contributed to "the component parts of price." For Smith, relative prices in a primitive society were determined by labor alone. "If among a nation of hunters, for example, it usually costs twice the labour to kill a beaver which it does to kill a deer, one beaver should naturally exchange for, or be worth two deer." But once land has been converted to private property and capital has arisen, prices are determined by wages, rents, and profits (or interest, in the modern sense). For the England of his time, Smith posited not the labor theory of value but a cost of production theory of price.

For Ricardo, Smith's distinction between the primitive and contemporary societies was unacceptable. According to him,

> Even in that early state to which Adam Smith refers, some capital, though possibly made and accumulated by the hunter himself, would be necessary to enable him to kill his game. Without some weapon, neither the beaver nor the deer could be destroyed, and therefore the value of these animals would be regulated, not solely by the time and labour necessary to their destruction, but also by the time and labour necessary for providing the hunter's capital, the weapon, by the aid of which their destruction was effected.[19]

But capital, while found in some form in even the most primitive social settings, was itself reducible to labor. Indeed the entire economic process by which goods are created and marketed, is ultimately, according to Ricardo, reducible to labor—and not less so for industrial societies than for primitive ones: "If we look to a state of society in which greater improvements have been made, and in which arts and commerce flourish, we shall still find that commodities vary in value conformably with this principle: in estimating the exchangeable value of stockings, for example, we shall find that their value, comparatively with other things, depends on the total quantity of labour necessary to manufacture them and bring them to market."[20]

Historians of economics do not agree on whether Ricardo's theory of value was a labor theory—that is, one in which the relative values of commodities are determined only by the relative quantities of labor necessary for their production. As Professor Stigler has noted, "A considerable number of historians of economics have given a flat affirmative answer to this question," but some "more careful historians of doctrine have recognized the several and important departures from a pure labor theory that Ricardo emphatically made."[21] Ricardo, for example, spoke at one point of labor "as being the foundation of all value, and the relative quantity of labour as *almost* exclusively determining the relative values of commodities." He also spoke of situations in which the ratio of fixed capital to labor varies between commodities: "This difference in the degree of durability of fixed capital, and this variety in the proportions in which the two sorts of capital may be combined, introduce another cause, besides the greater or less quantity of labour necessary to produce commodities, for the variations in their relative value—this cause is the rise or fall in the value of labour."[22] Based on this and other qualifications offered by Ricardo, Stigler concluded that there is "no basis for the belief that Ricardo had an *analytical* labor theory of value, for quantities of labor are *not* the only determinants of relative values."

Such a theory would have to reduce all obstacles to production to expenditures of labor or assert the irrelevance or nonexistence of nonlabor obstacles, and Ricardo does not embrace either view. On the other hand, there is no doubt that he held what may be called an *empirical* labor theory of value, that is, a theory that the relative quantities of labor required in production are the dominant determinants of relative values.[23]

Ricardo is often characterized as presenting a pessimistic outlook for society in general and for laborers in particular. There is some basis for this characterization, for Ricardo's emphasis was on the long run, and the prospects for long-run growth were not good. "At the heart of the Ricardian system," as Mark Blaug has noted, "is the notion that economic growth must sooner or later peter out owing to scarcity of natural resources."[24] Moreover wages in the long run would tend toward levels just sufficient "to enable the labourers, one with another, to subsist and to perpetuate their race, without either increase or diminution."[25] It was under the influence of Ricardian (and Malthusian) teachings on population and labor that wage theory became popularized in terms of the iron law of wages, while economics itself was widely known as the dismal science.

But the elements of pessimism underlying the Ricardian system have often been exaggerated. Most of the classical economists shared a vision of the long-term end to economic growth and the emergence of the stationary state. The difference between Smith and Ricardo on economic growth, and labor's role in it, is more one of emphasis than of fundamental doctrine. Ricardo agreed with Smith that wages may tend to be above their natural rate and, in an improving society, for an indefinite period may be constantly above it. And he was not pessimistic about the prospects for growth in the foreseeable future.[26] But he did not believe that all progress would necessarily benefit the workers in the short run. In particular, "the discovery and use of machinery may . . . be injurious to the labouring class, as some of their number . . . [may] be thrown out of employment."[27]

On the question of population and labor supply, Ricardo was much less pessimistic than Malthus, especially in terms of the ability of the laboring poor to change their own situation. Subsistence levels of living were not, he emphasized, determined once for all time by physical or biological needs but were culturally determined and influenced by the progress of civilization. It was possible, he believed, for the poor to raise their own standards gradually and to help ensure themselves against the greatest calamities associated with overpopulation: "The friends of humanity cannot but wish that in all countries the labouring classes should have a taste for comforts and enjoyments, and that they should be stimulated by all legal means in their exertions to procure them. There cannot be better security against a superabundant population."[28]

Ricardo is generally credited with being the first economist to use the marginalist approach, although the use of that term, as well as its general applicability beyond land economics and rent theory, came much later. The general theory of marginal productivity was implicit in Ricardo's theory of rent. As Mark Blaug has noted,

Ricardo had shown that the final dose of labor-and-capital on an intensively-used rent-yielding piece of land adds nothing to rent but consists solely of wages and interest, rent being due to the superior productivity of the intramarginal units. Wicksteed, Wicksell, and John Bates Clark . . . [later] realized that there is nothing unique about a no-rent margin; when land is the variable factor and labor-and-capital is the fixed factor, the margin will be a no-wage, no-interest margin. With that insight, the general marginal productivity theory of distribution was born, and to Ricardo's other accomplishments must . . . be added that of having invented marginal analysis.[29]

ECONOMIC THEORY VERSUS ECONOMIC POLICY

If it is generally true that "for over half a century Ricardo dominated economic thinking in Britain," there is one significant exception to that generalization.[30] This was in the failure of post-Ricardian economics to perpetuate what Schumpeter called "the Ricardian Vice": the tendency to pronounce upon policy questions on the basis of an analytical framework from which so much institutional data had been abstracted and in which so much was taken as given.[31] The tendency of nineteenth-century theorists to follow Ricardo's lead in such matters as the general neglect of the problem of maintaining aggregate demand, the emphasis on cost of production as the source of value and determinant of price, or the merits of deductive methodology over empirical or historical research was not matched in an extension or continuation of the marriage of theory and policy that had been characteristic of both the Smithian and Ricardian systems. On the contrary, the view came widely to be held that the economist's conclusions, "whatever be their generality and truth, do not authorize him in adding a single syllable of advice" on practical problems.[32]

The transition from the Ricardian vice was the result of a development occurring in economic thought during the second quarter of the nineteenth century, which would condition the discipline throughout the remainder of the century and which, in fact, has continued to exert some influence up to the present. This was the introduction of "explicit, systematic attempts to distinguish and separate off the 'positive' propositions of the 'science of political economy' from policy recommendations and ethical and political postulates, or doctrines advocating policy objectives," or, as it later came to be called, the art of political economy.[33]

Although the considerations and assumptions underlying this distinction probably received some implicit support from the tendencies of such earlier writers as Adam Smith to emphasize the natural character of the economic process and of Ricardo to speak about the laws of political economy, neither Smith nor Ricardo made any explicit distinction between economics as a science and economics as an art. On the contrary, Smith and other early writers called political economy a science while in fact defining it in terms that by late nineteenth-century standards would have made it an art.[34] While it is undoubtedly true that Ricardo's "emphatic, if methodologically unselfconscious abstractions did much to transform 'the simple system of natural liberty' into a set of simplificatory postulates or a neutral model," it is also true that Ricardo's economics was as clearly policy oriented as was Smith's and that his theory and his policy recommendations were mutually consistent and reinforcing.[35]

According to Sidgwick, the distinction between economics as a science and as an art was due "to the combined influence of Senior and J. S. Mill and cannot be traced further back."[36] In one of his earliest essays, John Stuart Mill criticized what he called "the vulgar notion of the nature and object of Political Economy. . . . That Political Economy is a science which teaches, or professes to teach, in what manner a nation may be made rich." Admitting that "this notion of which constitutes the science, is in some degree countenanced by the title and arrangement which Adam Smith gave to his invaluable work . . . *An Inquiry into the Nature and Causes of the Wealth of Nations,*" Mill's criticism was that this conception of political economy "confounds the essentially distinct, though closely connected, ideas of *science* and *art*." The first, he said, "deals in facts, the other in precepts. Science is a collection of *truths*; art, a body of *rules*, or directions for conduct. The language of science is, This is, or, This is not; This does, or does not happen. The language of art is, Do this; Avoid that. . . . If, therefore,

Political Economy be a science, it cannot be a collection of practical rules.[37] Mill then specified more fully the character of the science of political economy: "It does not treat of the whole of man's nature as modified by the social state, nor of the whole conduct of man in society. It is concerned with him solely as a being who desires to possess wealth. . . . It predicts only such of the phenomena of the social state as take place in consequence of the pursuit of wealth. It makes entire abstraction of every other human passion or motive."[38]

Mill's purpose was to explain, and perhaps to justify, the abstract method that Ricardo had employed. Political economy, he said, reasons "from assumptions, not from facts. It is built upon hypotheses, strictly analogous to those which, under the name of definitions, are the foundations of the other abstract sciences. . . . Political Economy, therefore, reasons from *assumed* premises—from premises which might be totally without foundation in fact. . . . The conclusions of Political Economy, consequently, like those of geometry, are only true, as the common phrase is, *in the abstract*; that is, they are only true under certain suppositions."[39]

This explicit recognition of the highly restrictive character of the assumptions on which the economist's reasoning was based, together with the strongly held belief in the necessity of such assumptions for rigorous analysis, provided the basis for the widely shared skepticism concerning the applicability of the economist's conclusions to questions of public policy. As Mill emphasized,

So far as it is known, or may be presumed, that the conduct of mankind in the pursuit of wealth is under the collateral influence of any other of the properties of our nature than the desire of obtaining the greatest quantity of wealth with the least labour and self-denial, the conclusions of Political Economy will so far fail of being applicable to the explanation or prediction of real events, until they are modified by a correct allowance for the degree of influence exercised by the other cause.[40]

The difficulties involved in taking into account these other causes—Mill elsewhere referred to them as "disturbing causes"—were great because of the "uncertainties inherent in the nature of these complex phenomena, and arising from the impossibility of being quite sure that all the circumstances of the particular case are known to us sufficiently in detail." Some of these circumstances might be the result of "some other law of human nature," in which case "the mere political economist, he who has studied no science but Political Economy, if he attempts to apply his science to practice, will fail."[41]

In his later work, Mill did not generally adhere to his own early and quite rigid distinction between economics as a science and as an art. He made it clear, for example, in the subtitle to his major work, *Prin-*

ciples of Political Economy with some of their applications to Social Philosophy, that he conceived of economics in a somewhat wider context than that of pure science. But his cautions and reservations concerning the difficulty of taking into account all of the special circumstances surrounding a particular case, and therefore of applying the principles of political economy to policy objectives, had a profound, lasting effect on nineteenth-century economics. Unless the economist undertook the responsibility to "sift and scrutinize the details of every specific experiment" in social policy, he "must rest contented to take no share in practical politics; to have no opinion, or to hold it with extreme modesty, on the applications which should be made of his doctrines to existing circumstances."[42]

A point related to the developments that led to a separation of the science of political economy from the art of applying it to concrete problems was the reinforcement of the idea that economic reasoning should be limited to cases in which "competition operates without restraint."[43]

Here, then, is a second reason for the economists' unwillingness to pronounce on policy questions. On the one hand, it was necessary, for analytical reasons, to postulate pure competition in order to produce order out of what would otherwise be chaos and to be able to reduce particular cases to "any assignable law." But none of the classical economists was so naive as not to be aware of the presence of monopolistic forces that interfered with or prevented competition from working itself out in the market, of the influence on the economic system of a host of nonmarket institutions, and of the force of custom. Nor were the greatest economists uninterested in problems, especially in the field of labor, for which the competitive model was obviously ill suited. Nassau Senior, who denied that the economist was entitled to "adding a single syllabus of advice" on practical problems, was perhaps the outstanding example of a leading figure in classical economics with a strong interest in policy questions, and he worked on virtually every aspect of contemporary labor problems. Probably his interest began with his desire to reform the poor law. His own appointment to the Poor Law Commission in 1832, where he "appears to have been the chief analytical force" and which he "carried . . . beyond the field of a mere Government inquiry into the sphere of social economics, was on the basis of his recommendation as a "practical Political Economist, who has written well on the subject."[44] The Poor Law Reform Act of 1834 was largely the result of the work of this commission and overcame what had long been some of Senior's principal objections to poor law relief—most importantly, by eliminating outdoor relief for the ablebodied and thereby drawing a distinction

between the laborer, who would thereafter be forced to seek his liveli-
hood in the market, and the pauper, who would be forced to work for
a minimal maintenance in an institutionalized setting.

Senior also served as a member and principal draftsman of the final
report of the Commission on the Distress of the Hand-Loom Weav-
ers. The report, submitted in 1841, contained an extensive analysis of
the economics of unemployment, together with a series of policy recommendations that included governmental promotion of education
and better housing for the laborers. Clearly Senior had found it
difficult to maintain in practice the division that he had posited between economics as a science and economics as an art, for the report
relied heavily on the analytical concepts and reasoning of economic
theory. Far from separating economic theory from practical problems, the work of Senior and others has convinced Stigler, at least,
that "the technical apparatus of the classical economics was best precisely in those areas, and on precisely those subjects, where the issues
were posed by concrete problems of the day."[45]

Clearly there is a paradox here. Senior denied the qualifications of
economists to speak on policy questions on the grounds that economics is a hypothetical and not a factual science. But later he applied
economic analysis to social problems and formulated policy proposals.
The explanation of this apparent inconsistency is that Senior, despite
his use of economics in analyzing such labor problems as the design
and administration of the poor laws, the effects of trade unions, and
technical change and unemployment, did not consider such activity to
be economics proper; rather it was part of the exercise of responsible
citizenship.[46]

Labor problems, like all other real-world problems, were not conceived of within a framework of labor economics, which might be
considered to be at one with the corpus of economic theory. On
the contrary, economics would remain a tight theoretical system, based on hypothetical premises and enjoying much of the supposed certainty of the physical sciences but clearly demarcated from
the pressing issues of the day. The problems of poverty and unemployment, economic growth and industrialization, conditions of work
and technological change stood largely apart from the economists'
theoretical systems.

The result was stultifying to the advance of economics: "There is a
considerable body of evidence that English economic thought in the
two decades before the publication of Jevons' *Theory of Political Economy* in 1871 had made very little progress." Checkland reports that
"contemporary opinion in the third quarter of the [nineteenth] century tended strongly to the view that political economy in England
seemed incapable of further substantial advance," and he attributes a

large part of this relative stagnation to the inability, or unwillingness, on the part of the classical economists to come to grips, as economists, with the social problems of the day. These areas were to be left to others—social scientists, social anthropologists and historians, economic journalists, and financiers, among others—who, with their new techniques, seemed able to tackle and solve society's problems.[47]

THE PRIMACY OF THE WAGE PROBLEM

From the standpoint of their formal theoretical systems, the classical economists approached the study of labor mainly in terms of its proportional share of the national income. For them, the question of what determined the general level of wages constituted the principal labor problem. The emphasis placed upon wages was undoubtedly the result of a number of forces. It reflected the Ricardian influence on the relative importance of distribution over production as the principal area of investigation for the economist. It was also a product of the economist's emphasis on the importance of market exchange as not only the basis of economic theory but also as the manifestation of an advanced economic society.[48]

The economy of England in the middle of the nineteenth century was a highly imperfect representation of the economist's model of a labor market. Many workers were in fact self-employed proprietors, artisans, and farmers, and many others received wages that were probably as much the result of custom as of competition. Also extramarket institutions, such as the poor laws, played a not insignificant role in distribution. On balance, it seems likely that the attention given by economists to the question of market wages was out of proportion to their actual importance as a proportion of the national income. But another factor probably counts heavily in explaining the primacy of the wage problem in classical economics: the implicit need, in an era of emerging class structure, to explain to the laboring class why it got what it did.

One of the most fundamental of the social changes that took place in England between the time of Adam Smith and that of the classical economists of the mid-nineteenth century was the emergence of a social class of laborers possessing a new capacity for political activity and other forms of activism.[49] In such a setting, the explanation of the factors involved in the determination of labor's share of the national income, and, even more importantly, of indicating the limits to which it might be raised, assumed a new importance. Despite his sympathy for the workers, it would not have occurred to Adam Smith to assert, as did Nassau Senior, that "the subject of wages" was "the most difficult and the most important of all the branches of political economy.[50] On the contrary, there is some reason to suppose that the whole question of distribution was something he added to his theory of value only after his contacts with the physiocrats in France.

Classical economic thought concerning wages centered upon the doctrine of the wages fund. It represented a theorem concerning the demand for labor rather than a theory of wages. In essence, the idea was that the demand for labor was limited by the amount of capital and would increase in proportion to it. Ricardo had defined capital as "that part of a wealth of a country which is employed in production, and consists of food, clothing, tools, raw materials, machinery, etc., necessary to give effect to labour." If the quantity of capital should increase, Ricardo added, "the market rate of wages will rise, for in proportion to the increase of capital will be the increase in the demand for labour; in proportion to the work to be done will be the demand for those who are to do it."[51]

These statements do not seem far wide of the ideas of Adam Smith on the subject, but there is a perhaps somewhat subtle yet very important difference, which affected the progress of political economy for many years to come. Smith had suggested the idea of the wages fund, or the demand for labor, but in his view it clearly was not a matter of capital alone. It also depended on revenue, or income, and was intimately associated with the idea of economic growth and industrial advancement. Following Ricardo, however, the emphasis came to be more and more narrowly focused on the proportions between capital and labor utilized in the productive process. Ricardo's disciple, James Mill, wrote: "Universally, then, we may affirm, other things remaining the same, that if the ratio which capital and population bear to one another remains the same, wages will remain the same; if the ratio which capital bears to population increases, wages will rise; if the ratio which population bears to capital increases, wages will fall."[52] James Mill's son, John Stuart, was more guarded, but did not deviate from his father's central position. The younger Mill's statement probably represents the fullest development and most mature of the classical thinking on the subject:

Wages, then, depend mainly upon the demand and supply of labour; or, as it is often expressed, on the proportion between population and capital. By population is here meant the number only of the labouring class, or rather of those who work for hire; and by capital only circulating capital, and not even the whole of that, but the part which is expended in the direct purchase of labour . . . wages not only depend upon the relative amount of capital and population, but cannot, under the rule of competition, be affected by anything else. Wages (meaning, of course, the general rate) cannot rise, but by an increase of the aggregate funds employed in hiring labourers, or by a diminution in the number of the competitors for hire; nor fall, except either by a diminution of the funds devoted to paying labour, or by an increase in the number of the labourers to be paid.[53]

Given the definition of capital that Mill has in mind here, there is nothing wrong with these statements in an ex post sense. Assuming that the number of laborers is given, wages cannot have risen, after the fact and in the aggregate, except by an increase in the funds expended upon labor. But the correctness of this reasoning rests upon its essentially tautological character. The more interesting question is what determines the increase or decrease in the annual expenditure upon labor. It is in an ex ante sense that Mill's statement presents a problem, for the classical economists saw the wages fund as predetermined both by a fixed labor-capital ratio and by the size of the capital stock.

Wages, according to the wages fund doctrine, are determined by the interaction of supply and demand. The classical economists, like the mercantilists, generally assumed a long-run labor supply curve that was infinitely elastic at the level of subsistence, so that the natural, or long-run, price of labor was a subsistence wage. By the nineteenth century, this was widely recognized to be a culturally, and not a biologically, determined level. In fact, the idea that the laboring poor might come to demand as customary a higher standard of living was frequently put forth as the best hope for their advancement. Presumably they would thereby voluntarily limit their fecundity pattern. But classical theory taught that market wages in the short run might be well above the subsistence level, however defined, depending on the buoyancy of the demand for labor, and it is precisely in this that the significance of the wages fund lies. The emphasis placed by the classical economists upon the wages fund represents a shift in focus from the natural rate of wages, which continued to be seen as a subsistence wage, to the market rate of wages and the related question of the possibility of labor's getting more than subsistence. Wage theory thereby came to be distinguished from population theory, with the interests of the economists increasingly upon the former because of its association with market processes. The failure of the wage fund theorists was, however, their inability to perceive the demand for labor in terms of market processes.

Despite the criticisms to which it has often been subjected, there are important elements of truth in the wages fund doctrine. For one, it helped to clarify the nature of capital as both an economic agent whose formation required an abstention from consumption and as a factor of production that contributed importantly to the demand for, and productivity of, labor. In this connection, the wage fund theorists were not ignorant of the significance of productivity. Senior especially emphasized that the size of the wages fund depended on the productivity of labor, which, in turn, depended on a number of factors: the laborer's skill, diligence, and strength; the climate and other natural factors; and the use of capital.[54]

All of these ideas, of course, are quite consistent with modern wage theory. What was new in the marginal productivity analysis of labor and capital, which is generally accorded the role of successor to the wages fund doctrine, was not the importance of productivity but the particular perspective from which the concept was viewed. The wages fund doctrine, to the extent that it was a theory of the demand for labor, was essentially macroeconomic in its focus.[55] The marginal productivity theory, on the other hand, is essentially microeconomic in its focus. It asks not about wages in the mass but rather about the wages of a particular employer. What has not been sufficiently emphasized by historians of economic thought is that the focus of neoclassical theory upon the margin was predicated on an earlier, or concomitant, shift in focus to the activities of the individual business firm. Like the wages fund doctrine, the marginal productivity theory relates only to the demand for labor, but it is the demand of an individual profit-maximizing business firm. On the supply side, the marginal productivity analysis added nothing new. In fact, given the same assumptions concerning the supply of labor under which the classical economists operated, the marginal productivity theory leads to the very conclusions of the classical economists: a subsistence wage rate. The marginal productivity theory teaches that employers will hire workers up to the point where the productivity of the last worker hired is equal to the wage rate, whatever that may be. Theoretically there is no reason why firms should not push employment to the point where marginal productivity is zero—except, of course, that a zero wage rate is not plausible. The point here is that the strength of the productivity theory over the wages fund doctrine is not so much in the difference in the conclusions to which it might lead as in the perspective from which it begins to reason. It starts by asking not what will be the division of national income between laborers and the recipients of other forms of income but rather how much labor will be hired by a profit-maximizing business firm. The focus is on the employment decision of the firm. This, in turn, leads to an analysis of wages based on the idea of a demand schedule for labor, which relates the numbers hired to the price of labor, a matter of primary importance to the development of a theory of wages but one never recognized as such by the wage fund theorists.

Had the classical economists paid more attention to the internal decisions and activities of business firms, they might have avoided some of the difficulties presented by the wages fund doctrine. By focusing more clearly on the question of what motivates an employer to hire labor, they would have been forced to consider the importance of labor's output, and its expected profitability, rather than placing so much emphasis upon the funds available in advance. This would have been appropriate, especially in the context of the increasing importance of the factory system and the extension and improved organization of capital markets that accompanied it. As a theory of employment at the level of the individual firm, the wages fund doctrine was not without relevance to the prefactory age. In the context of the putting-out system, for example, employment and wages to some considerable extent would be limited by the variable capital (raw materials and food, for example) that the merchant capitalist could supply to the cottagers in advance of their work's being completed and sold. But the extension of the market system, and especially of access to credit, made the wages fund doctrine increasingly anachronistic. Closer attention to activities within the firm might also have led to an earlier recognition of the substitutability of factors of production in an industrial system. One of the principal weaknesses of the wages fund doctrine was its reliance upon what seems an almost naive belief in the fixity of factor proportions in the economic process. A given increase in the quantity of labor demand was predicated on a proportional increase in the quantity of capital. Viewing labor and capital in terms of a rigid complementarity, the wages fund theorists failed to perceive the extent to which employers in an industrial economy substitute labor for capital and vice versa. And one of the key factors in a choice of that kind is clearly the price of the factor in relation to its productivity. Yet the price of labor, from the standpoint of the individual employer, was never systematically considered by the wage fund theorists. Here, probably, is the central weakness of the classical treatment not only of wages but of all forms of distribution. Concentrating on distributive shares of social class origins, they failed to perceive the idea of distribution as a phenomenon of market pricing. "The fundamental defect was clearly the failure to develop a theory of the prices of productive services."[56]

The passage of the wages fund doctrine and the emergence of modern wage theory came in connection with the increasing prominence of trade unions and bargaining power. As W. H. Hutt has pointed out, a theory of bargaining power arose alongside the classical theory of wages, but it was always more an attachment to rather than an integral part of wage theory.[57] The necessity for some attention to the question of collective bargaining and its influence on wages was mandated by the rise of trade unions in England. During the first half of the nineteenth century, the economist's emphasis, following Ricardo and Mill, remained largely on wages competitively determined. The emergence of an increasingly powerful trade union movement, however, was to make the competitive model less and less useful as a tool of analysis.

Jha has pointed to the necessary relevance of analysis to contemporary problems:

Perhaps all writing in economics . . . a very large part of it at any rate—in the last analysis is topical. . . . Contemporary economic problems suggest the subject, and the available framework of economic analysis provides the way in which the problem is approached and analyzed. Very often during the process of this scientific examination, the theoretical frames of the science, and its tools of analysis, receive an enlargement, refinement, or an overhaul.[58]

This sort of overhaul is what the trade union movement provided. Inquiries into the bargaining process provided the initial theoretical assaults on the classical theory of wages. It is precisely in the realm of the economist's study of labor that the English roots of the idea of imperfect competition are to be found.

THE CLASSICAL ECONOMISTS AND TRADE UNIONISM

As the industrial revolution in England progressed, industrial unrest became increasingly prominent. But during the first half—and to a lesser extent up until the last few decades—of the nineteenth century, the question of strikes was "generally disposed of by economists with a summary reference to the doctrine of the wage fund. Strikes could not increase the wage fund, therefore they could not enhance wages. If they should appear to raise the rate in any trade, this must be due either to a corresponding loss in the regularity of employment or to an equivalent loss in regularity or in rate, by some other trade or trades occupying a position of economical disadvantage. Hence strikes could not benefit the wage class."[59]

Commencing in the 1860s, however, a new idea began to enter theoretical discussions: the notion of indeterminacy. A procession of writers—Fleeming Jenkin, William Thornton, Francis D. Longe, Cliffe Leslie, even John Stuart Mill in 1869—gradually forced into economic theory a notion that had long been familiar to "the untutored mind of the workman": that unionism tends to introduce (or to increase) indeterminateness and that "within the range of its indeterminateness, trade unionism had a legitimate field of action, in the same way that there was a valid field for higgling in the indeterminateness of barter."[60]

Over the years, the focus of the economic writer shifted as a concomitant of the development of the discipline. Economics as a discipline developed as the focus shifted away from the philosophical-ethical or sociological-political toward the purely economic, an important

change for the economist's approach to the study of labor in the
nineteenth century. It explains, for example, why it was that "although economists from Adam Smith onwards had acknowledged the
part of trade unions in equalizing bargaining power as between individual workmen and employers, and despite growing criticism of
orthodoxy, it was long before trade unions gained more than grudg-
ing entry into economists' frames of reference."[61] Specifically
nineteenth-century economists have frequently been taken to task for
their failure to analyze trade unionism. Professor Alvin Hansen, for
example, has pointed to the tardiness with which economists came to
grips with the rise of organized labor, stating that "it was not until
Sidney and Beatrice Webb wrote their *Industrial Democracy* in 1897
that any serious economic analysis disclosing its role in a social democracy was made of this long-established institution."[62] He failed to add,
however, that when, in 1897, "serious economic analysis" of trade
unionism was undertaken by the Webbs, it was analysis quite outside
the accepted framework of economics and was the work of other than
professional economists. Analysis of unions was not yet considered to
be properly the undertaking of the economist. The Webbs were not
economists and their *Industrial Democracy* was not economic analysis, as
those terms were used at the time. How far their work was from the
economics of the day is indicated by their own words: "We analyse the
economic characteristics, not of combinations in the abstract in a
world of ideal competition, but of the actual Trade Unionism of the
present day, in the business world as we know it."[63] It is only because
of the work of the Webbs and others that the analysis of the economic
policies of trade unions later came to be included in the general study
of economics.

Wolman has noted that it was precisely in those areas with which
economists have traditionally been most concerned that the Webbs
fell short: "not in content but in the lesser emphasis they allot to the
efficiency of an economic system as the source of higher wages,
greater leisure, and advancing material standards of life."[64] It is not,
then, in economics, but "in the uncharted frontier region where History and Sociology meet" that the Webbs's most massive work was
done. Their forays into this uncharted region "revealed for the first
time the full significance of a world of movements and institutions
known, of course, to exist, but hardly thought deserving of systematic
exploration."[65] In "turning from theory to description and analysis of
institutions," as Lord Beveridge has noted, the Webbs were attempting "to place social science on a new basis." It is, indeed, in this attempt to reconstruct social science that the origins of the London
School of Economics and Political Science are to be found. Of the
school, Lord Beveridge noted that "it paid lip service to theory . . . but

its heart was elsewhere: in the study of institutions, where the heart of the Webbs was."[66]

It has seemed necessary to point out that the Webbs, as the first scholars to analyze trade unions scientifically, wanted to revolutionize social science in order to dispense with the notion that the failure of economists to pursue such analysis resulted from the economists' attitude toward unions. All too often, the alleged antipathy of the classical economists to the idea of unions is the implied reason for the so-called neglect of unions at the hands of the economists, whereas the Webbs's sympathies with unionism are well known. According to this view, economists of the period, conservative with respect to social change, frequently considered unions dangerous and unworkable. They were a conundrum for economics, therefore, until the work of the Webbs. In order to complete our review of the classical economist's study of labor, it is necessary now to look more closely at his attitude toward unions.

According to Professor Heckscher, laissez-faire had an eye to the human. The goal of the mercantilists, like that of the classical economists, had been the common good. But the common good had not been, as Bentham and the classical economists had it, the greatest happiness of the greatest number. Rather the individual was completely subordinated to the interests of the state. In this system, national wealth was not conceived of as the aggregate of individual wealth. The maximization of individual economic welfare was not, therefore, the goal of economic policy. In contrast, classical economics emerged in a period during which individual rights were being significantly advanced.

Classical competitive economic theory is not, however, predicated on merely the humanity or individuality of man; it is specifically toward man's role as a consumer that competitive economic theory is oriented. As Clair Wilcox has put it:

Competition is not an end in itself but a means to an end. The end which it serves is consumer welfare. . . . It is the purpose of the policy of maintaining competition to serve the interest of men as consumers rather than their interest as producers. The producer interest is a special interest that sets one group against another. The consumer interest is a general interest that all men have in common.[67]

The consumer interest may or may not be completely compatible with the public interest. The consumer, for example, may be indifferent about worker health and welfare or unconcerned with widespread unemployment or the evils of child labor. It is usually when consumer interests deviate from the public interest that, in a generally competitive society, departures from the policy of maintaining competition are effected. But it is the consumer-orientation of competitive economics that is the point at issue. In his revolt from mercantilism, Adam Smith stressed that consumption was the sole end and purpose of all production. That orientation was perpetuated by his successors. Thus, as Heckscher. points out, the classical economists sympathized with labor, but only to a point. They were indifferent to workers who did not add to the common good. And since unions interfered with attaining that end, classical economists looked at them as useless or even harmful.[68] The opposite was also true: economists were not popular with the working classes. And the dominant labor attitude throughout the nineteenth century remained, "If political economy was against the working classes, let the working classes be against political economy." The term *economist* to the workers covered "all middle class theorists on labor questions" and was the object of worker "hostility mingled with something akin to contempt."[69]

There was clearly much in the spirit and outlook of trade unionism that was antipathetic to the classical economists.[70] But to say categorically that they opposed trade unionism or regarded the interests of the consumer as always of the highest priority is not accurate. Adam Smith's sympathy with the worker has already been noted. "It is but equity," he held, "that they who feed, cloath and lodge the whole body of the people should have such a share of the produce of their own labour as to be themselves tolerably well fed, cloathed and lodged." Smith approved of state interference in industrial relations if labor would benefit: "When the regulation, therefore, is in favour of the workmen, it is always just and equitable; but it is sometimes otherwise when it is in favour of the masters."[71] Bentham in the *Manual of Political Economy* held that "opposition to machinery is well-grounded, if no care be taken to provide immediate employment for the discharged hands."[72] And for John Stuart Mill, "Trade unions were a normal element of the institutional pattern, and laws against them 'exhibit the infernal spirit of the slave master.' "[73] It appears, on balance, that the classical economists' opposition to trade unions is not nearly so clear-cut as it has seemed to some. Much of the popular political economy of the day, of course, went further in denunciation of unionism than the leading economists did. In any event, the failure of the classical economists to engage in the study of unionism relates not so much to the economists' attitudes toward unions as to their ideas on the nature of economics as an inquiry.

The classical economist's focus on the study of labor centered on the natural or long-run price of labor, deemed to be the result of competition and unaffected by bargaining institutions. That focus remained fundamentally unchanged through the impasse in wage theory that was marked by discussions of labor as a residual claimant and through the development of the so-called neoclassical economics toward the end of the nineteenth century. Even the development of the marginal productivity analysis did not represent a major change in this respect, for the approach of the economist to the study of labor was not fundamentally altered. There were, to be sure, changes. The economist's emphasis shifted from labor supply (away from population theory) to labor demand as a derived function of product demand. From a general analysis that was addressed to the question of the limits of wages as a whole, the economist shifted to a partial-equilibrium, microeconomic analysis of firm and industry demand. But neither the economist's conception of his discipline as a study of tendencies not his continuing emphasis on the long run was fundamentally changed.

It is indeed in a similarity of approach that we find the basis of the common aversion of both the classical and the neoclassical economists to an analysis of unionism. The neoclassical economist, forced by a recognition of the bargaining power possessed by trade unions to abandon the wages fund doctrine, was in fact no more concerned with analyzing unions than had been his predecessor, the wages fund theorist. And this was precisely the point of departure for the early labor economists: a shift in focus to the short run and a corresponding emphasis on institutional analysis and empirical research.

The economist's diffidence toward the study of unions can be explained by the common assumption that those institutions could affect only the market price. But the eclipse of classical wage theory was accompanied by the admission that unions might affect the natural price of labor, a matter of fundamental interest to the economic theorist. How far, indeed, institutional analysis was from neoclassical economics can be seen by examining the impact of unions on wage determination.

In the *Fortnightly Review* of May 1869, Mill acknowledged that unions could raise wages. And later that same year, he acknowledged the concept of indeterminacy, which had been introduced more or less explicitly by Jenkin and others somewhat earlier:

Between the two limits just indicated—the highest wages consistent with keeping up the capital of the country, and increasing it *pari passu* with the increase of people, and the lowest that will enable the labourers to keep up their numbers with an increase sufficient to provide labourers for the increase of employment—there is an intermediate region within which wages will range higher or lower according to what Adam Smith calls "the higgling of the market."[74]

If bargaining could affect only the market price, then the reason for the failure of the economists to undertake an analysis of the bargaining institution is obvious. The market price, as Ricardo said, tended toward the natural price. But the ability of unions to affect the long-run or natural price of labor, by compressing profits or whatever, is another matter. Here one is confronted with the tenacity of the classical methodology on the economics of the period. Where the Webbs set out to examine the economic characteristics of institutions, most economists grappled with abstract theories. Edgeworth's interest in unionism, for example, was confined to the search for ". . . a straightforward answer to the abstract question, what is the effect of combinations on contract in an otherwise perfect state of competition, as here supposed?" [75]

Edgeworth went on to say that in the face of indeterminacy of the wage bargain on theoretical grounds, there should appear the need for a principle of arbitration, with the latter, apparently, having little or nothing to do with economics. W. Stanley Jevons was more explicit. In *The State in Relation to Labour*, published in 1882, the year after Edgeworth's *Mathematical Psychics*, Jevons noted that the existence of unions alters the nature of the labor market. With unions, he wrote,

There is no longer competition among men and among employers. . . . The existence of combinations in trade disputes usually reduces them to a single contract bargain of the same indeterminate kind. . . . There may be no economic principle on which to decide the question. Mathematically speaking, the problem is an indeterminate one. [76]

Then he came close to removing the whole question of collective bargaining and industrial peace from economics: "It is obvious, then, that a trade dispute, especially when it has reached the acute phase of a strike, has little or nothing to do with economics. It is not a question of science."

What we have here is the old Ricardo-Mill tradition of the necessity of the competitive hypothesis to the economic method. If one great dogma of classical economics had been removed (the notion that unions could not permanently raise wages), there still remained another: the necessity of postulating competition in order to reduce cases to any assignable law. If, as was obviously the case with unions, the laws of supply and demand no longer applied, then it was not a question of science and had little or nothing to do with economics. In short, analysis of an institution that was by its very nature noncompetitive had no part in the economist's scientific frame of reference, however great might be his personal interest in it from the standpoint of social, political, or humanitarian considerations.

THE WORKER AND ECONOMIC PROGRESS

Although the classical economists did not, as we have seen, oppose trade unions to the extent that is often suggested and were, in some cases, favorably impressed with their advantages for society, it is certainly true that they failed to see in unions of workingmen the positive benefits discerned by early students of labor problems. In general, they were less impressed than were the early labor specialists with the possibility of improving the condition of the worker through extra-market means, either in the form of governmental policy or through institutional reforms, such as might lead to a redistribution of national income. Instead they saw distribution and production linked in such a way that the betterment of the workers depended mainly on economic growth achieved through competitive free enterprise. For them, the interests of both capitalists and workers were best realized in the steady growth of national output in the context of a free market economy.

A certain sense of optimism concerning the future of the worker runs through the classical analysis of the progress of the free market capitalistic economy. It is more pronounced with later writers such as John Stuart Mill or Alfred Marshall than with Malthus, Ricardo, or James Mill, but even the earlier analysts were not without hope. For Ricardo, these possibilities required for their realization an end to laws designed to alleviate poverty by redistributing existing income, because they ended only by interfering with economic incentives and, hence, the progress of economic growth.[77] Also required, Ricardo emphasized, was a receptiveness on the part of the working classes to the delights of "comforts and enjoyments" and the leisure to go with them. One of the most persistent themes in classical economics was the need for public policies that would help to induce the laboring classes to limit their numbers voluntarily. Toward this end, there was near-unanimous agreement on the merits of public support for education and cultural activities. The classical economists never deviated from Adam Smith's dictum that "the education of the common people requires . . . in a civilized and commercial society, the attention of the public."[78] Senior stressed that one of the principal ways in which government could and should fight both poverty and unemployment was to guarantee the existence of a good school system.[79] And several decades later, Alfred Marshall sounded the same theme.[80] Education was seen as more than a force that might ultimately help to control population growth by raising the aspirations of workers. Its positive role in economic growth in terms of its contribution toward enhancing the productive capacities of labor was also emphasized. The significance of human capital—of qualitative improvements in the human imputs in the economic process—was not lost on the classical economists. The "intellectual and moral capital of Great Britain," wrote Nassau Senior, "far exceeds all her material capital, not only in importance, but even in productiveness." "The bulk of the national revenue," he held, was "the result of personal capital, or, in other words, of education. It is not on the accidents of soil or climate, or on the existing accumulation of the material instruments of production, but on the quantity and the diffusion of this immaterial capital, that the wealth of a country depends." "Knowledge," he concluded, "has been called power; it is far more certainly wealth."[81]

The potential threat to the standard of living that was posed by unchecked population growth was never denied by even the most optimistic of the classical economists; it was, however, seen as best reduced by policies that would enhance the workers' understanding of the forces on which their future well-being depended. Thus education should not only make the workers more productive in a qualitatively improved sense; it should also help in maintaining a desirable balance between the increase of capital and that of labor.

Despite their hopes for the future, a number of nineteenth-century economists believed that the early English industrial revolution had not benefited the workers. "The increasing wealth of the nation," Malthus wrote in his first *Essay* in 1798, "has had little or no tendency to better the condition of the labouring poor. They have not, I believe, a greater command of the necessaries and conveniences of life; and a much greater proportion of them, than at the period of the Revolution, is employed in manufactories and crowded together in close and unwholesome rooms." Half a century later, this view was still being advanced. McCulloch concluded in 1859 that "there seems, on the whole, little room for doubting that the factory system operates unfavorably on the bulk of those engaged in it," and even Mill doubted whether progress had helped the workers.[82]

The question of the effects of early industrialization on the British worker's standard of living, or, more broadly, of its effects in reducing poverty generally, is a matter on which economic historians have not agreed.[83] Recent scholarship suggests, however, that at least until the middle of the nineteenth century, industrialization did not improve the workers' standard of living. While some upsurges may have resulted from the first stages of industrialization in the late eighteenth century, any general advances were quickly checked and, by the beginning of the nineteenth century, at best a leveling, and perhaps a decline, had set in. A. J. Taylor, after reviewing the evidence and arguments on both sides of the debate, has concluded that at least during the early decades of the nineteenth century, "the progress of the working class lagged increasingly behind that of the nation at large. Had working class incomes kept pace with the growth of the national income, the average worker could have expected to find himself some

50 percent better off in real terms in 1840 than thirty years earlier. Even the most sanguine of optimists would hardly claim that such was in fact the case."[84]

There can be no doubt that industrialization in England, as, indeed, in many if not most countries in which it has been achieved, was a socially harsh process. While Alfred Marshall could rightly stress, from the vantage point of the late nineteenth century, the increased earnings and increased leisure that had accrued to workers as a result of economic growth during the preceding one hundred years, the very real costs of that growth, borne heavily by the working classes, must not be overlooked. These costs are not totally reducible to monetary terms. The social changes attendant upon industrialization, such as the imposition of new and often strict forms of factory discipline and the changes in family life and family relationships attendant on the emergence of industrialization, probably also placed significant strains on the daily lives of the people. But even in strictly economic terms, there is little doubt that early industrialization in England was paid for to no small extent by the working classes. Wages long remained phenomena of custom as much as of market forces. "One important result of this," according to E. J. Hobsbawm, "was that employers almost certainly got their skilled labour in the nineteenth century at less than market cost." And the size of the resulting bonus accruing to employers was "at least as great as the bonus they had drawn from Professor Hamilton's 'profit inflation.'"[85] Although Hobsbawm is speaking only of skilled workers, it seems likely that his generalization would apply to unskilled workers as well, in view of both the imperfect state of early labor markets and the tendency for employers to act "always and everywhere in a sort of tacit, but constant and uniform combination, not to raise the wages of labour."[86] One analyst of this subject has concluded that "to a very considerable extent, Britain's industrialization was financed out of low wages, while the working classes were being exhorted to exercise self-restraint."[87]

The last point is of special importance. Before the Poor Law Reform Act of 1834, an important strand in the social fabric had been an attitude of benevolence toward the poor based on a combination of assumptions and beliefs having to do with traditional concepts of authority, responsibility, and charity. According to this view, which John Stuart Mill termed "the theory of dependence," the poor should be taken care of by the rich. In fact, for these higher classes, their duty was to help and guide the poor, making sure that they were well "fed, clothed, housed, spiritually edified, and innocently amused." The wealthy, he said, should "be *in loco parentis* to the poor, guiding and restraining them like children."[88]

Although not often explicitly articulated, this theory of dependence

underlay social policy toward the poor throughout the age of mercantilism. The process of industrialization in England during the late
eighteenth and early nineteenth centuries, however, was accompanied by the rise of what Reinhard Bendix has called an "entrepreneurial ideology" of which an important component was a change in
attitude toward poverty, and especially, toward the role of the worker
in society. The essence of the new ideology was the introduction into
social thought of two ideas, which "were clearly exemplified in the
everyday practice of employers, but which were, nevertheless, startling when stated as matters of principle. One was that the people
must depend upon themselves. The other was that the 'higher classes'
are not and, in fact, cannot be responsible for the employment of
the people or for the relief of the poor." [89]

The changed attitude was the result of the combined influence of
unsatisfactory experience with the poor law, continuing difficulties
with labor supply, and the writings of a number of social analysts and
commentators, importantly the Reverend Joseph Townsend and Edmund Burke.[90] But probably no other voice was more influential than
that of Thomas R. Malthus, whose *Essay on Population*, published in
1798, provided much of the rationale for the Poor Law Reform Act of
1834. Underlying both the Malthusian analysis and the reform legislation of 1834 was a notion quite foreign to centuries of social thought
on the problem of poverty: the major responsibility for poverty was
upon the poor themselves.

The central economic ideas of Malthus, based on the principle of
population pressing on subsistence, were by no means original. Adam
Smith and a number of earlier writers had already advanced the notion that mankind shared with the animal world the tendency to multiply up to limits defined by subsistence, an idea that was central to
classical wage theory and its conclusions concerning the subsistence
level of wages. But Malthus went further than his predecessors, and
most of his successors, in analyzing the causes of this phenomenon.
To Malthus, poverty was the result of excess population, which might
have been avoided had people exercised rational restraint by delaying
marriage until they could adequately support their families. In their
failure to do this—and their poverty was for him evidence of such
failure—Malthus discerned a pattern of behavior on the part of the
poor that was inconsistent with what he took to be the plan and wishes
of the Creator. If the wages of the laboring poor were insufficient to
support a family, Malthus insisted, they should remain single, and "if
they marry in this case, so far from fulfilling a duty to society, they are
plunging themselves into distress; . . . they are acting directly contrary
to the will of God, and bringing down upon themselves various diseases, which might all, or the greater part, have been avoided if they

had attended to the repeated admonitions which he gives by the general laws of nature to every being capable of reason."[91] What is important here is the emphasis Malthus placed on individual responsibility for poverty. For him, it was a private, not a social, problem.

Social and economic policy concerning poverty in nineteenth-century England by and large reflected Malthusian sentiments, which were eminently compatible with the rising individualism and utilitarianism of the time. Societal responsibility for poverty, the heritage of medieval canon law, thus gradually gave way to societal repressiveness toward the poor. The New Poor Law of 1834 abolished outdoor relief for the ablebodied and introduced new and harsher codes of conduct for the administration of the workhouses. The debtors' prisons and poorhouses of Victorian England were a reflection of the notion that poverty was essentially a failing of the individual against society.

Not all of social policy in mid-nineteenth-century England could be said to have reflected an entrepreneurial ideology without qualification. The reforms introduced under the various factory acts, for example, stand as testimony to some recognition of the evils of unregulated industrial activity. Nonetheless the prevailing mode of thought, reflected in classical economics no less than in social policy, was clearly on the side of the idea that the ultimate remedy for poverty lay in the habits and attitudes of the working people. The analyses and recommendations of various writers on the subject seemed, as Bendix had said, "to blend into one justification of industrial society which exonerated the entrepreneurs and placed the burden of guilt upon those who suffered most."[92]

The greatest failure of the classical economists' study of labor may well lie in their inability to explain the existence of widespread poverty and unemployment on grounds other than those having to do with behavior that was less than fully rational on the part of workers or other owners of factors of production. Thus low wages were seen as the result of an excess supply of labor, which the workers themselves must learn to control better; unemployment was the temporary result of some factors of production demanding too high a price; poverty was the result of some interaction of these forces or circumstances, but again, ultimately, the responsibility of the individual. What was lacking was an explanation or analysis of how the economic system itself might be responsible for these conditions.

THE MARXIAN CRITIQUE

4

The position of Karl Marx in the history of economic and social thought is somewhat paradoxical. He is generally considered one of the world's most powerful socialist thinkers, yet he contributed little to the theory of socialism; and although he stands as perhaps the severest and most trenchant critic of capitalism, he can be described as its discoverer. Although the classical economists from Smith through Mill had identified and analyzed the various institutions of a market economy, no one before Marx had systematized these as the capitalist mode of production. The institutions of capitalism for the classical economists were natural phenomena; for Marx, on the contrary, they constituted a particular economic system occupying a specific and limited time span in the stream of human history. Until the *Communist Manifesto* appeared, "No one had clearly seen this peculiar interdependence of class structure, technology, and general culture which is typical of the last two centuries of European and American social and economic history, and which has been called capitalism. Without Marx, Max Weber's investigations of the spirit of capitalism, [and] Werner Sombart's description of capitalist phenomena . . . [would not have been] possible." [1]

SOURCES AND INFLUENCES

Marx's debt to earlier thinkers was large. The socialist ideal dates at least from classical antiquity, and the concept of labor as both the ultimate source and measure of value was not only the basis of the teachings of the Schoolmen but also of the mercantilists and the classical economists as well. It was not Marx but John Stuart Mill who asserted that "labour alone is the primary means of production" and that "tools and materials, like other things, have originally cost nothing but labour." [2] Furthermore a number of the specific criticisms leveled by Marx at nineteenth-century capitalism had been made by other observers, both earlier and contemporary, including Sismondi, Proudhon, Rodbertus, the so-called Ricardian socialists such as William Thompson, Thomas Hodgskin, John Gray, and John Francis Bray, and even some of those, like Saint-Simon, Fourier, and Robert Owen, whom Marx and Engels dismissed as utopian. But although the socialist critique of capitalism is more extensive than the Marxian, Marx was the greatest and clearly the most influential of the socialist writers.

Probably the most important influence in the development of Marx's thought was the philosophy of Hegel, which contains the roots of both the Marxian conception of the economic process and the earliest of the specific criticisms Marx directed toward capitalism. The distinctive feature of Hegel's philosophy is that it provides "for the first time, a thoroughgoing attempt to view all philosophical problems and concepts, including the concept of reason itself, in essentially historical terms."[3] The historical unfolding of both ideas and institutional forms was the result of what Hegel termed a dialectic process in which each form, concept, or thesis carried its own negation or antithesis, producing, in turn, a synthesis or a new state of being or of mind.

In Hegelian terms, history is but the successive unfolding of new syntheses resulting from the conflicts or contradictions inherent in existing conditions at any point in time. For Hegel, the dominant force in this was the power of reason rather than of material forces. "Reason," he held, "is the Sovereign of the World. . . . Reason is *Substance,* as well as *Infinite Power. . . . It is the infinite complex of things,* their entire Essence and Truth."[4] Marx was never willing to accept the Hegelian primacy of mind over matter. "My dialectic method is not only different from the Hegelian," he insisted, "but is its direct opposite":

To Hegel, the life-process of the human brain, i.e., the process of thinking, which, under the name of "the Idea," he even transforms into an independent subject, is the demiurgos of the real world, and the real world is only the external, phenomenal form of "the Idea." With me, on the contrary, the ideal is nothing else than the material world reflected by the human mind, and translated into forms of thought. . . . The mystification which dialectic suffers in Hegel's hands . . . [is that] with him it is standing on its head. It must be turned right side up again, if you would discover the rational kernel within the mystical shell.[5]

The inversion of Hegel's position to reflect the primacy of material conditions, as well as his debt to Hegel for the idea of the dialectic, is well expressed in Marx's formulation of what has come to be known as dialectical materialism. Materialism in this sense does not mean a desire for a growing amount of material wealth but refers rather to "a philosophic view which holds that matter in motion is the fundamental constituent of the universe" rather than one in which the mind, spirit, or world of ideas was primary.[6] According to Marx,

In the social production of their material life, men enter into definite relations that are indispensable and independent of their wills; these relations of production correspond to a definite state of the development of their material forces of production.

The sum total of these relations of production makes up the economic structure of society—the real foundation on which arises a legal and political superstructure and to which correspond definite forms of social consciousness.

The mode of production of material life determines the social, political and intellectual life process in general. It is not the consciousness of men that determines their existence, but rather it is their social existence that determines their consciousness.

At a certain stage of their development, the material forces of production in society come into conflict with the existing relations of production or—what is but a legal expression of the same thing—with the property relations within which they have been at work before. . . . Then begins an epoch of social revolution. With the change of the economic foundation, the entire immense superstructure is more or less rapidly transformed.[7]

The Marxian debt to Hegel was not limited to the dialectical method. The importance of the concept of labor, so central to all of Marx's work and the factor that would bring him to a systematic study of political economy and the capitalist system, was also a legacy of his early study of Hegelian philosophy. According to Ernest Mandel, "Marx saw the Hegelian system as a veritable philosophy of labor."[8]

A second debt Marx owed to classical political economy, the teachings of which were readily amenable to a theory of labor exploitation. This was partly due to the legacy of Adam Smith. There was, first of all, the emphasis that Smith had placed on the view that labor was "the first price, the original purchase-money that was paid for all things," and that it was the means through which "all the wealth of the world was originally purchased."[9] A related, and perhaps even more fundamental, factor was the general failure of classical political economy, following Smith, to develop any well-reasoned analysis of the role of the capitalist or entrepreneur in the economic process. The passivity of the capitalist in the *Wealth of Nations,* coupled with Adam Smith's positive distrust of businessmen's motives, surely left the door open for the Marxian attack on the capitalist.[10] Smith's statement that in a developed economy, where capital has become a factor in the productive process, "the whole produce of labour does not always belong to the labourer" but rather that he "must in most cases share it with the owner of the stock which employs him" and his reference to both rent and profit as "deductions from the produce of labour" could hardly have presented a better invitation to a theory of labor exploitation.[11] As Marx himself noted, the "political economist tells us that everything is bought with labor and that capital is nothing but accumulated labor" and that "originally and in theory the *whole produce* of labor belongs to the worker. But at the same time he tells us that in actual fact what the worker gets is the smallest and utterly indispensable part of the product."[12]

Marx's anti-Hegelian insistence on the primacy of the material over immaterial forces was also easily reinforced, insofar as labor was concerned, by an idea he took from Adam Smith: that productive labor was labor that "realises itself in some particular subject or vendible commodity, which lasts for some time at least after that labour is past.

It is, as it were, a certain quantity of labour stocked and stored up to be employed, if necessary, upon some other occasion." For Marx, "Human labour creates value, but is not itself value. It becomes value only in its congealed state, when embodied in the form of some object. . . . Value must be expressed as having objective existence."[13]

According to Schumpeter, "Real understanding of [Marx's] economics begins with recognizing that, as a theorist, he was a pupil of Ricardo . . . his own argument evidently starts from Ricardo's propositions."[14] But the important word here is *starts*. Ricardo developed the labor theory of value beyond its Smithian origins in primitive society by insisting on its general applicability in an advanced capitalistic society. But Ricardo held only generally, not strictly, to the labor theory. Nor did he conceive of labor's exploitation in connection with it. Marx went much further in developing and adhering to a strict labor—as opposed to a multifactor cost-of-production—theory of value and a theory of labor exploitation. His starting points were the conclusions of classical political economy: that labor was both the basis and measure of value and that its own payment was given by its cost of production, or subsistence.

If the philosophy of Hegel and the political economy of Smith and Ricardo were the primary influences on Marx's thinking on the subject of labor, mention should also be made of the influence on Marx, especially the young Marx, of Friedrich Engels. Despite what must have been a mutually reinforcing influence exerted by Marx and Engels on each other during several decades of joint efforts, Engels's modesty, self-effacement, and deference to Marx to the end has obscured his contribution. But in fact it is to Engels that "credit is due for having been the first to urge Marx to take up the study of political economy and for having grasped, in a 'brilliant sketch,' the central importance of this science for communism." It is possible, according to Schumpeter, that "in the 1840's . . . [Engels] may even have helped to educate Marx in economics and in socialism, for at that time he was much further along."[15]

Whereas Marx's approach to the study of labor was through the rather abstract concept of alienation, with its roots in Hegelian philosophy, Engels had approached the subject through firsthand experience with the facts of industrial life. Sent to England by his family in 1842 to study the practical aspects of business affairs, Engels was quickly convinced of the deleterious effects of the factory system on English workers. After wide travels and extensive observation during a stay in England of twenty-one months, he published *The Condition of the Working Class in England* in 1845. Although hardly unbiased and written in highly polemical language as an unabashed indictment of English employers, this book stands as an impressive early effort to document the living and working conditions of English laborers. Although a number of inaccuracies have been discovered, Engels's treatment of such topics as town and factory life, labor market competition, Irish immigration, and working-class movements served a useful purpose that was being bypassed by most economists and others who might have been better equipped to undertake it.[16] Soon after the publication of Engels's book, the German economist and statistician Bruno Hildebrand, although he criticized Engels's work on a number of statistical, historical, and inferential points, nonetheless declared him to be "the most gifted and knowledgeable German writer on social problems."[17] And it was the judgment of Schumpeter that Engels's book, "however biased," was "a creditable piece of factual research, nourished by direct observation."[18]

Engels's analysis of the workings of the capitalist process undoubtedly influenced Marx, who at that time was starting his own study of economics. For example, Engels's discussion of commercial crises is based on the notion of the business cycle and foreshadows Marx's "reserve army of the unemployed." Having described the origins and processes of the commercial crisis, Engels concludes that

in due course depression gives way to boom. And so it goes on. English industry passes through a continuing series of cycles of boom and slump. Consequently English industry must always have a reserve of unemployed workers, except during the short period when the boom is at its height. The existence of such a reserve is essential in order that labour may be available to produce the great quantities of goods which are needed during the . . . boom. . . . The size of this reserve varies with the state of trade. When trade is good and more hands are wanted the number of workers in the pool of unemployed declines. . . . During a slump the reserve of unemployed swells to formidable dimensions.[19]

THE THEORY OF LABOR ALIENATION

Marx's early analysis of labor was undertaken largely within the framework of philosophy. Following Hegel, it is grounded in the concept of alienation, which is best developed in the *Economic and Philosophical Manuscripts,* a series of early essays written by Marx in 1844 but suppressed by him and not published until 1932.[20] Traces of the alienation theme appear also in the *Communist Manifesto,* written with Friedrich Engels in 1848, but the emphasis there is already shifting to the economic concept of exploitation. In *Capital,* the mature expression of Marxian thought, of which the first volume appeared in 1867, alienation is seldom mentioned and the emphasis is predominantly economic.

The concept of labor formed an important part of the Hegelian system of thought. Hegel held that the transference of potentiality into actuality, of the Idea into Existence, depended on "the Will—the activity of man in the widest sense. It is only by this activity that that Idea as well as abstract characteristics generally, are realized, actualized; . . . the motive power that puts them in operation, and gives them determinate existence, is the need, instinct, inclination, and passion of man." In this exertion of will, moreover, through which ideas were transformed into results, mankind realized its own individuality and identity.[21]

The Hegelian emphasis on the need for mankind "to find itself satisfied in its activity and labor" was an essential part of Marx's teaching. According to Marx, labor was *"life-activity, productive-life* itself," and "the whole character of a species . . . is contained in the character of its life activity." It was the consciousness of its life activity that set men apart from the animal world: "The animal is immediately one with its life activity. It does not distinguish itself from it." But man "makes his life activity itself the object of his will and of his consciousness." It followed that productive activity was itself but the activity in which consciousness was manifested.[22]

Work, then, constituted for Marx the essence of man's being as a species. As Eric Fromm has put it, for Marx man *"is* what he *does."*[23] "It is just in his work upon the objective world," according to Marx, "that man first really proves himself to be a *species being."*[24]

It was Marx's contention that under capitalism the worker was denied this identification with his product, and his labor was "estranged," resulting in the "alienation" of the worker. Despite his claim to the contrary, Marx never really explained the sources and nature of this alienation but simply assumed it as a fact of political economy and proceeded to examine its implications. At times, the concept of estrangement seems to describe the whole set of capitalist institutions and interrelationships, as in the following passage: "Now, therefore, we have to grasp the essential connection between private property, greed, and the separation of labor, capital, and landed property; between exchange and competition, value and the devaluation of men, monopoly and competition, etc.—the connection between this whole estrangement and the money system."[25]

This concept of estrangement or alienation, as E. G. West has pointed out, applies to the capitalists as well as to the workers and is inherent in an exchange economy.[26] Money, according to Marx, "constitutes true power and . . . gives me possession of alien objective essense. . . . The savage in his cave—a natural element which freely offers itself for his use and protection—feels himself no more a stranger, or rather feels himself to be just as much at home as a *fish* in water. But the cellar dwelling of the poor man is a hostile dwelling, 'an alien, restraining power which only gives itself up to him insofar as he gives up to it his blood and sweat.' " The difference was that the poor man did not own his cellar dwelling but was rather "in *someone else's* house, in the house of a *stranger* who daily lies in wait for him and throws him out if he does not pay his rent."[27] The economic inter-dependence characteristic of an exchange economy based on a division of labor and the use of money was for Marx a source of generalized estrangement: "Estrangement is manifested not only in the fact that *my* means of life belong to *someone else*, that *my* desire is the inaccessible possession of another, but also in the fact that everything is itself something *different* from itself, that my activity is *something else* and that, finally, (and this applies also to the capitalist), all is under the sway of *inhuman* power."[28]

Despite the inclusion of the capitalist as among those alienated by capitalism, it was the alienation of the worker with which Marx was most concerned and about which he was most explicit. Although Marx was not altogether clear on the ultimate source of the worker's alienation, he seems to attribute it to the paradox of labor's poverty amid growing national wealth—an "economic fact" that he asserts but on which he brings no empirical evidence to bear. "Do not let us," he begins by saying, "go back to a fictitious primordial condition as the political economist does, when he tries to explain. . . . We proceed from an economic fact *of the present.*"

The worker becomes all the poorer the more wealth he produces, the more his production increases in power and size. The worker becomes an ever cheaper commodity the more commodities he creates. With the *increasing value* of the world of things proceeds in direct proportion the devaluation of the world of men. Labor produces not only commodities: it produces itself and the worker as a *commodity*—and this in the same general proportion in which it produces commodities. This fact expresses merely that the object which labor produces—labor's product—confronts it as *something alien*, as a *power independent* of the producer. . . . So much does the appropriation of the object appear as estrangement that the more objects the worker produces the less he can possess and the more he falls under the sway of his product, capital.[29]

This concept of alienation is conceptually different from, and some-what narrower than, that resulting from the process of exchange gen-erally, for it is limited to the worker and is associated with his growing immiserization and subjugation to the power of capital, his own prod-uct. Marx elaborated on this kind of alienation:

Labor is *external* to the worker, i.e., it does not belong to his essential being; that in his work, therefore, he does not affirm himself but denies himself, does not feel content but unhappy. . . . The worker therefore only feels him-self outside his work, and in his work feels outside himself. He is at home when he is not working, and when he is working he is not at home. His labor is therefore not voluntary, but coerced; it is *forced labor*. . . . Lastly, the external character of labor for the worker appears in the fact that it is not his own, but someone else's, that it does not belong to him, that in it he belongs, not to himself, but to another.[30]

Marx's contention that labor's product "confronts it as something alien" only partially captures the essence of the worker's alienation, which he seems to imply is externalization: "The alienation of the worker in his product means not only that his labor becomes an object, an *external* existence, but that it exists *outside him*, independently, as something alien to him, and that it becomes a power on its own confronting him. It means that the life which he conferred on the object confronts him as something hostile and alien."[31] But alienation cannot be simply a matter of labor's product being embodied in a physical form external to the worker, for that is the case even in the fully free state of human production. A kind of externalization is inherent in Marx's description of free (noncapitalist) labor's objectification in its product, and in his statement that "An animal produces only itself, whilst man reproduces the whole of nature. An animal's product belongs immediately to its physical body, whilst man freely confronts his product." One cannot, after all, confront that which is not in some sense external.[32]

Closer to the essential meaning of the worker's alienation is Marx's comment that under capitalism the worker's product "becomes a power on its own confronting him." But labor's product cannot really be "a power on its own" for it is inanimate and must belong to someone. "If," Marx asks, "the product of labor is alien to me, if it confronts me as an alien power, to whom, then, does it belong? . . . To a being *other* than myself. Who is this being? . . . The alien being, to whom labor and the product of labor belongs, in whose service labor is done and for whose benefit the product of labor is provided, can only be a *man* himself. . . . Not the gods, not nature, but only man himself can be this alien power over man."[33]

Thus enters the capitalist, the owner of the product of labor. The source of the worker's alienation is not so much the externalization of labor's effort as it is the ownership of the (externalized) product of labor. The object of labor, according to Marx, is *"the objectification of man's species life; for he duplicates himself not only, as in consciousness, intellectually, but also actively, in reality, and therefore he contemplates himself in a world that he has created."* When his product is taken away from him, as is the case when it becomes the property of another, the worker is denied "his *species life*, his real objectivity as a member of the species." And the "immediate consequence of the fact that man is estranged from the product of his labor, from his life activity, from his species being is the *estrangement of man* from *man*. When man confronts himself, he confronts the *other* man."[34]

The confrontation by the worker of another in himself can perhaps best be understood in terms of the Hegelian dialectic, where "the finite, being radically. self-contradictory, involves its own self-suppression."[35] Estranged labor becomes, in the Marxian system of thought, a kind of Hegelian contradiction in which the alienated worker himself creates the forces responsible for his own alienation.[36] But to say that the worker, in his role as estranged labor, creates the relationship in which others stand to his production is to say, as Marx does, that the worker thereby creates private property, not only in the sense of capital or surplus value, but in the larger sense of the institutional arrangements through which the rights of ownership are established and maintained.[37]

There is clearly a contradiction here, for the existence of private property and its power over the worker was the originally postulated source of the worker's alienation. Marx himself recalls this: "True, it is as a result of . . . *private property* that we have obtained the concept of *alienated labor* . . . from political economy. But on analysis of this concept it becomes clear that though private property appears to be the source, the cause of alienated labor, it is rather its consequence. Later this relationship becomes reciprocal."[38]

Marx never resolved the contradiction into which he led himself. At one point he seeks to dismiss the problem as one of the "secrets" of private property: "Only at the last culmination of the development of private property does this, its secret, appear again, namely, that on the one hand it is the *product* of alienated labor, and that on the other it is the *means* by which labor alienated itself, the *realization of this alienation.*" Somewhat later, apparently unsatisfied himself with this formulation, he confronts the question directly: "We have accepted the estrangement of labor, its alienation, as a fact, and we have analyzed this fact. How, we now ask, does *man* come to *alienate,* to estrange, *his* labor? How is this estrangement rooted in the nature of human development?" But his response is a question-begging one and hardly satisfying: "We have already gone a long way toward the solution of this problem by *transforming* the question of the *origins of private property* into the question of the relation of alienated labor to the course of humanity's development. For when one speaks of private property one thinks of dealing with something external to man. When one speaks of labor, one is dealing directly with man himself. This new formulation already contains its solution."[39]

Whether because of his own lack of success in explaining the specific sources of alienation, or more generally because of its conceptual affinity with Hegelian philosophy (and hence with an early stage of his own intellectual development), and its absence in the literature of classical political economy, Marx never completed the analysis of alienation begun in the *Economic and Philosophic Manuscripts*. The first manuscript, "Estranged Labor," breaks off unfinished, and none of the others deals with the subject of alienation to a comparable extent. Marx did continue to emphasize the degradation of work under the capitalist mode of production, however. Perhaps the best illustration of Marx's mature thinking on the subject, in which alienation or estrangement is identified with exploitation and immiserization, is in *Capital*:

Within the capitalist system all methods for raising the social productiveness of labour are brought about at the cost of the individual labourer; all means for the development of production transform themselves into means of domination over, and exploitation of, the producers; they mutilate the labourer into a fragment of a man, degrade him to the level of an appendage of a machine, destroy every remnant of charm in his work and turn it into a hated toil; they estrange from him the intellectual potentialities of the labour process in the same proportion as science is incorporated in it as an independent power; they distort the conditions under which he works, subject him during the labour-process to a despotism the more hateful for its meanness; they transform his life-time into working-time and drag his wife and child beneath the wheels of the Juggernaut of capital. . . . It follows therefore that in proportion as capital accumulates, the lot of the labourer, be his payment high or low, must grow worse.[40]

Daniel Bell postulates that Marx eventually transformed the concept of alienation into the concept of exploitation. Bell holds that alienation was a theme of "the early Marx but not the *historical* Marx," who repudiated the concept of alienation: "The term, because of its Hegelian overtones, was, for him, too abstract. And, because it carried psychological echoes of ideas such as 'man's condition,' it was too 'idealistic.' Estrangement, for Marx, had to be rooted in concrete social activity; and Marx felt that he had found the answer in the idea of exploitation, the economic precipitate, so to speak, of alienation."[41] Bell, however, overstates the case. In *Capital,* Marx does not repudiate the concept of alienation; he simply fails to develop it. Although the later Marx says less about alienation than about exploitation, the concept of alienation remains important to his analysis and in a sense is the starting point of economic exploitation.

THE THEORY OF LABOR EXPLOITATION

The Marxian theory of exploitation begins with the classical theory of wages. Although Marx's analysis of wages went well beyond the standard classical formulation, especially in his treatment of cyclical movements of wages above and below equilibrium, his central proposition was that the wage rate was exactly what it was for the classical economists: the cost of production of labor. Citing the work of Petty, Vanderlint, Malthus, Turgot, and others, Marx starts with "the supposition that labour-power is bought and sold as its value. Its value, like that of all other commodities, is determined by the working time necessary to its production." The worker requires a given amount of goods and services for his maintenance: "Therefore the labour-time requisite for the production of labour-power reduces itself to that necessary for the production of those means of subsistence necessary for the maintenance of the labourer." Like Ricardo and Mill, Marx recognized that the level of subsistence was culturally and not biologically determined: "The number and extent of . . . so-called necessary wants as also the modes of satisfying them are themselves the product of historical development, and depend therefore to a great extent on the degree of civilisation of a country, more particularly on the condition under which, and consequently on the habits and degree of comfort in which, the class of free labourers has been formed."[42]

So far the Marxian position is perfectly compatible with the traditional classical formulation. As far as labor's exchange value is concerned—that is, its wage rate—Marx accepted the orthodox position. But for Marx, the determination of labor's exchange value was only part of the problem, since "the past labour that is embodied in the labour-power, and the living labour that it can call into action; the daily cost of maintaining it, and its daily expenditure in work, are two totally different things. The former determines the exchange-value of the labour-power, the latter is its use-value."[43]

It was precisely this difference between what labor cost the capitalist in the labor market—the wage rate—and what labor could produce in the workshop that constituted the exploitative element in Marx's analysis. Marx assumed that the socially necessary labor time needed for labor to produce an amount equivalent to its cost of production was less than the length of the working day. For him, the capitalist system was one in which the working day of the laborer was divided into two parts. The first, the time necessary for him to produce the value of his own level of subsistence, is independent of the capitalist system; the worker would have to work the same length of time to produce his necessary subsistence even were he to be self-employed. Under capitalism, where the capitalist lays out money in advance both for capital and labor power, the value of such labor power is merely reproduced.[44] It was the second portion of the working day, according to Marx, that offered the opportunity for exploitation. During this time the worker "creates no value for himself. He creates surplus value which, for the capitalist, has all the charms of a creation out of nothing. This portion of the working day, I name surplus labour-time, and to the labour expended during that time, I give the name of surplus-labour."[45]

Marx divided the net output of the economy into two parts, v (variable capital), representing the wage bill, and s (surplus), representing rent, interest, and profits. The difference between gross and net output he designated c (constant capital), representing plant and raw materials.[46] The ratio s/v represented, for Marx, "an exact expression for the degree of exploitation of labour-power by capital, or of the labourer by the capitalist."[47]

It is the position of Joan Robinson that the Marxian concept of exploitation, based as it is on the division of the working day, "has no meaning as applied to individual industries . . . [since] in a specialized industrial economy, it would take any group of workers more time than there is to produce for themselves the goods which they consume. The division must be conceived as applying to the output of the economy as a whole."[48] But although a macroeconomic view of Marxian exploitation can be sustained, it is an exaggeration to say that Marxian exploitation is meaningless at the level of the individual industry.[49] First, Marx himself accommodates Robinson's objection by noting that since the efforts of the individual worker form "part of a system, based on the social division of labour, he does not directly produce the actual necessaries which he himself consumes; he produces instead a particular commodity, yarn for example, whose value is equal to the value of those necessaries or of the money with which they can be bought."[50] The macroeconomic view of exploitation also suffers from a failure to recognize that Marxian exploitation is, as Thomas Sowell has rightly emphasized, "exploitation of man by man, not of one factor of production by another. There is no real issue of relative contributions of labour and capital in the Marxian system, which argues precisely that capital itself is created by labour, and therefore is not to be regarded as a contribution of its legal proprietor at all."[51]

But perhaps the greatest weakness of a macroeconomic interpretation of Marxian exploitation is its failure to recognize that the distinguishing feature of Marxian exploitation is its independence from the market process and its association with the internal operations of the business firm. From a strictly economic standpoint, the labor market was, for Marx, exactly what it was for the most laissez-faire of the classical economists: "a very Eden of the innate rights of man."

There alone rule Freedom, Equality, Property and Bentham. Freedom, because both buyer and seller of a commodity, say of labour-power, are constrained only by their own free will. They contract as free agents, and the agreement they come to, is but the form in which they give legal expression to their common will. Equality, because each enters into relation with the other . . . and they exchange equivalent for equivalent. Property, because each disposes only of what is his own. And Bentham, because each looks only to himself."[52]

There is, no doubt, a strong element of typically sardonic Marxian humor in this description of the labor market, but there can be no doubt about Marx's holding generally to classical teaching on the workings of exchange. "The circumstance," he says elsewhere, "that on the one hand the daily sustenance of labour-power costs only half a day's labour, while on the other hand the very same labour-power can work during a whole day, that consequently the value which its use during one day creates, is double what he pays for that use, this circumstance is, without doubt, a piece of good luck for the buyer, but by no means an injury to the seller." Throughout his analysis of exploitation, Marx insists that "the laws that regulate the exchange of commodities, have been in no way violated. Equivalent has been exchanged for equivalent. For the capitalist as buyer paid for each commodity . . . and the labour-power, its full value."[53]

The divorce of exploitation from market exchange makes the Marxian use of this concept quite different from that of its employment in more recent economic literature. For Pigou and Robinson, for example, exploitation is a function of the structure of the labor market and its imperfections.[54] For Marx, exploitation has nothing to do with the sphere of exchange or with buying and selling; it is therefore quite independent of market structure. Rather it is the result of the consumption (as distinct from the purchase) of labor power by the capitalist or his realization of labor's "value in use."

Having paid service to the laws of exchange, with labor receiving its full value in the market, Marx temporarily abandons the market in favor of the sphere of the internal operations of the firm. "The consumption of labour-power," he notes, "is at one and the same time the production of commodities and of surplus value," but this consumption "is completed, as in the case of every other commodity, outside the limits of the market or of the sphere of circulation." Let us, he therefore says, "take leave for a time of this noisy sphere, where everything takes place on the surface and in view of all men, and . . . [proceed] into the hidden abode of production . . . Here we shall see, not only how capital produces, but how capital is produced. We shall at last force the secret of profit-making."

The source of exploitation in the Marxian scheme lies in the difference between labor's exchange value, given by its cost of production and realized in the labor market, and its use value, determined by its ability to produce useful commodities and belonging, after labor's sale, to the capitalist. "The seller of labour-power," Marx wrote, "like the seller of any other commodity, realises its exchange-value, and parts with its use-value. He cannot take the one without giving the other. The use-value of labour-power, or in other words, labour, belongs just as little to its seller, as the use-value of oil after it has been sold belongs to the dealer who has sold it. The owner of the money has paid the value of a day's labour-power; his, therefore, is the use of it for a day; a day's labour belongs to him."[55]

This emphasis on the use value (as distinct from exchange value) of labor, on the consumption (as distinct from the purchase) of labor power by the capitalist, and on the realm of production (as distinct from the realm of exchange)—on the internal operations of the business firm—is a distinguishing but too-seldom-noticed characteristic of Marxian economics. Had Marx limited himself to market operations, he could not have constructed the theory of exploitation while staying within the framework of classical economics. He stayed within that framework by ascribing to the market precisely those characteristics and results to which Smith, Ricardo, and Mill could have subscribed, but by going beyond or behind the market into the internal operation of the capitalist enterprise. In the Marxian system, the laborer finds in the labor market fair value for his necessary labor time—let us say six hours' worth of labor per day. But he "finds, *in the workshop*, the means of production necessary for working, not only six, but during twelve hours." The production of surplus value, the basis of Marxian exploitation, was thus independent of the realm of exchange, which, for the orthodox classical economists, was the beginning and the end of economic activity. The production of surplus value was, as Marx noted, "entirely confined to the sphere of production."[56]

For Marx, the production of surplus value was not the same as its realization by the capitalist. According to him, it encompassed a second process:

The entire mass of commodities, the total product . . . must be sold. If this is not done, or only partly accomplished, or only at prices which are below the prices of production, the laborer has been none the less exploited, but his exploitation does not realise much for the capitalist. It may yield no surplus value at all for him or only realise a portion of the produced surplus value, or it may even mean a partial or complete loss of his capital. The conditions of direct exploitation and those of the realisation of surplus value are not identical. They are separated logically as well as by time and space.[57]

Thus although Marxian exploitation and the production of surplus value are independent of the exchange process, the capitalist's profits from that exploitation are dependent upon market activity.

To say, moreover, that the market was for Marx what it was for the economists of the orthodox classical tradition is to limit ourselves to its economic characteristics. The phenomenon of market purchase and sale remained for Marx a source of alienation and estrangement. Marx refers often in *Capital* to "alienation by sale," and despite the fact that Marx sometimes used *alienate* as no more than a formal transfer by sale, it is clear that the process of exchange itself, if not exploitative in the formal sense of denying the worker his full value or full cost, was nonetheless a demeaning and dehumanizing phenomenon for Marx.[58] It is, moreover, the essential basis of exploitation in that "the labourer, on quitting the process [of production], is what he was on entering it, a source of wealth but devoid of all means of making that wealth his own."

Since, before entering on the process, his own labour has already been alienated from himself by the sale of his labour-power, has been appropriated by the capitalist and incorporated with capital, it must, during the process, be realised in a product that does not belong to him. . . . The labourer therefore constantly produces material, objective wealth, but in the form of capital, of an alien power that dominates and exploits him.[59]

Although the laws of exchange or competition in the labor market ensured, for Marx no less than for the orthodox economists, that labor would be paid its full value as determined by its cost of production, the tendency of capitalist production was, according to Marx, to reduce that part of the working day necessary for the worker's subsistence. "Since the production of surplus-value is the chief end and aim of capitalist production," it followed that the purpose of the capitalist would be best served by efforts "to shorten that part of the working day, during which the workman must labour for his own benefit, and by that very shortening, to lengthen the other part of the day, during which he is at liberty to work gratis for the capitalist."[60] Part of the lengthening of the time during which surplus value might be created was held by Marx to be the result of coercive work rules, which lengthened the workday considerably, usurping "the time for growth, development, and healthy maintenance of the [worker's] body," stealing "the time required for the consumption of fresh air and sunlight," and reducing "the sound sleep needed for the restoration, reparation, refreshment of the bodily powers."[61]

But it was not alone the lengthening of the working day that was productive of surplus value. More than most other economists of the nineteenth century, Marx was sensitive to the dynamic character of capitalist methods of production. The capitalist of the Marxian model is constantly seeking to expand his enterprise and to revolutionize its methods, a necessary component of his search for surplus value since, by increasing labor's productivity through new and improved methods of production, he can shorten that portion of the workday in which the worker produces the value of his own subsistence.[62]

Marx noted that the tendency of modern industry, especially manufacturing, with its growing emphasis on division of labor, was to increase the productiveness of labor at the expense of the individual laborer, converting him "into a crippled monstrosity, by forcing his detail dexterity at the expense of a world of productive capabilities and instincts." He quoted with approval Adam Smith's remarks concerning the adverse effects of division of labor on the individual workman, despite its economic advantages. To the role of machinery in modern industry Marx gave special emphasis. Not only did the machine increase the productiveness of labor in general and thereby reduce the socially necessary labor time required for the worker's subsistence. It also "dispenses with muscular power . . . [and] becomes a means of employing labourers of slight muscular strength . . . the labour of women and children was, therefore, the first thing sought for by capitalists who use machinery."[63] This property of the machine made it, for Marx, a special source of exploitation. Before the advent of the machine,

the value of labour power was determined, not only by the labour-time necessary to maintain the individual adult labourer, but also by that necessary to maintain his family. Machinery, by throwing every member of that family on to the labour market, spreads the value of the man's labour-power over his whole family. It thus depreciates his labour-power. To purchase the labour-power of a family of four workers may, perhaps, cost more than it formerly did to purchase the labour-power of the head of the family, but, in return, four days' labour takes the place of one, and their price falls in proportion to the excess of the surplus-labour of four over the surplus-labour of one. In order that the family may live, four people must now, not only labour, but expend surplus-labour for the capitalist. Thus we see, that machinery, while augmenting the human material that forms the principal object of capital's exploiting power, at the same time raises the degree of exploitation.[64]

Machinery also affected the relative bargaining positions of capitalist and worker. Previously the worker and capitalist each had a commodity (labor power and money and the means of production) to exchange. "But now the capitalist buys children and young persons under age. Previously, the workman sold his own labour-power, which he disposes of nominally as a free agent. Now he sells wife and child. He has become a slave dealer."[65]

But while raising the productivity of labor, machinery ultimately displaced labor; that, indeed, was its paradox. Surplus value, Marx held, derived only from variable capital invested in labor power. But machinery, in substituting for human labor, reduced the ratio of variable to constant capital. As Marx put it, "However much the use of machinery may increase the surplus-labour at the expense of the necessary labour by heightening the productiveness of labour, it is clear that it attains this result, only by diminishing the number of workmen employed by a given amount of capital. It converts what was formerly variable capital, invested in labour-power, into machinery, which, being constant capital, does not produce surplus-value."[66] This is one of the contradictions of capitalism that Marx believed would lead to its demise. That capitalism contains the seeds of its own destruction is, of course, inherent in the Marxian view of history, grounded in the Hegelian dialectic.

LABOR AS A FORCE IN HISTORY

For Marx, the beginning and the end of the capitalist system are defined in relation to the concept of labor. The origins of capitalism he placed in the bringing together of a comparatively large number of individual employees. The end of the capitalist system would come with the socialization of labor, the beginnings of which were already evident in cooperatives and labor unions, and with the eventual overthrow of the bourgeois capitalist state by the proletariat, the wage-earning class. "The first step in the revolution by the working class," according to the *Communist Manifesto,* "is to raise the proletariat to the position of ruling class, to establish democracy."[67] And if the origins and the demise of capitalist production both lay with labor, so too was labor to be the propelling force through which the transition to socialism would be effected.

The historical role of labor in the Marxian system is best seen in terms of its role not as an economic factor of production but as a social class. "The history of all hitherto existing society," the *Communist Manifesto* teaches, "is the history of class struggles," most recently between the bourgeoisie and the proletariat, representatives of capital and labor.[68] Not only has society come to consist of these two classes, but the proletariat itself is growing as a result of its incorporation of smaller businessmen as capitalist production proceeds.

The lower strata of the middle class—the small shopkeepers, and retired tradesmen generally, the handicraftsmen and peasants—all these sink gradually into the proletariat, partly because their diminutive capital does not suffice for the scale on which modern industry is carried on, and is swamped in the competition with the large capitalists, partly because their specialized skill is rendered worthless by new methods of production. Thus the proletariat is recruited from all classes of the population.[69]

The capitalist of the Marxian model is above all a capital accumulator. The Marxian business firm is a growth-oriented organization, which is forced by competition to expand. As Marx put it, "The development of capitalist production makes it constantly necessary to keep increasing the amount of the capital laid out in a given industrial undertaking, and competition . . . compels . . . [the capitalist] to keep constantly extending his capital, in order to preserve it, but extend it he cannot except by means of progressive accumulation."[70] The Marxian capitalist thus is not only a profit seeker but also a profit user; he constantly plows back his profits into further capital acquisition.

The nature of competition is different in the Marxian model from that of the models of traditional economics in that it leads openly and directly to monopoly or, at least, to a tendency toward monopoly through the progressive elimination of smaller and less successful firms. According to Marx, one of the "immanent laws of capitalist production itself" was "the centralisation of capital. One capitalist always kills many." The result was not only a "constantly diminishing number of the magnates of capital, who usurp and monopolise all advantages" which modern economic growth might under other social arrangements be producing, but also the swelling of the ranks of the proletariat with the dispossessed former capitalists. The working class, Marx emphasized, was "a class always increasing in numbers."[71]

The growing size of the working class, together with its increasing instability of employment—the result of periodic crises and the cyclical phases of the business cycle—made it a formidable foe. As its numbers increase, so too "grows the mass of misery, oppression, slavery, degradation, exploitation; but with this too grows the revolt of the working-class, a class . . . disciplined, united, organised by the very mechanism of the process of capitalist production itself." The system ends when "the monopoly of capital becomes a fetter upon the mode of production, which has sprung up and flourished along with, and under it. Centralization of the means of production and socialisation of labour at last reach a point where they become incompatible with their capitalist integument. This integument is burst asunder. The knell of capitalist private property sounds. The expropriators are expropriated."[72]

Following the overthrow of capitalist authority there arises a temporary dictatorship of the proletariat. During this period, the workers use their newly gained political power "to wrest, by degrees, all capital from the bourgeoisie, to centralize all instruments of production in the hands of the state, *i.e.*, of the proletariat organized as the ruling class; and to increase the total of productive forces as rapidly as possible." Although the dictatorship of the proletariat may last for an extended time, the working class, too, will ultimately disappear in the classless socialist state. There all production will have been "concentrated in the hands of a vast association of the whole nation . . . in which the free development of each is the condition for the free development of all."[73] In such a setting, the goal of communism will be achieved: from each according to his ability, to each according to his need.

A POSTSCRIPT ON MARXIAN ECONOMICS

Marx was a better macroeconomic than a microeconomic theorist. His perception of capitalism as a changing form of economic organization, propelled by business firms for whom capital accumulation and growth are characteristic goals, was well ahead of that of most of his contemporaries. His analysis of the problems of economic concentration, periodic deficiencies of aggregate demand, and economic crises and unemployment, as well as his exhaustive studies of the movements of wage rates, presaged the direction that much of economic analysis would take only many years later. But in terms of price or value theory, Marx's standing is much lower with economists. It was in that limited framework that Marx could be dismissed some years ago by Paul A. Samuelson as "a minor post-Ricardian."[74]

The fundamental weakness of Marxian theory, as economic theory, is its basis in a set of principles that were already being subjected to widespread criticism at the time he wrote: the notion that labor alone was the source of value and that cost of production was the sole regulator of price. The classical theory of wages was widely discredited by the 1860s, and a number of analysts were at work on a new approach—an approach which would reject the classical labor theory of value.

Marx could not have accepted a nonlabor theory of value, for to do so would have destroyed the basis of his entire theoretical system. He wanted a theory of value not as an explanation of price—he himself acknowledged at several points that price and value diverged, an acknowledgment that has led to a substantial body of literature on the so-called "transformation problem"—but rather as a basis for a theory of exploitation. Had the conclusion of classical wage theory, the tendency toward a subsistence wage for the worker, not been available as his starting point, he could not have constructed the theory of exploitation, which is so central to his system. For example, had the conclusion of neoclassical theory, which is that labor receives a wage equal to its marginal product, been Marx's starting point, his analysis, say, of the effect of the role of machinery on the worker's productivity and all of his conclusions would have been quite different.

It is not in formal economic analysis so much as in historical-sociological inquiry that Marx's contribution to the study of labor rests. His early insights on labor's alienation in modern industry stand as a useful starting point for more recent work on the subject, yet the element of hope that his analysis suggests for the future of the working classes has inspired countless workers in newly developing economies. In this regard, Schumpeter has noted, Marxism is a religion no less than a system of economics, and Marx the prophet is undoubtedly more appealing, and his position more secure, than Marx the economist.[75]

MARGINALISM AND THE FOUNDATIONS OF MODERN WAGE THEORY

The classical theory of wages, centering on the doctrine of the wages fund, came under increasing attack in the 1860s and following the publication of W. T. Thornton's *On Labour* was explicitly repudiated by John Stuart Mill in 1869.[1] Mill's recantation did not, however, signal the end of the classical doctrine. In both England and America, at the hands of such prominent figures as J. E. Cairnes and F. W. Taussig, efforts continued for more than two decades to revive and sustain the theory. These efforts would ultimately be unsuccessful, but the debate over the wages fund theory in the 1870s and 1880s represents an important chapter in the history of economics, especially for American economics, for the debate was primarily an American one, and it was "the central focus of theoretical discussion among American economists during what can be regarded as the coming of age of analytical economics in the United States."[2] The debate over the wages fund also produced the key concepts of the marginal productivity theory, which, by the end of the century, had become established as the accepted approach to the problem of distribution.

THE WAGES FUND CONTROVERSY

J. E. Cairnes's *Leading Principles of Political Economy*, although published in 1874, four years after Jevons's introduction of the concept of marginal utility, is generally regarded as "the last statement of the classical system of ideas . . . its cost-of-production theory of value, its reformulation of the Wages-Fund doctrine, and, above all, its unqualified acceptance of what is called 'the great Malthusian difficulty' stamp . . . [it is] as broadly representative, as far as any single work can be, of classical political economy."[3]

But to describe Cairnes as the last of the classical economists is not to imply that he was insensitive to the realities of the industrial world in England in the 1870s. Concerning the labor market, for example, Cairnes admitted that competition was not fully free and that the notion that labor "may be shifted about from one occupation to another in search of the highest remuneration, is a mere figment of the economist's brain, without foundation in fact." He also acknowledged that "industrial skill is not a thing to be acquired in a moment, and that which a man possesses is the result, in general, of considerable time and outlay devoted to its acquisition." Moreover there were "limitations imposed by social circumstances on the free competition of labor."[4] But Cairnes held that in order to achieve what he called "an effective industrial competition," it was not necessary that every worker should be fully capable of entering any given occupation so long as a certain number were able to do so. For each type of occupation, there would be, Cairnes argued, a number of workers whose abilities, education, and, possibly, social position, would qualify them for employment therein.

It was Cairnes's position that although competition between industrial groupings was absent, the workers within such groups constituted an effective competitive market. This preserved, within each noncompeting group, the cost-of-production principle of value advanced by the earlier economists. To the problem of exchange between noncompeting groups, Cairnes applied the principle of reciprocal demand, which had earlier been developed by John Stuart Mill in his analysis of the determination of values in international trade.[5] Thus, for Cairnes, one part of the wage problem— determining relative wages from a microeconomic point of view—was subsumed in the general problem of value: " 'Relative wages and profits' . . . follow the same laws which govern the exchange value of commodities . . . wages and profits, regarded as relative phenomena, are governed by Cost of Production, where the producers are in effective competition with one another, and, where they are not, by Reciprocal Demand."[6] But the theory of value, based on cost and demand, was only a partial solution to the problem of wage determination. According to Cairnes,

What the doctrine of value reveals to us on this subject is the causes which determine the *relative* remuneration of laborers as among themselves, and that of capitalists as among themselves. It tells us why some classes of workmen and some classes of capitalists receive the same or equivalent remuneration, while in other cases inequality in various degrees prevails; but it tells us nothing as to what determines the positive remuneration which any class of capitalists or of labourers receives, nor as to the causes on which depend the average well-being of all classes.[7]

In dealing with the macroeconomic problem of the general level of wages, Cairnes fell back on the concept of the wages fund, although, as Marshall later noted, "he did so only by explaining away so much which is characteristic of the doctrine, that there is very little left in it to justify its title."[8] One of Cairnes's modifications to the classical theory was the emphasis he placed on industrial structure: "The aggregate amount of wealth appropriated to the laboring population in any country varies, not simply with the progress of the national capital, but with this latter circumstance taken in connection with the character of the national industries, the rest being also, within certain narrow limits, modified by the supply of labor. In other words, it appears that the same amount of capital will yield under different circumstances Wages-funds of different dimensions, and will consequently be capable of supporting populations of different magnitudes." Also, he insisted, the wages fund did not necessarily determine the long-run economic position of the wage-earning class, since "there is nothing in the nature of things which restricts the laboring population to this fund for their support." In their role as laborers, it was to the wages fund to which the workers must look. But Cairnes held that "they may help production otherwise than by their labor: they may save, and thus become themselves the owners of capital, and profits may thus be brought to aid the Wages fund."[9]

Cairnes took issue with what he took to be the unnecessarily rigid interpretations of the wages fund doctrine of such critics as Longe and Thornton. He quoted Thornton, who had argued that the wages fund theory assumed that "capitalists put aside a portion of their means with a determination that, whatever happens, they shall be spent in wages," and went on to say, with some scorn, that "the doctrine, as I understand it, makes no such assumptions; nor am I, in holding it, bound to maintain any such absurdity."[10] Thornton had agreed that "every employer possesses a certain amount of money, whether his own or borrowed, out of which all his expenses must be met, if met at all." But, he asked, "is there any law fixing the amount of his domestic expenditure, and thereby fixing likewise the balance available for his industrial operation? May he not spend more or less on his family and himself, according to his fancy—in the one case having more, in the other less, left for the conduct of his business? And of what is left, does he or can he determine beforehand how much shall be laid out on buildings, how much on materials, how much on labor?"[11] Cairnes's answer was that the wages fund theory involved no predetermination as rigid as that which Thornton had suggested.[12]

On the question of the influence of trade unions on wages, Cairnes was less dogmatic than most earlier defenders of the wages fund had been. While holding that the power of unions to raise wages was limited, except at the expense of other workers or at a cost in unemployment, he nonetheless acknowledged that in favorable economic circumstances in certain industries, where profits were above the minimum necessary for continued production, trade unions might more quickly bring real gains to the workers than could the slower market process. Because of lags in the workings out of competition, Cairnes wrote, "Laborers may be excluded from all share in the prosperity of which the entire fruits are appropriated by their employers. If, then, laborers have the power, as we have seen they have, of shortening or of annihilating altogether this interval, why may they not use it? It seems to me that there is here a perfectly legitimate field for Trades-Union action."[13]

Despite these qualifications, however, there can be no doubt about

Cairnes's attachment to the fundamental assumptions underlying the doctrine of the wages fund: that the amount available for the payment of wages was limited by capital assets, not only for the economy as a whole but for the typical business firm as well. Cairnes assumed, as did the earlier classical economists, that "the hiring of labor for productive purposes is an incident of the investment of capital" and not an alternative to it.[14] The fundamental defect of the classical system, the failure to recognize the essential fact of substitutability between capital and labor, was perpetuated in Cairnes's system.

The debate over the wages fund concerned the concept and nature of the business firm, and the resolution of the problem, culminating in the formulation of the marginal productivity theory, produced a theory of production and distribution applicable to all hired factors of production. R. D. Collison Black has argued that the marginalist revolution in economic science established "the concept of economizing behavior . . . [as] an essential part of the core" of economics but noted that "with the classical economists this was not so."[15] This may be an overstatement of the differences between the classical and neoclassical economists, but it contains important elements of truth. The classical economists' conception of the businessman can probably fairly be said to be that of accumulator, interested in the growth of his wealth and employing it toward that end, while the neoclassical conception was of the businessman as a maximizer, deciding on the best combination among the choices open to him. The distinction is between getting more and getting most. For both the classical and the neoclassical economists, the search for profits was the prime business motive, but for the classical economists, this effort was limited by the ownership of wealth. Cairnes was in the classical tradition when he approached wage theory by emphasizing "the amount of wealth spent in the hiring of labor."[16] The neoclassical economists would have agreed with him that "a capitalist engages and pays a workman from precisely the same motives which lead him to purchase raw material, a factory, or a machine," and that the capitalist "invests his wealth productively in order to obtain a profit on the portion of his means so employed," but they did not give to the ownership of wealth the emphasis that Cairnes and the classical economists did.[17] According to Cairnes, the amount of the capitalist's investment will be determined by "the amount of his total means; . . . , his character and disposition as affected by the temptation to immediate enjoyment on the one hand, and by the prospect of future aggrandizement on the other; [and] the opportunities of making profit. Alter any of these conditions—his total means, his character, or his opportunities of making profit, and the effect will be an alteration in the amount of his investment."[18]

For Cairnes, the profit motive was limited by other considerations, especially the ownership of capital. Mark Blaug has asserted that one of the weaknesses of the classical economists' reasoning was that "they had no theory of the firm," meaning, presumably, that they failed to see the possibilities of factor substitutions within the firm.[19] There is a theory of the firm implicit in Cairnes's remarks, but the conception is of the firm as an owner of assets, first of all, and a hirer of factors of production only within the limits imposed by its wealth position. It was this view of the firm, and the related question of the businessman's motivation in hiring both capital and labor, that provided an important part of the final challenge to the wages fund doctrine.

One of the most effective and influential carriers of that challenge was Francis A. Walker. In a long review of the literature on the wages fund theory in 1875, Walker noted that "the present situation is somewhat chaotic" and that "much, at least, of the structure of the economists lies hopelessly broken upon the ground." He began his analysis by raising the question as to "whether it is worth while to attempt to repair the ruin; whether any economical purpose is to be served by reconstructing the wage-fund" theory. He concluded by asserting that the theory was without validity under any circumstances and that "the term itself should be abandoned."[20]

Walker's attack centered on the notion that wages were paid out of capital: "Wages are really paid out of the product of current industry; and that product bears no constant relation to existing capital." He began his analysis by asking what motivates a business firm to hire labor. It was not, he contended, an employer's purpose to dispense a certain fund for the benefit of the wage earners but rather to earn profits for himself through the sale of labor's produce; that is, "wages bear a clear and direct relation to the product."[21]

Walker denied even the most tenuous connection between capital and wages, insisting that it was labor's current product that accounted for its wages. He acknowledged that in England wages had often been advanced out of capital, but the economic history of the United States suggested a totally different pattern: "From the first settlement of the Colonies down to the discovery of gold in California, laborers, whether in agriculture or in manufactures, were as a rule hired by the year and paid at the end of the year." After reviewing a large collection of accounts from the books of farmers in different sections of the country as late as 1851, which showed certain advances and charges to the hired help, including cash for personal expenses and bills for bookmakers, grocers, apothecaries, doctors, and tax collectors, he wrote: "Yet in general the amount of such advances does not exceed one third, and it rarely reaches one half, of the stipulated wages of the year." It was thus erroneous to refer to wages thus paid as coming from capital. "At the time these contracts were made the wealth which was to pay these wages was not in existence. At the time these services were rendered, that wealth was not in existence. It came into existence only as the result of those contracts and the rendering of those services."[22] His study of New England manufacturing plants suggested that yearly payments at the end of the year were common until the mid-1850s.

Walker placed strong emphasis upon labor's positive contributions to economic growth and development, especially in newer countries. He disagreed with the wages fund doctrine, instead insisting, "Other things do not and cannot remain the same when population . . . increases or decreases. Production, that one essential thing, changes at once. . . . So far is it from being true that, capital remaining the same, an increase of population implies a decrease of wages, the effect may be exactly the reverse; and Americans have seen the process going on over large sections of country for long periods of time." It was not alone in new and rapidly expanding economies, according to Walker, that the wages fund doctrine was invalid. Even in older and more fully populated countries, the classical theory was faulty "for it excludes altogether the contribution which the newcomer, the additional laborer, makes to the production of the community."[23]

The wage-fund doctrine regards him as a pure addition to the divisor, without recognizing the fact that his labor must also add something to the dividend. . . . [Even in the more populated counties] he still contributes something, and that something, however small it may be, helps to swell the amount that can be paid in wages. It is simply inconceivable that the earth should ever be so crowded with population that another able-bodied workman could add positively nothing in production.[24]

In his refutation of the wages fund doctrine, Walker anticipated many elements of the marginal productivity theory. This is true not only of his emphasis on the worker's contribution to production as the basis for his wages but also on the emphasis he placed on labor's efficiency and the means through which it could be increased. Walker stressed that labor productivity, and hence the level of wages, depended on "industrial aptitudes of the people, their intelligence, sobriety, and thrift; elements which the wage-fund theory peremptorily excludes from the problem of the present rate of wages, making the *number* of laborers the sole divisor of a predetermined dividend."[25] New and improved equipment and work processes were at the heart of increased productivity and, as such, should contribute to increased wages.

Walker nevertheless failed to develop a viable theory of wages. His own positive theory, which he articulated in his *Political Economy* and which is commonly referred to as the residual claimant theory, failed to gain wide acceptance, possibly because it "came dangerously close

. . . to asserting the absurdity that each factor gets what is left over after the others have taken their shares." In the history of wage theory, Walker stands as an effective critic of the weaknesses of the classical doctrine, especially its limited understanding of the nature of the business firm under capitalistic organization, "around whose various ideas and expression much of the distribution discussed revolved" for a number of years.[26] He anticipated but failed to develop the intimate connection between wages and productivity upon which modern wage theory would be built.

The last major defender of the classical theory of wages in Anglo-American economics was Frank W. Taussig, whose *Wages and Capital* was published in 1896. One year earlier, he had remarked that "courage is required to intimate that there can be any degree of truth in . . . [the wage fund theory] whatever," and a good part of *Wages and Capital* was devoted to outlining the criticisms that had been directed toward it.[27] Taussig believed that "the old doctrine of the wages fund had a solid basis in its conception, incomplete yet in essentials just, of the payment of present labor from past product," yet he had to conclude that "in its relation to other economic questions, whether practical or theoretical, the whole wages fund controversy was of comparatively little significance."[28]

Practical questions—on strikes, trade unions, combinations—invariably arise as to particular wages, not as to wages at large; while it is only to the questions of wages at large that general reasoning as to wages and capital can apply. So far as the deeper problems of distribution are concerned, it appeared again that these have little to do with the general wages fund. . . . In fact, the wages fund doctrine, or what there is of truth in it, has to do rather with production than with distribution. It serves to describe the process by which the real income of the community emerges from a prolonged process of production.[29]

As a recent student of the subject has noted, "Taussig deeply regretted the complete eclipse of the wage-fund theory and felt that it contained certain truths which economic theory and policy could neglect only to their serious detriment, but when it came down to the nub, there was only one truth that Taussig could insist upon—that production takes time—and Bohm-Bawerk had already given that proposition a degree of vigor that no revival of the wage-fund doctrine could have done."[30] Taussig's masterful analysis of the wages fund, intended as a means of preserving its essential truths, proved instead to be its final eulogy.

MARGINALISM AND THE PRODUCTIVITY OF LABOR

According to Thomas S. Kuhn, the development of scientific thought involves occasional discontinuities associated with a new way of approaching or defining a problem, to which he has applied the term *paradigm*. To qualify as a paradigm, a particular scientific achievement must be "sufficiently unprecedented to attract an enduring group of adherents away from competing modes of scientific activity" and must also be "sufficiently open-ended to leave all sorts of problems for the redefined group of practitioners to resolve."[31] The achievements of Artistotle, Ptolemy, Newton, and Lavoisier are but a few examples of paradigmatic works in Kuhn's sense of the term. According to him, the emergence of paradigms importantly affects the subsequent development of a scientific field: "When . . . an individual or group first produces a synthesis able to attract most of the next generation's practitioners, the older schools gradually disappear." Some take up the new mode; those who do not are eventually ignored by their peers. The result is thus "a new and more rigid definition of the field . . . it is sometimes just its reception of a paradigm that transforms a group previously interested merely in the study of nature into a profession or, at least, a discipline."[32]

To some extent, the field of economics underwent such a paradigmatic experience in the closing decades of the nineteenth century, with the development of the marginal utility theory and, somewhat later, that of marginal productivity. What is often called the marginalist revolution in economics refers to "the nearly simultaneous but completely independent discovery in the early 1870's by Jevons, Menger and Walras of the principal of diminishing marginal utility as the fundamental building block of a new kind of static microeconomics." Yet *revolution* may be an exaggeration of actual developments. The work of Jevons, Menger, and Walras—and John Bates Clark, who can be credited with independent discovery of marginal utility in the United States—was anticipated in varying degrees by Gossen, von Thünen, Longfield, and even Ricardo. As Mark Blaug has noted, "There is as much marginalism in Ricardo as in Jevons or Walras, but it is applied to different things."[33] Second, the new theories found acceptance only gradually and never fully displaced the older approach. It is, indeed, the position of Professor Stigler that although "the marginal utility revolution of the 1870's replaced the individual economic agent as a sociological or historical datum by the utility-maximizing individual . . . the essential elements of the classical theory were affected in no respect."[34] This is close to the view earlier expressed by Wesley Mitchell that Jevons, Menger, Walras, and J. B. Clark did not produce a new approach to economic theory but merely "a new variety of the Ricardian species. The utility theorists and the cost theorists held the same conception of human behavior, they worked at the same problems, and employed the same methods . . .

the two lines of analysis were so much alike that they harmonized admirably when Marshall incorporated both into a single framework."[35]

There is merit in these qualifications, for the history of economics from the *Wealth of Nations* to the present day displays a remarkable consistency built on the fundamental concept of self-interest. The utility-maximizing consumer of Jevons's theory is not fundamentally different in character from the worker who, in Adam Smith's schema, sought to maximize the net satisfactions from his job. There was, nevertheless, a consequence of lasting significance coming out of the work on marginal utility, and its essence is contained in T. W. Hutchison's comment that what proved in the end to be important about marginal utility was "the adjective rather than the noun."[36] What the marginalist approach to economic analysis meant most fundamentally was a redefinition of the economic problem. Rather than analyzing the causes of the increase in a nation's wealth or the macrodistribution of this wealth among landlords, laborers, and capitalists, for the marginalist or neoclassical approach, "pricing and resource allocation with fixed supplies of the factors of production became *the* economic problem, setting aside all questions about changes in the quantity and quality of productive resources through time."[37] Constrained maximization, in short, became the accepted mode of economic reasoning.

According to Frank Knight, "The greatest improvement introduced by the marginal utility viewpoint came in the field of distribution theory" as a result of the extension of its fundamental principles to the problem of the pricing of the factors of production.[38] This occurred with the development of the marginal productivity theory, in the closing years of the nineteenth century, and while a full history of this development would include the contributions of von Thünen, Wicksteed, Stuart Wood, and others, it was primarily the achievement of John Bates Clark. Clark was one of a number of American economists whose doctoral work in economics was undertaken in Germany and whose early approach to economics was conditioned by exposure to the historical economists then predominant in Germany. His first book, *The Philosophy of Wealth* (1885), reflected many of the criticisms toward traditional theory that had been advanced by the German historical school. Economic theory, according to Clark, was defective in its premises: "The better elements of human nature were a forgotten factor . . . [and] a degraded conception of human nature vitiated the theory of the distribution of wealth."[39] Also, Clark held, the received theory (which he often called "Ricardian") was defective in its treatment of competition:

Competition is no longer adequate to account for the phenomena of social industry. . . . Competition of the individualistic type is rapidly passing out of

existence. . . . Individual competition, the great regulator of the former era
has, in important fields, practically disappeared. It ought to disappear; it was
in its latter days, incapable of working justice. The alternative regulator is
moral force, and this is already in action. . . . The present state of industrial
society is transitional and chaotic.[40]

In the labor market, especially, competition of the old individualistic
variety could no longer be assumed. On the contrary, the actual
workings out of competition over time had produced, Clark held,
collective action by both labor and capital.[41]

Clark never lost his early interest in the dynamic institutional
changes brought about under industrial capitalism, and he returned
to this question in his *Essentials of Economic Theory* (1907). But the high
regard in which he is held in the history of economic thought rests
almost solely on his *Distribution of Wealth*, and the contrast between
that book and his earlier *Philosophy of Wealth* could hardly be greater.
In his *Distribution*, the first full and comprehensive statement of the
theory of marginal productivity, Clark eschewed his earlier emphasis
on historical and institutional analysis. His purpose was "to show that
the distribution of the income of society is controlled by a natural law,
and that this law, if it worked without friction, would give to every
agent of production the amount of wealth which that agent creates."
His method was to abstract from the dynamic changes of the real
world by showing "to what rates the market prices of goods, the wages
of labor and the interest on capital would conform, if the changes that
are going on in the industrial world and in the character of its activities were to cease." He planned to show that "in the midst of all
changes there are at work forces that fix rates to which, at any one
moment, wages and interest tend to conform."[42]

Clark's starting point was the proposition that so far as natural laws
were undisturbed, the share of income going to any productive agent
would be measured by that agent's actual product. Thus "the entire
study of distribution" was but "a study of *specific production.*"[43] He ob-
jected to the classical distinction between production and distribution
and insisted on the essential unity of these processes. Clark's theory of
wage determination was built on both Ricardian rent theory and the
marginal utility theory of value. There are, Clark noted, "two permanent entities combined in the industry of the world," capital and
labor, both of which "have an unlimited power of bodily transmuta-
tion." Moreover in contrast to the fixity of proportions between capital and labor, the underlying premise of classical wage theory, Clark
emphasized that "there is often appreciable elasticity in the amount of
labor that can be employed in connection with a stock [of capital]."[44]
The classical theory of diminishing returns had been built on the assumption of the fixity of land. Clark generalized from this by sub-

stituting capital for land and asking what the result would be of increasing the number of laborers. Let us imagine, he suggested, a representative community.

Give, now, to this isolated community a hundred million dollars' worth of capital, and introduce gradually a corresponding force of workers. Put a thousand laborers into the rich environment that these conditions afford, and their product *per capita* will be enormous. Their work will be aided by capital to the extent of a hundred thousand dollars per man. This sum will take such forms as the workers can best use, and a profusion of the available tools, machines, materials, etc., will be at every laborer's hand. . . . Add, now, a second thousand workers to the force; and, with the appliances at their service changed in form—as they must be—to adapt them to the uses of the larger number of men, the output per man will be smaller than before. This second increment of labor has at its disposal capital amounting to only half a hundred thousand dollars per man; and this it has taken from the men who were formerly using it. In using capital, the new force of workers goes share in share with the force that was already in the field. Where one of the original workers had an elaborate machine, he now has a cheaper and less efficient one; and the new workers by his side also have machines of the cheaper variety. This reduction in the efficiency of the instrument that the original worker used must be taken into account, in estimating how much the new worker can add to the product of industry.[45]

The addition of workers has caused both the new and the original workers to work with inferior capital equipment, and the new worker therefore "brings into existence less wealth than did one of the first division of laborers."[46] We must, however, Clark went on to say, "be careful as to the arithmetic of the change:

The product that can be attributed to this second increment of labor is, of course, not all that it creates *by the aid of the capital that the earlier division of workers has surrendered to it*; it is only what its presence adds to the product previously created. With a thousand workers using the whole capital, the product was four units of value; with two thousand, it is four plus; and the plus quantity, whatever it is, measures the product that is attributable to the second increment of labor only. There is a minus quantity to be taken into account in calculating the product that is attributable to the final unit of labor.[47]

It was the final unit of labor, according to Clark, that was determinate so far as wages were concerned. With the increment of labor that is "the last one that the isolated society contains, we have the law of wages."

The last composite unit of labor . . . has created its own distinguishable product. This is less than the product that was attributable to any of the earlier divisions; but, now that this section of the laboring force is in the field, no division is effectively worth any more than is this one. If any earlier section of the working force were to demand more than the last one produces, the employer could discharge it and put into its place the last section of men. What he would lose by the departure of any body of a thousand men, is measured by the product that was brought into existence by the last body that was set working. Each unit of labor, then, is worth to its employer what the last unit produces.[48]

Clark's work integrated the classical theory of diminishing returns with the neoclassical theory of marginal pricing—the notion that competitive prices are determined at the margin by the contribution, either to utility or to production, of the final unit or agent. The theory applied equally to all factors of production and effectively brought together the concepts of production and distribution, fully incorporating the concept of labor into the competitive market schema. The competition by and for labor would tend to force the wage rate to an equality with labor's marginal productivity. If the wage rate exceeded marginal productivity, competition between workers, unemployed because profit-maximizing entrepreneurs would not hire agents whose costs exceeded their contribution to production, would tend to force wages down. Conversely if wages fell short of marginal productivity, the competition would be by employers, who would try to outbid each other for laborers whose contribution to production exceeded their costs, thus forcing wages up. Marginal productivity, therefore (in Clark's terminology it was *final productivity*), was the key to the natural law of wages that he had sought.

Although he specifically eschewed any consideration of distributive justice as lying "outside of our inquiry, for it is a matter of pure ethics," there was clearly an implied ethic, especially for an individualistic society, in Clark's conclusion that "if each productive function is paid according to the amount of its product, then each man gets what he himself produces," and later critics would with some justification be able to charge the *Distribution of Wealth* with a pro-property bias, however unintended.[49] Clark followed Locke in asserting that "for nothing, if not to protect property, does the state exist. Hence a state which should force a workman to leave behind him in the mill property that was his by right of creation, would fail at a critical point." He felt that the state's function was adequately fulfilled in an economic organization of competitive capitalism, whose laws he had discovered, since "property is protected at the point of its origin, if actual wages are the whole product of labor, if interest is the product of capital, and if profit is the product of a coordinating [entrepreneurial] act."[50]

THE MARSHALLIAN SYNTHESIS

The concept of marginal productivity extended and complemented that of marginal utility; together they integrated the theory of pricing of the factors of production, and thereby the problem of distribution, with the theory of the pricing of final goods and services. Neither concept, however, represented a complete theory of price, despite the claims advanced by some contemporaries who saw the new approach as replacing the classical doctrine. According to that doctrine, value was based on cost of production commonly expressed in terms of labor. The limitations of the newer theories were recognized and emphasized by Alfred Marshall, the dominant figure in economics during the late nineteenth and early twentieth centuries. Marshall held that marginal utility—of which he himself was an independent co-discoverer—and marginal productivity had useful contributions to make to economic understanding, but he insisted that they did not destroy the validity of the older doctrines. He extended economic knowledge and teaching so far and in so many ways that a commentator in the 1920s remarked that to the extent that "there is today any generally accepted body of economic doctrines, it is largely what Marshall made it."[51] Surely a major part of his achievement was the integration of the newer theories and approaches of his own time with the classical doctrine of Ricardo and Mill.

Marshall began his analysis of wages by noting that "the alert business man is ever seeking for the most profitable application of his resources, and endeavouring to make use of each . . . agent of production up to that margin, or limit, at which he would gain by transferring a small part of his expenditure to some other agent." The businessman was thus the "medium through which the principle of substitution so adjusts the employment of each agent that, in its marginal application, its cost is proportionate to the additional net product resulting from its use." So far, Marshall seems to be adopting a position very close to Clark's, but he stopped short of it by denying that marginal productivity could be advanced as a theory of wages, charging that "there is no valid ground for any such pretension."[52]

Marshall pointed out that the marginal productivity of labor, the extra output that could be sold for a profit as the result of hiring an additional worker, related only to the firm's demand for labor and said nothing about the question of labor supply. Yet the supply of labor, as the classical economists had emphasized, was an important part, albeit for Marshall only a part, of wage determination. In rejecting the claims of the utility theorists to have replaced the Ricardian cost of production theory of price, Marshall had noted the one-sidedness of both schools: "We might as reasonably dispute whether it is the upper or the under blade of a pair of scissors that cuts a piece of paper, as whether value is governed by utility or cost of production." According to Marshall, a truly scientific account of price determination would always emphasize the joint action of demand and supply but would note that changes in demand could often be effected more rapidly than changes in supply. Thus, *"as a general rule*, the shorter the period which we are considering, the greater must be the share of our attention which is given to the influence of demand on value; and the longer the period, the more important will be the influence of cost of production on value."[53]

In his analysis of wages, Marshall continued his emphasis on the joint action of demand and supply. The concept of marginal productivity was important because it illuminated the conditions underlying the firm's demand for labor. But the classical economists had not entirely erred when they emphasized the importance of both the quantity and quality of labor. According to Marshall:

Demand and supply exert coordinate influences on wages; neither has a claim to predominance. . . . Wages tend to equal the net product of labour; its marginal productivity rules the demand-price for it; and, on the other side, wages tend to retain a close though indirect and intricate relation with the cost of rearing, training and sustaining the energy of efficient labour. The various elements of the problem mutually determine (in the sense of governing) one another; and incidentally this secures that supply-price and demand-price tend to equality; wages are not governed by demand-price nor by supply-price, but by the whole set of causes which govern demand and supply.[54]

In the long run under static conditions, Marshall believed that the cost of production theory of the classical economists achieved validity, even in the case of labor, because of a

tendency towards a position of normal equilibrium, in which the supply of each of these agents shall stand in such a relation to the demand for its services, as to give to those who have provided the supply a sufficient reward for their efforts and sacrifices. If the economic conditions of the country remained stationary sufficiently long, this tendency would realize itself in such an adjustment of supply to demand, that both machines and human beings would earn generally an amount that corresponded fairly with their cost of rearing and training.[55]

But Marshall, ever alert to the dynamics of change, was unwilling to tarry long in so static a world. "As it is," he added, "the economic conditions of the country are constantly changing, and the point of adjustment of normal demand and supply in relation to labour is constantly being shifted."[56]

There is a certain ambivalence in Marshall's approach to the study of labor (which extends to his whole analysis). He was more sensitive than most of his predecessors in England to changing economic processes and institutions, yet his concept of equilibrium of economic forces ultimately shaped his vision of the economic process.

Marshall came to the study of economics with a strong sense of social reform, and in the *Principles* wrote that "the dominant aim of economics in the present generation is to contribute to a solution of social problems."[57] His *Principles* began and ended on a note of concern for the problem of poverty and the possibility of the economic betterment of the large masses of people. In his approach to labor problems and labor markets, he often came close to the arguments and criticisms of economic theory later advanced by the so-called institutional economists. He acknowledged that the labor market was a highly abstract concept and that terms such as *the wages of labor in general* had little meaning in relation to actual problems: "In fact there is no such thing in modern civilization as a general rate of wages. Each of a hundred or more groups of workers has its own wage problem, its own set of special causes, natural and artificial, controlling the supply-price, and limiting the numbers of its members; each has its own demand-price governed by the need that other agents of production have of its services."[58]

Like the German historical economists and the American institutionalists, Marshall acknowledged the changing character of economic life and institutions and insisted that the principles he was articulating were not valid for all times and places. He noted the inequalities of bargaining power that often characterized conflicts between capital and labor, as well as the growing influence of trade unionism, an institution that he described as "more full of interest and instruction than almost anything else in English history."[59] He noted that "the term 'competition' has gathered about it evil savour, and has come to imply a certain selfishness and indifference to the well-being of others," and held that it was "not well suited to describe the special characteristics of industrial life in the modern age."[60] Yet despite these qualifications, they remained just that: qualifications to Marshall's essentially deterministic analysis of economic life based on the synthesis of classical and neoclassical supply and demand theory. Despite the limitations of the concept of competition and despite the growing importance of nonmarket forces such as the labor union and the large-scale enterprise enjoying substantial economic power, the essence of the Marshallian system was the workings of competitive supply and demand. "[N]o matter how heavily overlaid with illustrative material," as Homan has noted, Marshall's *"Principles* bears the imprint of his early bent for 'pure' theory."[61]

Thus in the Marshallian system, despite frequent deferences to institutional complexities and realities, the study of labor was ultimately subsumed and embedded in competitive market reasoning. Marshall succeeded in preserving the essential insights of the classical cost-of-production theorists by showing their relevance to the concept of labor supply, and of reconciling and synthesizing these with the newer insights into the nature of the firm's demand for labor which the marginal productivity theory offered. But it would remain for others to develop the institutional analysis of labor problems.

"We tend," writes Neil Chamberlain of John R. Commons, "to think of Commons as being a labor economist, but both in his public and teaching roles, he ventured into an amazing variety of fields."[1] Not only did Commons's interests within economics encompass much more than the study of labor—he taught and wrote as well on such subjects as industrial organization and control, taxation, monetary policy, and price theory—but also he frequently ventured outside economics altogether into law, history, sociology, political science, public administration, and other fields. In this respect, there is a strong similarity between Commons and Adam Smith, whom we tend also to think of as an economist although, in fact, he was not really an economist at all since the term had little meaning in his day. He was a professor of moral philosophy, and there is scant mention in the *Wealth of Nations* of the economist's method of approach or the limits of his field. It is clear, however, that Smith's conception of political economy was a broad one and one with which Commons could readily have agreed: "a branch of the science of a statesman or legislator . . . [which] proposes to enrich both the people and the state."[2] Commons may be thought of as a labor economist in precisely the same way that we tend to think of Smith as an economist: as a founding father of that which the term later came to mean. The term *labor economics* nowhere appears in Commons's labor writings, and for approximately the same reason that *economics* was not used by Smith. For both economics and labor economics, the term acquired meaning and the discipline took shape only after certain early workers directed attention to the need for specialized study in what had been part of a larger field. In the case of labor economics, the term did not become widespread in the United States until after the publication of Solomon Blum's text by that title in 1925. By that time, Commons's primary interests had shifted away from labor studies and toward the enunciation of his theory of institutional economics. Earlier references, including those made by Commons, are to labor problems.

The difference between these terms is not merely one of semantics. The emergence of the term *labor economics* is to be viewed as at one with the efforts of the students of labor to integrate more fully with general economics and to identify more closely with the economist's approach. This development, belonging primarily to the 1920s and 1930s, marks a definite shift from the earlier period, when references to labor problems were rather more clearly characterized by the absence of economic analysis and theoretical constructions. It is during this earlier period of focus on labor problems, encompassing roughly the last two decades of the nineteenth and the first two decades of the twentieth centuries, that the study of labor first emerged as a field of specialization within the economics departments of American universities.

THE BACKGROUND AND THE ENVIRONMENT

During the early and middle years of the nineteenth century, political economy in England was attuned to the dominant economic problems of the day and was accorded a wide following by all but the working classes. It can probably fairly be said that at no other time or place has there been such popular interest in the subject. In contrast, public interest in the United States during the years before the Civil War was dominated by political issues. Even such economic issues as the controversies surrounding the First and Second Banks of the United States, the question of protection in international trade, or the disposal of public lands seemed to be dominated by political, frequently sectional, considerations. But in the decades following the Civil War, economic issues gained the ascendancy.[3] Whether the problem was railroads, public utility regulation, manufacturing combinations or trusts, labor unrest, agrarian discontent, or the older but continuing problems of the monetary standard and the tariff, questions of economic policy were central topics of the day.

During the 1850s, the English historian Macaulay had predicted that the boasted American immunity from the social upheavals of Europe would cease as soon as great manufacturing centers arose, with large numbers of workers who would sometimes be unemployed. "Then," he had written, "your institutions will fairly be brought to the test." He continued, "Distress everywhere makes the laborer mutinous and discontented, and inclines him to listen with eagerness to agitators who tell him that it is a monstrous iniquity that one man should have a million, while another cannot get a full meal."[4] To many observers of the 1870s and 1880s, that time appeared to have come. During the 1870s, a large-scale labor movement first became evident in the United States, highlighted in 1877 by the national strikes against the railroads in protest over a reduction in wages. Violence ensued, and federal troops were used for the first time in a labor dispute. By the 1880s, American unionism, not yet consistently manifesting the characteristics of what Robert Hoxie would later call "business unionism" and viewed generally as a menacing foreign conspiracy, appeared to be a major economic problem. The mid-1880s saw great gains in union membership, as well as violence, capped by the Haymarket Square riots in Chicago in 1886. Some states had established labor bureaus in the 1870s, but it was not until the mid-1880s that the federal government took its first halting steps in the area of labor relations. In 1883 Congress held extensive hearings on the relations between capital and labor and the following year established the Bureau of Labor in the Department of Interior. Four years later, the bureau was incorporated into the newly organized (but not yet cabinet-level) Department of Labor.[5]

In all the turbulence surrounding the growth of organized labor in the United States during these years, professional economics had little to say and excited little interest. Amasa Walker, the author of a widely used text, wrote that "although desirable that the instructor should be familiar with the subject himself, it is by no means indispensable." Another leading textbook author of the period, Arthur L. Perry of Williams College, claimed to have gained full insight into the field through perusal of Bastiat's *Harmonies Economiques*: "I had scarcely read a dozen pages in that remarkable book, when, closing it, and giving myself to an hour's reflection, the field of political economy in all its outlines and landmarks lay before my mind, just as it does today." And Richard T. Ely, an undergraduate at Columbia during the early 1870s, recalled that among his classmates, economics was known as "dry bones" and was generally regarded as a "finished product."[6]

But if the academic study of economics was poorly regarded, there was nonetheless an increasing interest in economic problems. This relates to the contrast mentioned earlier between England and the United States. In England, where political economy first developed as an academic subject, the subject as taught was in step with the dominant economic needs of the times. Thus the doctrine of free trade proved efficacious to an island nation that was the seat of an empire of largely undeveloped economies and was, both in terms of resources and institutions, ideally suited to manufacturing, especially at a time when real costs of food production were declining in newly opened lands and advancements in ocean transport were making their speedy importation a possibility. Later the Malthusian doctrine and its logical extension, the emphasis on restraints on the birthrate, appealed to the relatively highly populated country, whose needs were for capital deepening, especially when the capital needed to be generated largely within the domestic economy by forgoing consumption.

The circumstances and patterns of development of the United States were quite different from those of England, and while many of the assumptions and teachings of classical political economy were accepted in this country as elsewhere, there were always important reservations. Thus the Malthusian doctrine of the tendency of the population to outstrip the means of production was modified, where it was not entirely rejected. As early as 1838, Francis Bowen, who taught economics (in addition to philosophy) at Harvard College, took issue with the Malthusian conclusions: "In this country, we are not obliged to render life in an almshouse more irksome and uncomfortable than it need be, through fear that it may become a favorite place of abode for the suffering poor. . . . We may admit the [Malthusian] principle, but in our own case, deny the application."[7]

It was, indeed, in the applications that American interest centered. The English doctrines often seemed at variance, however, with the needs of the United States. "The peculiar situation of our own land," wrote Bowen, "is sufficient to qualify materially the force of the general maxims established by European writers," and he called for "a work which shall bear the same relation to American institutions that the writings of Malthus and Ricardo do to those of England."[8]

There were attempts, such as Bowen's own *American Political Economy,* but no general or analytical work of the first order was produced in the United States, and the European classics went unrivaled. Bowen's successor at Harvard, Charles F. Dunbar, reviewing the first century of the progress of American economics, wrote in 1876 that "the United States have, thus far, done nothing towards developing the theory of political economy, notwithstanding their vast and immediate interest in its practical applications."[9] Indeed the leading textbooks, such as those by Perry and Amasa Walker, offered nothing new.

If it was on practical applications or problems that the best American work was done, this cannot be said of the economist's study of labor, at least until the work of Francis A. Walker in the late 1870s. On the so-called labor question, a topic of much discussion at the time, American economists during the 1860s and early 1870s were at one with the English classicists. If the Americans modified the Malthusian population thesis or the free trade doctrine as it applied in international affairs, they nonetheless wholeheartedly accepted the most doctrinaire of the classical views concerning wages and labor. The principle of laissez-faire and the doctrine of individual rights and responsibilities seemed nowhere so firmly entrenched as in the orthodox American economists' references to the wage bargain. Perry, who held that strikes were "false in theory" and "pernicious in practice," held also that "the limits of legislative action are pretty narrow. Capital and labor should both have the utmost liberty of action."[10]

By and large, both the popular and professional economists dealt with the labor question by attempting "to convince the worker that he was better off than he had ever been before, that the capitalist was his ally and benefactor, and that therefore he should remain quiescent and abstain from economic or political action designed to alter the *status quo.*"[11] The idea that the worker was disadvantaged in the wage bargain, an idea subscribed to by Adam Smith, was generally denied. So too was the idea of an inherent conflict between capital and labor.

Smith had pointed out that "what are the common wages of labour depends everywhere upon the contract usually made between those two parties, whose interests are by no means the same. The workmen desire to get as much, the masters to give as little as possible."[12] The American laissez-faire economists were less inclined to emphasize this competitive nature of the wage bargain and stressed instead its complementary aspects. This was frequently reinforced by explicit theological references, which were less typical of English writers and which served, if anything, to give even stronger justification for the policy of laissez-faire in labor matters in the United States than had been the case in England. Perry, for example, took issue with those who regarded

the laborer as at a disadvantage compared with capital, because the laborer must at once dispose of his product or starve; which seems to me a superficial view of the relation, because capital submits to an instant loss when it declines to employ labor. Capital does not like to lose its profit any more than the laborer likes to lose his bread. In a true and general view, the one is under just as much pressure to employ laborers, as the other is to get employment. They come together of necessity into a relation of mutual dependence which God has ordained, and which, though man may temporarily disturb it, he can never overthrow.[13]

Amasa Walker asserted that any belief in the inevitable antagonism between capital and labor "blasphemes against the harmonies of providence—is sightless before the glorious order of man and nature." Simon Newcomb warned labor that if capitalists were not free to act as they saw fit, without interference from labor, then capital would disappear and all would be the poorer.[14]

SOME NEW VOICES

These economists were products of American training. Their approach to the study of labor was conditioned by their adherence both to the English classical doctrines concerning wages and labor and to the political extension of these doctrines, an attitude of laissez-faire toward the labor market. Beginning around 1880, however, there began to return to this country from Germany a group of young American economists—Jacob Hollander aptly referred to them as economic investigators—trained in German research methods, imbued with German ideals of political action, and "tingling with the possibilities of the historical method in economic science." They were determined to put new marrow into what they called the "dry bones" of "the old political economy." It was the coincidence of the appearance of this group, and the appearance of the specific issues to which they immediately began to address themselves, that accounted for the remarkable progress made in empirical economics in the United States during the next several decades: in public finance, transportation, labor, immigration, cooperation, the tariff, and other applied fields.

It is important to note the complementary aspect of this combination of economic problems and academic economists seeking problems to investigate. Had the economists been products of the American training of the day, they might have eschewed consideration of many of the problems that demanded attention, especially in the field of labor. If, on the other hand, these German-trained investigators had arrived on the scene a decade or so earlier, they would probably not have been successful in securing positions. The return of these men to America and their subsequent academic and public activities marked the end of American apathy toward economic study and the beginning of sustained economic inquiry in the United States.[15] Henceforth the academic study of general economics and the continuing interest in special economic problems would be much less imperfectly joined.

These German-trained economists included many who advanced the study of labor in the United States: Richmond Mayo Smith, Henry W. Farnam, Henry Carter Adams, John Bates Clark, and Henry Rogers Seager, among others. In connection with the incorporation of labor studies into the field of economics, however, none played a role of greater significance than Richard T. Ely, who published the first book on the labor movement by an American academic economist.[16] It was Ely who first interested John R. Commons in the study of labor at Johns Hopkins University, and it was Ely who later brought him to the University of Wisconsin to establish what became for many years the leading center for American labor economics. Ely's approach, largely empirical and historical, gave early labor studies their most common characteristic. There is, then, much justification for Philip Taft's assertion that "the study of labor, or labor economics as it was at one time not unjustly called, may be said to have begun with the publication of Ely's book in 1886."[17] Mark Perlman has called that book, *The Labor Movement in America*, "the pioneer effort in the field" and noted that it "attracted a great number of able, socially conscious students to the study of economics. In point of fact, it is probably this book, written by a leading professional economist, that explains why the history of American unionism became associated initially with economics rather than with political science or history."[18]

In ascribing to Ely this role of pioneer and founder, however, certain qualifications are in order. The association of labor history with economics rather than with history departments is due surely as much (if not more) to a preference on the part of American historians for political as opposed to economic history than to the fact that a leading professional economist was interested in labor history.[19] So wide were Ely's interests that only a fraction of the topics on which he wrote could be said to belong to the realm of economics. If Ely's labor writings brought Commons to his seminars at Johns Hopkins, and thereby, in a sense, labor history to economics, then no less did his writings on the problems of cities attract to his seminars students such as Albion Small. But problems of municipal administration, Ely's interests notwithstanding, did not become a part of economics, and Small, Edward A. Ross, Frederick Jackson Turner, and several others among Ely's students became professors not of economics but of sociology and history. Indeed so flexible were the boundaries of the social sciences in the United States during the closing decades of the nineteenth century (and perhaps nowhere was this flexibility so prominent as in the seminars at Johns Hopkins which were conducted jointly by Ely and the historian Herbert Baxter Adams), that it is doubtful that any one book could have had a decisive influence in delimiting those fields.

Nor was Ely the only economist discussing labor problems at this time. In the early 1880s, Carroll D. Wright had castigated economists for their neglect of the labor question. And Francis A. Walker in 1879 had chided the profession for its neglect of the historical method and practical problems, pointing out that this neglect had "cost the science of economics public regard, especially among the laboring classes."[20] But in 1886, the same year in which Ely's book appeared, Henry Carter Adams was speaking on "The Labor Problem" at Cornell University, and Richmond Mayo Smith of Columbia University was writing, in an article on labor statistics prepared for the first issue of the *Political Science Quarterly*, that "the burning question in political economy, at the present time, is that of the distribution of wealth, especially in respect to the so-called laboring class."[21] Many economists thus were beginning to concern themselves in a new way with the labor question. Indeed they could hardly have failed to do so, so much was the topic in the forefront of public discussion. Moreover as studies in social problems of current interest, college classes in labor frequently were found not in economics departments during the 1880s but rather in departments of social science, an early forerunner of sociology, or, quite often, in departments of ethics. Much of what encompassed the labor question consisted, it was thought, not only of economic but also of ethical considerations. Carroll Wright provides an example: "The presence of crime works a direct injury upon the welfare of the workingman in many ways. It costs him more to live because of it; it disturbs his sense of justice because the convict works at the same occupation which furnishes his support; but, while the labor reformer cries for the abolition of convict labor, the political economy of the labor question cries for the reduction of the number of criminals by the prevention of crime as the surest and most permanent remedy for whatever evils may grow out of the practice of employing convicts in productive labor."[22]

In the face of such considerations it is not surprising to note that the earliest instruction in American universities, embodying much of what later came to be called labor problems, was instruction not in economics at all, but rather in what might be called social pathology and social reform. One of the first in an American university to give instruction in social problems was the Reverend Francis Greenwood Peabody of Harvard University. He began instructing in ethics or moral philosophy in the Divinity School in 1879, and during the early 1880s, he, along with Graham Taylor, who taught social economics at Chicago Theological Seminary, and Franklin B. Sanborn, who taught social science at Cornell University, were giving the only college courses devoted exclusively to social problems.

The fact that the earliest courses dealing with social problems emerged in departments of ethics rather than economics reflects the development of these fields during the nineteenth century. With Adam Smith, no sharp line divided analysis from policy recommendations, and the spirit of social progress permeated his work. But increasingly during the nineteenth century, the effort of economists was to make theirs a positive science, and "the problems of progress were separated from those of political economy and became associated under the newer term of Utilitarianism":

This line of division, by which ethics became a theory of social progress, while economics was reduced to a theory of the production of material goods, was strengthened by the popular belief that the pursuit of wealth was the source of moral and political degeneration. Economists were not to be blamed for not seeing the economic causes of social progress, at a time when money getting was supposed to be the root of all evil. They assumed, as did everyone else, that the motive power of progress lay in other fields than economics—in ethics and religion. . . . They readily assented—yes, even demanded—that all problems of social reform should be handed over to ethics, so that economics could be made a positive science after the model of the physical sciences. Problems of what is, it was claimed with apparently many good reasons, should be separated from problems relating to what ought to be.[23]

The study of what is in contrast to what ought to be is thus frequently given as the province of the nineteenth-century economist. Indeed this demarcation of economics was an inseparable part of its growth as an independent discipline. However, the nineteenth-century economist was less concerned with what was than with what, given certain assumptions, would be in the long run. The study of what is involves some empiricism, which was generally lacking in the classical and neoclassical economics. But those who first taught labor problems in American universities were not economists and were not concerned with the economist's avowal of the positive and disavowal of the normative. They began to concern themselves not only with what ought to be but also with what is. Nor is this latter a coincidence. What Schumpeter said of the later scholastics of the Middle Ages applies as well to these early students of labor: "Preoccupation with the ethics of pricing . . . is precisely one of the strongest motivations a man can possibly have for analyzing actual market mechanisms."[24] Sanborn, a leader in the social science movement, who was brought to Cornell University by Andrew Dickson White specifically for the purpose of giving "a course of practical instruction calculated to fit young men to discuss intelligently important social questions," held that "to learn patiently what *is*—to promote diligently what *should be*—this is the double duty of all the social sciences, of which political economy is one."[25] The Reverend Francis Greenwood Peabody, who taught the only course devoted to social problems at Harvard University during the eighties, first in the Divinity School and later in the Department of Social Ethics, stressed the moral aspects of social problems. In a letter to Sanborn, he wrote:

I was led to my subject by a somewhat different road from most of those who deal with it. As a teacher of ethics I became aware of the chasm which exists between such abstract study and the practical application of moral ideals; and it seemed to me possible to approach the theory of ethics inductively through the analysis of great moral movements, which could be easily characterized and from which principles could be deduced. I studied thus with my class the problems of Charity, Divorce, the Indians, the Labor Question, Intemperance, with results of surprising interest. My class, under our elective method, grew from ten to fifty and was made up from five departments of the university. Each student made written reports of personal observation of some institution of charity or reform; and from these data thus collected I endeavored in each case to draw out the ethical principles involved. The results of the examination showed that the students felt a living interest in the subjects treated, and I think they will be more public spirited as citizens and more discreet as reformers by even this slight opportunity for research.[26]

These, then, are some of the qualifications that must be made to the generally tenable expression of Philip Taft and others that the study of labor began with Richard T. Ely, for it is clear that even before the work of Ely, some attention was being paid in American universities to the study of labor problems. There was, moreover, a tradition in the teaching of labor problems that included the inductive approach, the rejection of laissez-faire economics, and the espousal of an active movement for social reform. Since labor problems had been taught as part of the social reform movement, what Ely and the other early economists working in the field of labor really did, in moving the study of labor into economics departments, was not only to demarcate a new area of specialization but also to join the movement for social reform in the area of capital-labor relations. The early labor economists swept aside the long-held and widespread notion, expressed by Perry, that "political economy has no concern with questions of moral right . . . the grounds of morals and economy are independent and incommensurable."[27] Ely held otherwise and wrote that "a wider diffusion of sound ethics is an economic requirement of the times."[28] It is not the case that, as individuals, the orthodox theorists were less concerned with questions of ethics and morality, nor were they less humanitarian than the early students of labor. But whereas most theorists maintained that the noneconomic aspects of a problem must not be confused with the economic, Ely held that the economic and ethical aspects were inseparably intertwined. The new political economy, he wrote, was based on a recognition of the close relationships between ethics and economic life.[29]

Although this feature changed in later years, the emphasis on ethics and reform is one of the most conspicuous features in both the writings and the activities of the early students of labor. Very early in his career, and very much in the tradition of those reformers who taught labor problems before him, John R. Commons wrote: "From the state and the family, as the two fundamental institutions of society, we advance to the social problems of the day. To all of these Christian ethics should be applied."[30] Participation in a charity organization would, he felt, be of particular significance to the student of social problems because such an organization "touches every social problem—the problem of labor, of the unemployed, of long hours, of women and children workers, of city government. . . . Such a position furnishes the best possible opportunity for laboratory work in the science of sociology; it is the doorway to a real knowledge of social problems."[31]

Commons's reforming activities spanned his life's work. At Wisconsin, he sponsored three great reform programs of national significance. One put the regulation of public utilities under the control of a public commission. Another created the Wisconsin Industrial Commission, which had the power to make and enforce safety regulations. The third gave Wisconsin the first unemployment insurance program in the United States.[32] Of these reform activities, stretching over his thirty active years at Wisconsin, Commons has written, "I was trying to save capitalism by making it good."[33] He was interested, that is, not only in describing what is but also in helping to bring about what he thought should be.

An important part of the explanation for the emphasis on social action that marked the work of the early students of labor stems from the heritage of their German training. But the temper and the spirit that these economists brought to the study of labor problems was very close to that infused into the subject by its earlier students, the teachers of Christian ethics. Moreover the emphasis on reform long continued to be a prominent feature of the economists' study of labor. The reform element was central in the definition of the labor problem put forward by Edward W. Bemis, one of Ely's early students, who taught and wrote on labor subjects at the University of Chicago in the 1890s. He believed that the problem was whether the improvement in the condition of workers has kept pace with the advance of society and if it has not, how could it and "a more harmonious adjustment of the relation between labor and capital be established." [34]

Again manifesting the labor economists' preoccupation with reform, the authors of the first, and for many years the most widely used, textbook on labor problems, Thomas Sewall Adams and Helen L. Sumner, divided their work into two parts, "Evils" and "Remedies." The text closed with these words: "The hope of the hour is in specific social reform." [35] This preoccupation with social reform accounts not only for the labor economists' interest in social legislation but also for their preoccupation with organized labor. They viewed the labor union as an engine of possible relief from poverty wages, child labor, aspects of the sweating system, and other social and economic problems.

The economists who returned from Germany were too original and independent as thinkers to have brought with them an undiluted brand of German *Historismus* or *Kathedersozialismus*. While rejecting the most extreme of the German positions, they never, on the other hand, fully rejected the English or Austrian influence. Ely was careful to distinguish between the English masters of economics and "the teachings of the smaller men who followed after them, and who, pushing things to apparently logical conclusions, omitted necessary qualifications, and exaggerated greatly their errors." [36] Seager, who studied both at Berlin and at Vienna and who thus had the benefit of working directly under both Schmoller and Menger, showed in an early paper how he "preferred the Austrian line of attack upon theoretical problems." [37] One must, on the whole, reject the idea of a massive importation of German ideas into the body of American economic thought as a result of the dominant positions attained by the German-trained economists. Indeed some of the influences in economic thought frequently considered as German are traceable, ultimately, to America. Thus Friedrich List, one of the first in Germany to dispute the relevance of Adam Smith's postulates to his country, was influenced by his travels in America and by the American economist Daniel Raymond.[38]

It is not surprising that there should have been cross-fertilization in economic thought between America and Germany. Nor is it surprising that American students, when confronted with economic problems which they deemed to exceed the capacity of the analytical tools at hand, should have turned to Germany for training, for the political and economic problems they faced were quite similar. Sectionalism was a common issue to both, and their economic problems—incipient industrialism and difficult issues of public policy, including the banking system, public finance, bimetallism, and the tariff—were similar.[39] In sum, American economic thought in general and the American economists' approach to the study of labor were fundamentally affected by the training received by American economists in Germany, and it is important to note the special qualities that experience imparted.

Nineteenth-century German thought was characterized by an emphasis on facts and by a way of looking at complex phenomena that can perhaps best be described as organic and evolutionary. When Richmond Mayo Smith said in 1886 that "the new method in political economy is historical, comparative, and statistical," he was eminently in the German tradition.[40] Nineteenth-century German thought was best attuned to problems requiring "fundamentally organic thinking [and] development."[41] That is why, for example, long before the work of the Webbs, when the English economists were assuming away, as given, the societal and institutional developments, the best work on English trade unions was done not by English but by German scholars, notably Brentano, Held, and Bernreither, and why Beatrice Webb, while working on *Industrial Democracy,* wrote of it in her diary: "I doubt whether the English reading public will understand or be impressed; if there is to be a *succes d'estime,* that appreciation will come from Germany."[42]

German thought was also characterized by a rejection of classical individualism in favor of an active intervention by the political state. The reaction against eighteenth- and nineteenth-century liberalism, which accorded a position of primacy to the beneficial aspects of unhindered individualism, "found its most striking expression in the new German Empire with its imposing development of scientific research."[43] Nineteenth-century philosophical thought in Germany manifested clearly the difference between the English and the German conceptions of freedom and progress. In England, the dominant school of thought was represented by the hedonists—Hobbes, Hume, Locke, Bentham, and others—for whom the self-seeking individual was the motive power in society, which could ensure "the greatest happiness for the greatest number." Freedom in these terms meant freedom from the restrictions of the state. The state, with few exceptions, could only impede the progress made possible through laissez-faire and individualism. But in Germany, where the philosophical line was from Kant through Fichte to Hegel, progress was seen as following upon the introduction of an extraindividual force: the state. Thus freedom in the Hegelian system was viewed as the ability of the individual to identify with "the duties and responsibilities invested in him by the state, which, for Hegel, is the highest of all social institutions." [44] Ely, who wrote that "reformation of our state life must precede any solution of the labor problem," owed his views of the state largely to Schmoller, who held that "the State is the grandest existing ethical institution for the education of the human race." [45] Ely put the following sentences into the prospectus that he drew up as a platform for the American Economic Association: "We regard the state as an educational and ethical agency whose positive aid is an indispensable condition of human progress. While we recognize the necessity of individual initiative in industrial life, we hold that the doctrine of *laissez-faire* is unsafe in politics and unsound in morals; and that it suggests an inadequate explanation of the relations between the state and the citizens." [46] This condemnation of laissez-faire, however, was not included in the statement of principles of the association. It was feared that many of the members of the profession would be alienated by so strong a rejection of laissez-faire. The adopted statement of principles opens, however, with the assertion, "We regard the state as an agency whose positive assistance is one of the indispensable conditions of human progress." [47]

Much of what later characterized the American economists' approach to the study of labor—a historical and comparative approach to the study of labor institutions and organizations, an inductive study of labor's actual economic position and of the effects of labor's policies, an espousal of the ideal of an interventionist state in labor matters, and an emphasis on the actions of groups rather than of individuals—all derived at least in part from the German heritage.

Perhaps the most obvious manifestation of the German influence on the American economists' study of labor was the emphasis on historical research. The sustained study of labor in the United States began as a study in labor history. Ely has said that he found his master in Karl Knies, who "conceived of economics as belonging neither to the natural nor to the mental sciences, but to the group of historical disciplines which have for their object the study of man in society in terms of its historical growth." [48] Although Ely's *Labor Movement in America* was not entirely a historical treatment, it was largely so, and his dissatisfaction with that aspect and his hopes for historical research on a grander scale was a prominent feature of the book.[49] Much of what might be called the larger work in labor, that which went beyond the teaching of labor courses and the writing of texts on labor problems and which embodied the most fruitful original research, continued for many years to be in the field of labor history.

THE ECONOMISTS AND ORGANIZED LABOR

Ely's departure from the economist's earlier, almost exclusive, concern with the formulation of a long-run theory of wages and his espousal of the analysis of the actual workings of trade unionism was sufficiently significant for Philip Taft to assert that labor economics began with his book in 1886.

The Labor Movement in America opened by asserting that the labor movement "is acquiring new meaning in our times. A marvelous war is now being waged in the heart of modern civilization. Millions are engaged in it. The welfare of humanity depends on its issue."[50] Ely proceeded to a description of early communistic societies in America and traced the origins and growth of organized labor in the United States. Knowledge of the early period, especially from 1800 to 1850, had always been scant, and Ely's research into these years represented pathbreaking efforts. Then followed three largely sympathetic chapters on various aspects of organized labor, five on socialism and internationalism, and a concluding chapter, "Remedies," in which Ely eschewed any "simple, easily applied formula which will cure social evils." He offered instead "a few suggestions, scarcely more than hints, which may be useful to the reader, enabling him to contribute to a better utilization of the world's experience, and of established rules of moral conduct." Essentially, he concluded, there are "four chief agencies through which we must work for the amelioration of the laboring class, as well as of all classes of society. These are the labor organization, the school, the State, and the Church."[51]

Ely was particularly optimistic concerning the aims and methods of organized labor. What Hoxie later called the uplift character of the Knights of Labor meshed well with the Christian socialism that was so much a part of Ely's early writings. He asserted that the Knights of Labor "was established on truly scientific principles, which involved either an intuitive perception of the nature of industrial progress, or a wonderful acquaintance with the laws of economic society." Writing, as he did, at the apex of the power of the Knights, Ely could not have foreseen their early downfall. Ironically, however, some of Ely's arguments favoring the organization of the Knights came close to those used fifty years later by the organizers of the CIO: "The invention of new machinery and the improvement in technical processes have weakened the position of unions composed exclusively of mechanics of a single trade." The organization of the Knights of Labor on inclusive lines, Ely felt, accorded well not only with "the laws of economic society" but was, moreover, "in line with the precepts of Christianity. The strong help·to bear the infirmities of the weak, and no grander conception of human brotherhood than that which they profess, characterizes any movement of our times." In short, said Ely, "the labor movement . . . is the strongest force outside the Christian Church making for the practical recognition of human brotherhood."[52]

Such unqualified support of trade unions, regarded as monopolies in economic theory, was offensive to conservative, orthodox economists. (Indeed Ely himself, as early as 1900, pointed out that he no longer held some of the views expressed in the book.)[53] The less restrained among leading orthodox economists, such as Simon Newcomb, accused Ely of "an intensity of bias and a bitterness toward all classes of society, except one, to which it would be hard to find a parallel elsewhere than in the ravings of an anarchist or the dreams of a socialist."[54] J. Laurence Laughlin was more restrained, but without mentioning him by name, questioned Ely's judgment and approach and even whether such studies as his ought to be the concern of the economist.[55] Here we can see beginning to manifest itself a division between labor students and many economic theorists that continued for several decades. Labor specialists on the whole have been strong advocates of unionism, while economic theorists, perhaps reflecting the individualistic bias of classical and neoclassical economics, have generally been more likely to stress the monopoly aspects of unions. W. H. Hutt, for example, has asserted that "the interests of the unionists were almost universally antagonistic to those of the laboring masses. Had historians of the trade union movement been orthodox economic theorists they might have laid the strongest emphasis on this point. As it happens, however, they have been practically without exception persons with an undisguised hostility to orthodox theory; and this may account for their failure to stress what might have struck other economists most forcibly."[56]

Hutt is representative of those economists who stand on the far side of individualism. Nonetheless the points he makes illustrate the cleavage between economic theorists and labor economists. One must, for example, take with some caution Joseph Dorfman's assertion that "the fact that labor economists were not given to blanket endorsement of the labor movement derived not only from their loose formal ties to it, but also from their very broad interests and their close contacts and working relationships with the rest of the profession."[57] Dorfman may be correct when he referred to labor economists' failure to give "blanket endorsement" to the labor movement, but they did generally give approval and positive encouragement. Paul Brissenden, in his 1926 review of Solomon Blum's *Labor Economics,* reported that Blum had once told him that he wished there were "some way in which a college professor could *do something* for the labor movement." "Here," added Brissenden, "is that something. It puts the labor movement, as well as students of the labor movement, deeply in his debt." Brissenden was not in any sense implying that Blum's text was an apologia for organized labor. On the contrary, it was, he pointed out, "a carefully pondered, closely reasoned, philosophical analysis of the conditions under which the modern wage earner lives, bargains, strikes—and of the state's allocation of rights and privileges to wage earner and employer groups respectively."[58] But that Blum was generally favorably disposed toward trade unionism is hardly to be doubted.

The generally sympathetic views of labor economists toward labor unions is partly the reason why labor courses long dwelt heavily on organized labor and why economists (usually theorists), less sympathetic with the aims of trade unionism or with the idea of collectivism in general, often challenged that approach. Edward H. Chamberlin, for example, asserted during the 1950s that courses in labor generally focused on trade unions, paying little attention "to the unorganized sector and to the possible means of alleviating the lot of the *really* underprivileged by means other than collective action."[59]

It should not be supposed either that Professor Chamberlin's charge was an isolated case, or that the alienation of many economic theorists, effected partly by the espousal by labor economists generally of the aims of organized labor, is a recent development. Ely, for example, not only attracted to economic study such men as John R. Commons, Edward Bemis, Albion Small, and Monsignor John A. Ryan, but he alienated others such as Simon Newcomb and J. Laurence Laughlin. As early as 1899, John R. Commons alluded to divisions among economists.[60]

On the whole, the generally sympathetic attitude that the early students of labor brought to their analyses of trade unions impaired their relationships with the rest of the profession. As Professor Dunlop has remarked, "industrial relations specialists became somewhat suspect by more othodox academic colleagues."[61]

EARLY RESEARCH IN LABOR PROBLEMS

Ely's *Labor Movement in America* resulted partly from the work of the graduate students in his and Herbert B. Adams's joint seminars in history and political economy at Johns Hopkins University, and throughout the 1880s and 1890s the kind of work originally sponsored by those seminars; detailed empirical investigations of a limited aspect of a particular problem, frequently of current topical or historical interest, resulted in the publication of numerous monographs and articles.[62] Many of these were published by the Johns Hopkins University in a series, Studies in Historical and Political Science, and, in later years, in similar series undertaken by the University of Wisconsin and other institutions.

A perhaps more important outlet for publications resulting from such studies was offered by the new professional journals. The year 1886 saw the launching of both the *Political Science Quarterly* and the *Quarterly Journal of Economics*. Six years later, the *Journal of Political Economy* appeared on the scene, devoted, in the words of J. Laurence Laughlin, its first editor, "largely to a study of practical problems of economics, finance, and statistics."[63] Although the *American Economic Review* did not appear until 1911, the American Economic Association began its *Publications* in 1886. The articles published soon reflected the renaissance of economic study that was taking place in this country generally, and, more particularly, the new concern with social problems. In the latter category, the study of labor occupied a prominent place.

The constitution of the American Economic Association (1886) states that "the conflict of labor and capital has brought into prominence a vast number of social problems, whose solution requires the united efforts, each in its own sphere, of the church, of the state, and of science." The bylaws of the association called for the organization of seven standing committees, the first of which was on labor, chaired by Ely. A resolution listed ten topics that were "suggested to the chairmen of the standing committees, as proper subjects for reports." Those in the field of labor included "The Effect of Half-Time Working on the Laborer," "The Normal Working Day," "Employment of Women in Factories," and "Effect of Transportation on the Laborer."[64]

The boundaries of the emerging field of labor economics become discernible by looking at the kinds of questions relating to labor with which economists were concerning themselves. The first few volumes of the *Quarterly Journal of Economics* commencing in 1886, included the following articles on labor:

An Historical Sketch of the Knights of Labor

Action Under Labor Arbitration Acts

Legislation for Labor Arbitration

The South-western Strike of 1886

Occupations of Immigrants
Wage Statistics and the Next Census
The Unemployed in American Cities
Industrial Arbitration: Its Methods and Limitations
Insurance of the Unemployed
Co-operative Stores in the United States

The first issue of the *Journal of Political Economy* carried no article in
the field of labor, but soon thereafter a number were forthcoming.
Volume two, for example, spanning the years 1893–94, listed the fol-
lowing titles:
Convention of the American Federation of Labor
Apprentice System in the Building Trades
German Labor Colonies and the Unemployed
The Homestead Strike
Conference of State Bureaus of Labor Statistics
The Chicago Strike of July, 1894
Trade Unionism and the Evolution of the Type-Setting Machine
Immigration
Similarly, early issues of the *Political Science Quarterly* carried the fol-
lowing titles, among others:
American Labor Statistics
The Taxation of Labor
The National Bureau of Labor, and Industrial Depressions
The Benefit Features of American Trades Unions
Control of Immigration
The State and the Poor
Italian Immigration into the United States

A review of the work then being done in the field of labor in the
United States shows a number of emerging trends. There was, first of
all, a continuing concern with what Francis A. Walker called "the
Wages Question." Ely, in his *Past and Present of Political Economy*
(1884), had criticized Cairnes's attempts to rescue the Ricardian concept of "the natural rate of wages" by reference to "disturbing causes"
and "non-competing groups." "If equality of wages means anything of
value at all," Ely said, "it must denote some approximation in real life
to the absolute equality called for. What are the facts of the case?" According to Ely, the facts were

that unequal wages for similar services are not only paid in places not remote
from one another, but even in the same city or town. . . . Any reader who still
believes that, somehow or other, the theory of equal wages may be true,

should consult a document like the *Annual Report* of the Massachusetts Bureau of Statistics of Labor, for 1883, and ascertain the number of rates of wages paid to unskilled labor in a single state. . . . the daily wages of ordinary laborers engaged in the manufacture of boots and shoes varied from seventy-five cents to two dollars, seven different rates being mentioned, differing from one another by almost two hundred per cent. And yet a comparison is made between the accuracy of political economy and physics.[65]

Ely made no appeal for the reconstruction of the theory or a search for what might be called a short-run theory of wages, as some labor economists later urged. Rather he rejected the theory out of hand in favor of a search for the facts of the case. At this time studies, admittedly crude, were being undertaken of wages in particular industries, as well as analyses of and recommendations for the improvement of the collection of wage statistics. In 1886, Richmond Mayo Smith reported that although one national and fifteen state bureaus of labor statistics had been organized in order "to investigate the earnings of American labor, the fundamental question of the labor problem," only the Massachusetts bureau, headed by Carroll D. Wright, had made "any really systematic effort to determine the wages of the laboring class, with completeness and accuracy."[66]

Most of the studies on wages reflected the feeling that wages were increasingly the result of conscious (as opposed to competitive) forces. As Franklin Giddings put it: "There are two sets of forces operating with reference to the rate of wages. One set is composed of the forces of competition. Their action is automatic. Their resultant is mechanical equilibrium. The other forces are self-conscious forces of human feeling and opinion. They set up a standard of justice, and take form in moral judgments, appeals to reason, the policy of labor organization, legislation and administration."[67]

Later studies attempted to define the forces making for wage rates and differentials, but the early work concentrated mainly on reporting the differentials. There also began to appear studies of particular unions or, frequently, of particular strikes. These were often historical in approach and sympathetic in tone. The outstanding characteristic of most of these studies, whether of unions, strikes, or wages, was their particularity to plants, firms, industries, or regions. This undoubtedly reflects an aversion of the early students to the generality of the rejected theory of wages. Thus the theory of marginal productivity, which was developing in these years, is useful in explaining why the general level of wages differs over time or over space. It would be difficult to explain why wages are higher now than in 1850, or higher in the United States than in India, without reference to productivity. But the theory sheds little light on why wages in firm A are higher than in firm B for a particular type of labor in a particular locale. Indeed it was the existence of such differences that resulted in the rejection of the theory by the students of labor. The labor students thus turned to the particular, an emphasis that lasted a number of years. As recently as the late 1950s, Lloyd G. Reynolds pointed out that whereas "aggregative theorists frequently make assumptions about general wage movements which are unrealistic in terms of wage determining institutions at the plant level," at the other extreme, he said, "labor economists tend to focus on wage determination in the plant or industry in isolation from general forces of change in the economy."[68] It is only fair to add that Professor Reynolds was at the time attempting to bridge the gap between these two approaches.

The articles written during the closing years of the nineteenth century also reflect a substantial concern with the issue of maintaining industrial peace and, more fundamentally, industrial goodwill. A good deal of attention was paid to the aims and methods of arbitration and conciliation and to the merits of protective labor legislation. Frequently social experiments in European countries were the subject of special studies. Much attention focused also on current and recent strikes, with emphasis on the economic losses imposed by idleness.

There were studies of particular aspects of unions. Edward Bemis, for example, felt in 1887 that "so little is known of the means other than strikes which our American labor organizations are using to elevate and help their members" that he undertook a survey of the benefit features, other than strike benefits, of forty-four unions. He found that a portion of union funds had been paid as strike benefits in recent years and that nonstrike benefits were on the increase. He concluded that "the good is replacing the bad in the ranks of united labor. The experience of England gives good ground to expect that with the growth of our labor organizations most of their abuses will disappear and conservatism become the rule."[69] Other studies traced the histories of particular unions or covered other special aspects, such as apprenticeship rules and union attitudes toward the introduction of new machinery, examined workers' cooperatives, and featured reports on immigration.

Perhaps the most striking characteristic of these articles and special studies was their empirical character. The search for what is in the economic sphere was clearly their common denominator and gave to the writings of the period the largest share of whatever they possessed of a cohesive approach. Questions of what should be were not, to be sure, lacking. Frequently these combined with a rejection, on the part of the students of labor, of the consumer orientation of classical and neoclassical economics in favor of a new concern for the worker. Thus Bemis, writing on the coal miners' strike in the 1894 *Outlook,* wrote, "If any strike was ever justified, this one is. . . . Why should not all citizens give aid moral and even financial, to this effort of our miners, not to raise their standard of life, but to prevent its falling still lower, until absolute want stares them in the face?" And Harry A. Millis, in a 1914 article on the minimum wage, asserted: "The public has no claim to products and services at prices not sufficient to keep the average worker in a fair state of health and efficiency. Consumers should not be subsidized to the sacrifice of those who, through their employers, serve them. Especially is this so in those cases where the consumers are materially better off than the laborers."[70]

No one work drew together the multiplicity of studies on labor into a consistent or coherent whole until Emile Levasseur's *American Workman* appeared in 1898. The Frenchman's work might justly be called the first textbook on American labor and one that proved to be in several ways a prototype of the book that became for many years the standard text in American labor courses, that by Adams and Sumner.

One area in which Levasseur's influence is evident is in the recognized plurality and multiplicity inherent in the very phrase *labor problems*. He cited a number of changes that had occurred—among them, "the transformation of small manufacturing and the growth of the unit of industry, the regulation and inspection of factories, the employment of machinery and manual labor, the work of women and children, the competition between native and imported labor, apprenticeship and manual training"—and noted "they are often spoken of collectively as *the labor question* or *the social question*, but they are really distinct problems, for the most part, incapable of settlement by a single solution. While we are not to lose sight of the bonds that unite them, we must study them one at a time, and, where it is possible, the special solution of each problem."[71]

Five years later, Adams and Sumner, reflecting also the uplift or reform spirit noted earlier, wrote largely in the same vein: "In a very general and abstract sense there is such a thing as *the* labor problem, which may be defined as the problem of improving the conditions of employment of the wage-earning classes . . . [but] there is no one labor problem whose solution would carry with it the settlement of all others. . . . The consequence is that when we begin to study the labor problem it divides up into a number of evils and abuses . . . for each of which in turn a number of practical remedies are in use or under active consideration."[72]

The scope of Levasseur's investigations may be gathered from the topics of his chapters: food of workmen, clothing, lodging, loan and building associations, savings and insurance, real wages and the workingman's budget of income and expenditure, the accumulation of fortunes and American democracy, tariff, poor relief, conciliation and arbitration, socialism, labor laws, labor organizations, wages of men, wages of women and children, sweating, immigration, strikes, and crises.[73]

That the first book-length treatment of American labor problems should have been the work of a foreigner appears to be somewhat of an anomaly and is undoubtedly related to the fact that special courses in labor were slow in emerging in the United States. The appearance of the Adams and Sumner text in 1905 reflects, in a sense, the definite establishment of the field of labor problems within economics departments.

THE EMERGENCE OF LABOR COURSES

Until the 1880s, no college or university in the United States offered as political economy anything approaching labor problems. Indeed, "in 1876, according to Laughlin's study, made in 1892, of the teaching of political economy, there were thirty-eight colleges and universities teaching political economy, of which only three colleges offered as many as two courses in the subject, and these in each case consisted of an elementary and an advanced course."[74]

During the 1880s, courses in social ethics or in social science began to treat of questions touching labor. The social ethics approach to labor problems was led by Francis G. Peabody and Graham Taylor, and was generally taught in divinity schools, although the ethical approach—sometimes called Christian sociology—was prominent also in the early works of Ely and Commons and was the point of departure as well for Albion Small and the Sociology Department of the University of Chicago.[75] The social science approach envisioned the emergence of a synthetic discipline, the subject matter of which would be all of the many forces and factors forming society and social policy. This approach took its name from Henry C. Carey's *The Principles of Social Science,* published in three volumes from 1858 through 1860. The American Social Science Association was organized in 1865, and thereafter courses of instruction multiplied rapidly.

By the 1890s, the term *social science* had largely been displaced by *sociology,* although many professors of the subject still held an inclusive view of the discipline. It was during the 1890s that instruction in labor problems began to emerge as the province of the sociologist, although frequently the sociologists were members of economics departments. Thus Edward Cummings became a member of the Harvard University Economics Department in 1892 and began to teach a new course as, "The Social and Economic Condition of Workingmen in the United States and in Other Countries."[76] Cummings was clearly the labor specialist at Harvard during the 1890s, reviewing books on the subject and writing articles on labor for the *Quarterly Journal of*

Economics. His designation, however, was officially assistant professor of sociology. At the University of Chicago during the 1890s, Albion Small treated trade unions, among other institutions, in his sociology classes, and a course entitled "The Labor Movement" was taught as a sociology-anthropology course.[77] The economics department, headed by J. Laurence Laughlin, treated of labor only peripherally. The University of Chicago was founded in 1892, but it was not until 1900— when Katherine Bement Davis analyzed causes affecting the standard of living and wages—that a doctoral dissertation was done in the field of labor.[78] Indeed two of the most prominent labor specialists who were graduate students in economics at Chicago during the 1890s, Robert F. Hoxie and Harry A. Millis, did their dissertations on other than labor—Hoxie on "An Analysis of the Concepts of Demand and Supply in their Relation to Market Price" and Millis on the "History of the Finances of the City of Chicago."

Beginning in 1900, separate courses in labor, taught as courses in economics, emerged and began to multiply rapidly. At Johns Hopkins University, where interest in the study of labor had fallen off after Ely's departure for Wisconsin in 1892, the first course in labor problems, taught by W. F. Willoughby, appeared in 1900. No course in labor was listed for the following year, but in June 1902, a gift of fifteen hundred dollars "for the purpose of instituting a systematic investigation into the history, activities, and influence of labor organizations in the United States" turned the Economics Seminary, conducted for the most advanced graduate students by Jacob Hollander and George E. Barnett, in the direction of sustained labor studies, and for many years thereafter Johns Hopkins University was the source of some of the most fruitful and influential labor studies in the United States.[79]

At Columbia University during the 1880s and 1890s, Richmond Mayo Smith taught a comprehensive course, "Practical Political Economy," which "embraced three main divisions: 'modern problems'; 'money and trade,' or the problem of exchange; and 'labor and capital' or the problems of distribution." When he died in 1901, the course was abolished, and the section on distribution was split into two parts: "Labor Problems" and "Trust and Corporation Problems." In 1902, the appointment of Henry R. Seager firmly established labor problems as a field of specialization at Columbia.[80]

Cornell University established courses in social science with the appointment of Franklin Sanborn in 1884. These treated certain aspects of the labor problem (specifically prison labor, immigration, and pauperism) along with many other topics. In 1885–1886, Henry Carter Adams, a member of the economics department, taught a course, "Unsettled Questions in Political Economy," in which "the questions that received attention were—Theory of Free Competition, Social Reform (Including Factory Legislation, Trade Unions, Socialism, The Labor Question, etc.) the Railroad Question, Free Trade or Protection, and Commercial Crises."[81] Adams's views on labor were offensive to one of the university's major benefactors, Henry W. Sage, and he lost his position at Cornell the following year and went to the University of Michigan. No separate course in labor developed in the economics department at Cornell until 1904–1905, when Robert F. Hoxie established the field with a course entitled "Problems of Organized Labor," which he described as focusing on "conditions of employment, methods of industrial bargaining and remuneration, the economic claims and legal status of labor, considered mainly in connection with the growth, policies, and activities of labor unions."[82] Hoxie remained at Cornell for only two years before returning to the University of Chicago, and during the next decade, although labor problems continued to be taught there (successively by Frank Fetter, Alvin S. Johnson, and Robert A. Campbell), Cornell does not seem to have had a labor specialist, at least before Sumner Slichter's tenure there during the 1920s. Perhaps for this reason, Cornell did not become the center of much original work in labor in this early period nor did it attract graduate students in the specialty.

A similar situation developed at Harvard University. During the 1890s, Edward Cummings, a sociologist, taught "The Labor Question in Europe and the United States: The Social and Economic Conditions of Workingmen." By 1900, Cummings was no longer teaching at Harvard, and the course was offered by a Mr. Willoughby. E. Dana Durand taught it in 1901–1902, and in 1902 it passed to William Z. Ripley—for the first time called "Labor Problems." Because Ripley's interests covered so much more than labor, and probably also because railroad problems seem to have been his strongest interest, Harvard University developed no labor specialist until much later, and was not an important center for labor studies.

At the University of Chicago, Veblen in 1900 dropped his course on agricultural problems and began to lecture on the economics of workingmen, but it was Hoxie's return to Chicago in 1906 that established that institution's eminence as a center for labor studies. During the decade between Hoxie's return to Chicago and his untimely death in 1916, he became one of the leading students of American unionism, and his influence was significant in attracting to Chicago many of the ablest future labor economists.

At the University of Wisconsin, the arrival of John R. Commons in 1904 soon established that institution as the leading center for labor study. No other single scholar turned as many graduate students in the direction of labor studies as did Commons. A partial list of his students includes David J. Saposs, Edwin Witte, Ira Cross, Theresa McMahon, Paul S. Taylor, Don Lescohier, John B. and Irene Osgood Andrews, Helen L. Sumner, Arthur J. Altmeyer, Ewan Clague, Stewart Schrimshaw, Katherine Lenroot, William M. Leiserson, Selig Perlman, John A. Fitch, Philip Taft, Alvin H. Hansen, and Sumner H. Slichter.[83] Nor did any other institution ever have five specialists working in labor at the same time. Commons described the curriculum in this way:

My teaching on labor subjects, beginning in 1904, with twenty-five or thirty students, was expanded and specialized during the years, until, in order to keep down my hours of teaching, I contrived a two-year sequence for juniors and seniors. The courses were mainly lectures. The sequence and specialization were labor unions, labor legislation, labor management, immigration. Eventually it was possible to turn over these specialized courses to my own former graduates, until we had, including myself, five specialists as colleagues in the one field of labor within the economics department.[84]

This review of the large number of universities that instituted courses in labor problems between 1900 and 1905 illustrates the pertinence of Henry Seager's comment upon the appearance of the first American text, Adams and Sumner's *Labor Problems*. A textbook on labor problems "was so urgently needed," he wrote, "that even a mediocre performance in this field would have been welcome to teachers of the subject." He did not hesitate to add that the work was, in fact, "a highly creditable production" and that it deserved to "rank as one of the important recent contributions to American economic literature."[85]

No other text in the field of labor has had so lasting an impact as the Adams and Sumner text. What Samuelson's text has been to introductory economics since the 1950s, Adams and Sumner's was to the study of labor through the 1920s. Others emulated it, but none readily displaced it. Not only was the Adams and Sumner text the first and long the dominant one in the field of labor problems, it also anticipated in its focus and approach what later came to be called the institutionalist method in economic analysis.[86]

LABOR ECONOMICS AND THE INSTITUTIONALIST MOVEMENT

The term *institutional economics,* long common in the language and literature of social science and evocative of the work of such figures as John R. Commons, Wesley C. Mitchell, Thorstein Veblen, Robert F. Hoxie, Morris A. Copeland, Clarence E. Ayres, and others refers generally to various efforts, especially during the 1920s and 1930s, to infuse economic theory with a greater realism than is (or was held to be) afforded by reasoning in purely market terms. For most institutionalists, the institutions of capitalism, in addition to the competitive market, and the data of both economic history and of contemporary economic life, have been the stuff of an improved economic science.[1] The development of labor economics as an applied field, especially in the interwar period, was fundamentally affected by, and in turn affected, the institutionalist movement.

INSTITUTIONALISM FORESHADOWED

Thomas S. Adams and Helen L. Sumner's *Labor Problems,* published in 1905, was the first and long the dominant text in the field and importantly conditioned its subsequent development.

In the introduction, Adams and Sumner gave a short statement of the nature of capitalistic enterprise and of the institutions that lay at the heart of the problems to be discussed: "These, then, are what may be called the fundamental factors of the modern labor problem—the wage system, the permanent status of the wage earning class, the factory system—with all which that implies—and the extreme concentration and control of wealth in the hands of a very small proportion of the population." The authors also pointed out that "capitalism, the separation of the industrial classes, and the labor problem are the products of progress itself . . . the growing pains of youth and not the signs of approaching decay."[2] However, whatever inherent optimism was thus expressed in the future of the capitalistic system was tempered by a concern for the short run, one of the most conspicuous features of the early labor writings and one that persisted for some time. The classical and neoclassical theorists, in addition to passing over or eliminating short-run influences on the workings out of economic laws, frequently tended to ignore as well the short-run costs of long-run progress. Automation is a case in point. Perhaps because the experience of the nineteenth century so spectacularly demonstrated that increased real income through higher demand for labor followed on the introduction of new machinery and precluded any long-run adverse effects on aggregate employment, the temptation to ignore the short-run social costs of technological change is understandable. Thus economic theorists too often treat automation as simply the source of added output through a changing production function. But to suggest that the issue might have more than one side does not put one in the futile position of a neo-Luddite. A generation before Keynes felt it necessary to remind his profession that in the long run we are all dead and that we have to live and deal with short-run problems, Adams and Sumner made essentially the same point (and their words, now seventy-five years old, are not without relevance for today's world with its consciousness of the threat of technological unemployment so evident in much collective bargaining):

Of course, it avails nothing to the man who is thrust aside or maimed by the car of progress, to be told that his suffering is a mere incident in the upward march of society. This truth, indeed, carries with it a supplementary lesson of the gravest consequence: society must learn to minimize the unfortunate incidents of progress, and systematically compensate those who are injured literally for humanity's sake, because it is just this incidental and temporary destructiveness of progress that accounts for the gravest economic and social evils of our epoch. Moreover, society must learn to restrain the capricious plunging, the unnecessary deviations of our figurative vehicle; and as invention crowds upon invention, and revolutionary methods replace those to which we are accustomed and to which we have accommodated ourselves,—in a word, as progress becomes more rapid, social regulation must increase.[3]

The Adams and Sumner text was directed less to an analysis of the impact of labor problems on the economy than to a description of their impact on individuals. Relatively little attention was paid to the macroeconomic effects of labor problems—for example, the impact of the union on the general level of wages and prices or the effects of organized labor's policies on the country's balance of international payments. Nor does the fact of relative weakness of unions in those days, or relative unconcern with macroeconomic problems generally, afford the whole answer to this neglect, for there was little attention directed to questions of allocative efficiency on the microeconomic side. Rather the focus of the problems approach was the individual.[4]

The origins of the problems approach to the study of labor lay largely in the heritage of social reform, for this approach clearly relates to the first scientific efforts toward eliminating poverty, efforts that were designed to attack poverty at its roots in favor of the earlier reliance on charity. The scope of the first text on labor problems is evident from a quick reading of its chapter titles: Book 1, "Evils," contained four chapters—"Woman and Child Labor," "Immigration," "The Sweating System," and "Poverty, Earnings and Unemployment." Book 2, "Remedies," included chapters on "Strikes and Boycotts," "Labor Organizations and Employers' Associations," "The Agencies of Industrial Peace," "Profit Sharing," "Cooperation," "Industrial Education," "Labor Laws," and "The Material Progress of the Wage Earning Classes." The treatment was largely descriptive and

factual, frequently with historical overtones. There were few references to the existing economic theory, which, according to Henry
Seager, constituted one of the book's major weaknesses: "Even for
students who come to the book fresh from a general course in economics, a brief outline of the theory of wages would be valuable, and
for others it is well nigh indispensable. Without it readers are almost
certain to lose their bearings among the mass of details presented in
the body of the book, and to ascribe quite undue importance to such
factors as trade unions, or such facts as are peculiar to American experience during the last century."[5] But here is precisely where the
significance of the short-run point of view lies. The productivity theory
may be an acceptable, even indispensable, part of the explanation for
long-term changes in wages, but Adams and Sumner were trying to
get at the facts of the case. They stated in their preface that "where it
was necessary, we have sacrificed both interest and general social
philosophy in order to present concrete facts." Their interest in the
short run necessarily precluded their attention to traditional wage
theory, which assumes away the very matters they were trying to explain. As Melvin Reder has noted, "For short run purposes, an economic wage theory will probably never prove satisfactory. In a given
year, wage rates are determined by the whole range of forces
economists call institutional."[6]

It is manifestly clear that Adams and Sumner were not unaware of
the dangers of a plethora of facts and that facts by themselves tell
nothing. But their hope evidently was that, in lieu of the type of
model analysis ordinarily associated with economic theory, a coherence could be gained by focusing on the relevant institutions: the
wage system, the capitalized form of modern industry, the factory
system, and the permanency of the wage earning class.[7]

Like the institutionalism that developed a generation later, the approach taken by Adams and Sumner can be viewed as largely re-
pudiating the existing economic theory. Perhaps Seager was mistaken
in the notion that the failure of the text to refer to wage theory was a
regrettable omission. A case can also be made for viewing it as a conscious attempt to find, in the analysis of the institutions that were both
the cause and embodiment of the various labor problems, an ordering of otherwise unmanageable details that would serve as an alternative to the ordering or structuring provided by economic theory.

The view that Adams and Sumner were attempting to find an alternative for orthodox wage theory, and one that would be a short-run
explanation, is further supported by their discussion of bargaining
theory in a section of the chapter on organizations, "The Economic
Justification of Labor Organizations." Given the various imperfections of the labor market, they say, "the bargain between the employer

and the laborer is indeterminate so far as the semi-impersonal or objective forces of the market are concerned, and consequently within certain limits the seller will get more or less according as his power of higgling is great or little." [8] And in their discussions of how these limits are fixed, discussions very much in the tradition of the Webbs, Adams and Sumner take a path of analysis that can only be described as theoretical:

With a proper understanding of the terms, however, it is not misleading to say that under ordinary circumstances the minimum wage of the laborer will be determined by the standard of life of his time and trade. . . . On the other hand, the maximum limit, the highest offer of the employer, can not exceed the net value which the laborer is capable of adding to the output of the establishment. In other words, the upper limit is fixed by the productivity of the worker. [9]

It is not, then, altogether true that Adams and Sumner omitted any treatment of the theory of wages. They clearly state that productivity fixes the upper limit of the wage bargain, although they fail to relate this to a demand for labor. Similarly the standard of living (by which they mean something akin to the worker's own estimate of the opportunity cost of his accepting a specific employment) determines the lower limit, although they do not specifically relate this to the supply of labor. In any event, it appears that the bargain theory of wages was more acceptable to these early labor students than was the orthodox theory largely because it was a short-run theory grounded in economic institutions and practices deemed important in contemporary economic life. Nor was this feature to change significantly through several decades of labor studies.

A NEW SPECIALTY

"In the field of labor," Joseph Dorfman has written, "the period from 1918 to 1929 presented a paradox: while organized labor was declining in both strength and numbers, a new specialty, labor economics, achieved acceptance and began to produce a distinct body of theoretical and empirical literature." [10] Dorfman's designation of labor economics as a new specialty is interesting. Theorizing about labor as an abstract concept had long been a central feature of economic theory, particularly after Adam Smith made labor the first price that was paid for all things and Ricardo made distribution of relative shares the leading question for theoretical economics. The post-Ricardian classical and neoclassical economists generally eschewed any study of labor institutions as being outside the scope of science, but, the founders of the American Economic Association recognized the necessity for institutional and factual labor studies by economists as early as 1886.

Indeed with the rapid multiplication of courses and literature relating to labor institutions and the various labor problems associated with industrialization, which particularly marked the last years of the nineteenth century and the first years of the twentieth, labor study by economists was a well-established field before World War I. What appears to be new about the new specialty of labor economics in the 1920s is the wedding of these two earlier interests in the study of labor: the study of wage theory plus the study of wage institutions and wage problems. The result was the "distinct body of theoretical and empirical literature" to which Professor Dorfman has referred.

One must not exaggerate the extent to which empiricism and theory merged in this period, however, for the alliance was frequently uneasy. True, Solomon Blum, in the first text to be entitled *Labor Economics,* did include a chapter on wage theory and, throughout the work, achieved a "coherence and integration of subject matter . . . [which was] a distinct improvement upon nearly all of the earlier texts."[11] Those earlier texts, consistently modeled on Adams and Sumner, had paid little heed to orthodox wage theory and made no efforts to integrate that theory with empiricism. The authors of the earlier texts concentrated generally on reporting, in a somewhat sequential manner, specific labor problems and on offering suggested remedies for them—the latter frequently built around increased governmental action or the actions of labor unions. Blum's work differed in that it attempted a greater integration of economic analysis and paid less attention to the evils befalling individual workers in an industrial system. A more specific distinction between Blum's *Labor Economics* and the earlier labor problems texts was his inclusion of a chapter entitled "Theories of Wages." This, one might suppose, should be a good illustration of Professor Dorfman's characterization of labor economics as a new specialty. Indeed Blum's work is prominently featured by Dorfman as representative of the body of theoretical and empirical literature that began to be produced by the labor students during the 1920s. But the plurality in the chapter title— "Theories of Wages"—is significant.

"Why," asked Barbara Wootton of labor economists in 1926, "is it necessary always to summarize theories of wages that are now universally discarded? In other branches of economics, dead theories are left to rot, except in treatises (other than textbooks) which have a special reason for disinterring them."[12] A partial answer to this question, one suspects, is that in many other branches of economics, the received theory was deemed to be adequate for the task at hand. But if the weaknesses of the theory are to be stressed, is it not useful to emphasize the ephemeral character of other particular theories? As Richard Lester put it in the first edition of his *Economics of Labor,* "A study of the weaknesses in such theories should help to develop a healthy skepticism and should aid in understanding how economic doctrines evolve and change with changes in economic structure and economic institutions."[13]

So it was with Blum. After explaining and dismissing the wages fund theory, Blum considered the marginal productivity theory. He found that "the thesis that the wage is determined by the productivity of labor" was "tautological and logically unsound, as well as lacking in practical applicability" and that it was usually associated with an un-critical deification of the competitive system." Blum then criticized the failure of economic theory to come to grips with the problem of monopoly other than as an exception to pure competition.[14]

Despite Blum's criticisms of orthodox wage theory, his was still a book more clearly approaching economics (as that term is usually un-derstood) than was the Adams and Sumner text. One sees emerging with Blum a limited search for tools of economic analysis satisfactory to the task at hand. Blum's approach, conditioned by his teachers, Jacob Hollander and George Barnett at Johns Hopkins University, was marked by no mere rejection of economic theory in favor of what Ely called "the facts of the case." It was, rather, marked by a dissatis-faction with the state of economic theory as it may be applied to the facts of the case and by suggestions, however tentative and incom-plete, for improvement. Blum's advice to the economist, to the effect that he surrender certain doctrines stemming from orthodox eco-nomic analysis and "devote himself to the factual considerations sur-rounding trade unions, monopoly, and the actual practices involved in the use of credit," did not mean that he thought such pursuits would suffice in lieu of a theory of wages. A study of the factual con-siderations would be merely a necessary antecedent to an adequate theory. That Blum well appreciated the distinction between the theo-retical and the merely descriptive is evident from his dismissal of the bargain theory as a theory of wages. It was, according to him, "little more than a statement of the unionists' positions . . . less a theory in the true sense than a description of practical methods in the field of wage adjustment." It could not "become a complete theory of wages or even the cornerstone of such a theory, because it does not answer, or even ask, the questions whence the wages are paid, and to what limits wages can rightfully be raised."[15] One finds, then, with Blum a rekindled interest in the kinds of questions that the classical and neo-classical economists had raised, as well as a continuing interest in the institutional approach.

Blum's criticism of economic theory—a criticism of the answers provided rather than of the questions asked—offers only one of the caveats that were suggested earlier concerning too facile an acceptance of the idea of the merging of theory and empiricism that began, for the field of labor, with the labor economics of the 1920s and 1930s. Another is suggested by the continued dominance of the Wisconsin school. The "Specialists in Industrial Relations" to whose work and influence Dorfman referred when he spoke of the "body of theoretical and empirical literature" that was produced during the twenties included, in addition to Blum, George E. Barnett, Norman J. Ware, Leo Wolman, Paul H. Douglas, Isador Lubin, and Sumner H. Slichter. The trouble with this listing as representative of the twenties is that it seriously understates the influence of John R. Commons and the University of Wisconsin. Indeed, only one of these, Slichter, studied under Commons even for the M.A., and then took his doctorate at the University of Chicago. Had Johns Hopkins University in fact been as dominant a center for labor studies as it is dominant in the background of Dorfman's choice of leading labor specialists during the twenties (Barnett, Blum and Wolman were all products of Johns Hopkins and most of the others were probably closer to the Johns Hopkins approach to labor studies than to the Wisconsin approach), then trends in labor history, as well as in labor economics in general, might have been quite different from what in fact they were. For, as we shall have occasion to note at greater length below, there was a marked difference between the Wisconsin (Commons-Perlman) and the Johns Hopkins (Hollander-Barnett) approaches to the study of labor.

A third warning against overstating the extent to which the labor specialists moved closer to economic theory comes from one whose own work was eminently in the tradition of both theory and empiricism, and who was himself a representative contributor to the emerging body of theoretical and empirical literature, Paul H. Douglas. In his presidential address before the American Economic Association in 1948, Douglas charged the profession with "scientific schizophrenia" in the study of labor and wages: "I have known professors, who teaching both theory and labor economics, have instilled the pure doctrine of John Bates Clark during one hour, and then during the next hour have taught as economic gospel the bargain theories of Sidney and Beatrice Webb."[16]

Despite these qualifications concerning the extent to which the students of labor began increasingly to espouse economic analysis, it is nonetheless true that the labor economics of the years following World War I was sufficiently different from the problems approach to the study of labor that had characterized the prewar years to constitute in essentials a new discipline.[17]

FROM PROBLEMS TO PROCESSES

One of the most striking features of the books in the labor field written after World War I is their rejection of the emphasis on the evils associated with the use of labor in an industrial system, which had characterized the problems approach to labor studies before the war. "The approach of the subject heretofore," wrote Willard Atkins and Harold Lasswell in 1924, "has been too pathological. We have analyzed various symptoms of disease in the social body—poverty, strikes, boycotts, lockouts, gunmen—and have examined various remedies. . . we have specialized in splints and bandages without the prerequisite course in general anatomy. . . . Just as an understanding of the composition and functioning of the human organism is a condition precedent to the efficient treatment of bodily disease, so is an understanding of the composition and functioning of the working population a necessary preliminary to the diagnosis and treatment of the diseases of the social body." [18]

This viewpoint was shared and perpetuated by other writers. In the 1920s and 1930s, students of labor attempted to broaden their focus from the problems of labor as those of merely one social group toward a larger view that would see many of those particular problems as both partial and transitory in the broad process of social change. In an early distinction between labor problems and labor economics, Dale Yoder wrote in 1933, "Labor problems, in so far as they are not merely situations which some individual or small group desires to change, are maladjustments in the functioning of the processes which form the subject matter of labor economics. They are, so to speak, the pathological phases of these processes . . . which processes are not operating in a manner satisfactory to those participating in and directly dependent upon their functioning." Labor economics, on the other hand, was coming to be both more sharply distinguished from labor problems and more closely aligned with general economics than was the case before World War I: "Labor economics . . . is that phase which describes and explains the particular function of laborers in the economic process. . . . Labor economics is not at all different, either in the viewpoint it uses or in the basic nature of the phenomena it studies, from any other division of economics. It is merely one of several such divisions." [19]

Clearly the economist's study of labor was coming to be increasingly oriented toward the traditional viewpoint of the economist, that embodying the economy at large. The tendency was increasingly away from the mere enumeration of specific problems of one group—labor—followed by recommended solutions for these problems. Nor is it the case that the labor economists of the interwar period were any less concerned with labor problems or were any less reform oriented in their outlook than had been their predecessors. What distinguishes the labor economics approach of 1925 from the labor problems approach of 1905 is the effort in the later period to make the study of labor problems subordinate to and only a part of the study of basic economic processes.

Part of the explanation of this transition lies in the fact that as time passed, it became increasingly clear that not only were labor problems a permanent feature of the industrial process—when solutions were presented for some, others would appear—but also that each generation had its own problems. The basic economic processes, in which the problems had their genesis, however, were coming to be recognized as much less ephemeral than many of the specific problems.

As an important part of their reporting specific labor problems, the early students of labor had placed heavy emphasis on fact gathering. But labor economics, reflecting the newer emphasis was

concerned primarily with principles, secondarily with facts. That is not because facts are unimportant in labor economics. They are vitally important . . . [but] facts change with great rapidity. . . . In the study of either general or specific labor questions, there can be no substitute for complete, accurate, and detailed factual information as a basis for analysis and decision. But the facts themselves cannot be anticipated, and those already collected, while helpful for purposes of interpretation, often do not apply to the current problem. It is different with principles.[20]

The transition from labor problems to labor economics, the growing integration of problems with the more basic economic processes, and the increasing emphasis on principles in contrast to factual descriptions indicate a number of changes, changes of degree (rather than of kind). The emergence of labor economics, for example, did not replace the study of labor problems; labor economics without references to particular problem areas is unthinkable—as, indeed, is the whole of economics. The terms labor problems and labor economics were used jointly, and alternatively, for at least forty years, and are, albeit less frequently, so used today. The most exhaustive synthesis of the field produced during these years, the three volume series entitled *The Economics of Labor* by Harry A. Millis and Royal E. Montgomery, centered around three major problem areas: (1) wages, hours of work, and living standards, (2) unemployment, work accidents, and disease, and (3) trade unionism. It is the integration of those problems with the broader forces and processes of economic life that demarcates the labor economics texts from the earlier volumes on labor problems.

One of the chief means by which labor problems were more closely integrated with the economic process was a growing emphasis on research in collective bargaining, which had become increasingly significant after World War I. Indeed both the paucity of collective bargaining in the prewar period and the identity in the public mind of the concept of labor with that of struggle is at one with the concept of labor study as that of problems. After the war, when collective bargaining had been more or less regularized "in a number of industries—men's and women's clothing, printing, coal mining, construction and the railroads," empirical research focusing on the bargaining relationships increasingly occurred. "These were largely industry studies, stressing formal structure, procedures, and working rules."[21]

I noted earlier Joseph Dorfman's characterization of the emergence of labor economics as a paradox in a period when organized labor was declining. What must be kept in mind, however, is that an important part of the transition to labor economics consisted in the shift from labor problems to labor or industrial relations. The paradox to which Dorfman referred is partially resolved, it appears, by relating the development of labor economics (from labor problems) less to developments in the growth of organized labor than to those in industrial management following World War I. Thus although union membership was not increasing during the 1920s, by the end of the decade industrial relations "had achieved a more or less firm pattern in a number of industries." Nor was the growth of industrial relations during the 1920s alone a matter of unionism. The decade was one of significant advance in the techniques of scientific management and in the growth of company unions. It is possible that their use helped foster peaceful relations in much of industry, at least in comparison with earlier periods in our history. If organized labor did not grow during the 1920s, at least the concept of the inevitability of some kind of employer-employee relations was replacing the older view of labor problems as temporary evils calling for specific and permanent correction. This was an important component in the shift to labor economics. Paul Brissenden wrote in 1926 that students were recognizing

the interdependence of labor problems on the one hand and problems of industrial administration . . . important evidence of the partially accomplished substitution of the notion of an integrated series of relationships for the atomistic notion of a more or less unrelated series of problems, each of which may be called a labor problem.

Stress on *relations* (buyer-seller, employer-employee, etc.) means stress on transactions which necessarily arise from those relations. In labor economics this means that attention must be centered upon the individual and collective bargains (wage contracts and trade agreements) made by and between employer and employee or between unions of employers and unions of employees.[22]

The increasing attention paid to labor relations and collective bargaining also relates to the emphasis so far placed on the integration of labor study with the economic process rather than with economic theory during this period. Although the interwar years were generally marked by a growing interest in wage theory, this does not mean that there was an uncritical acceptance of the tools of economic analysis by the students of labor. On the contrary, although there were important exceptions, a significant gap continued to exist between labor economics and economic theory.

THE LABOR ECONOMISTS AND ECONOMIC THEORY

"The existence in America of . . . flourishing areas of applied economics—such as labor economics and industrial relations [has] meant," according to Professor Samuelson, "that economists with an empirical bent could follow their inclination without necessarily cutting themselves off from the body of economic theory."[23] Dorfman has also referred to labor economists in terms of "their close contacts and working relationships with the rest of the profession," in contrast, say with agricultural economics or home economics as fields "so specialized as to have little or nothing to do with the main body of economic theory."[24] To what extent are these views valid for the interwar years, the formative period of the new specialty of labor economics?

A first observation must be that the earliest labor economists were generally unequivocal in their rejection of economic theory. One of the most important reasons was what the labor economists considered to be the individualist bias in the classical model as well as the neoclassical theory of marginal utility. As Eric Roll has written: "In nearly all classical literature, economic analysis was allied with an historical view of the structure of society which underlay the whole economic process. In its place was put a view of society as an agglomeration of individuals. The subjective theory of value (even in its earlier cost-of-production form) is only compatible with an individualist view of society and in some of the more extreme formulations becomes even 'atomistic.' "[25]

The concern of the new economic theory with the behavior of the individual has been referred to as "a sign of the progress of liberal political philosophy."[26] One qualification that ought to be made, however, concerning the liberal political philosophy is that it frequently fell short of including the laborer. Edgar Furniss, for example, detected the exclusion of the laborer from the rising individualism that characterized English (as opposed to Continental) mercantilism.[27]

The rise of trade unionism in the nineteenth century, both in England and the United States, may be viewed as an attempt on the part of laborers to accomplish on a group basis what could not be done individually. Workers believed that they were being denied the economic benefits that the classical political economists associated with economic liberalism. Laborers seeking to unionize were trying to acquire an increased share in the fruits of an economic system that was becoming increasingly concentrated and monopolistic but that had as its conceptual and ideological basis the individualism of classical liberalism.

Perhaps in response to these trends, the early students of labor attempted to restructure economic theory on a group basis. One of the most striking features common to all of the early labor students was their dissatisfaction with economic theory. "The economy," wrote Ely, "does not consist simply of a sum of individuals, nor does the national economic life—which it is the province of the political economist to investigate—mean a sum of individual economies. This notion, the fictitious assumption of the classical individualistic political economy, holds only of men living in an isolated barbarous condition, which is a low, mean state of independence." Similarly John R. Commons's efforts to restructure economic theory were based on the idea of "collective action in control, liberation and expansion of individual action," and he frequently contrasted his approach with that of "the older science of individualistic economics."[28] All of Commons's key conceptual tools—transactions, due process, going concerns, custom, and so forth—embody the idea of group action in control of individual action. The writings and activities of the Webbs also reflect not only their desire to effect social reform but also their rejection of economic theory and their desire "to place social science on a new basis."[29] Robert F. Hoxie's interest in trade unionism was an outgrowth of his efforts to reform economic theory. "It seems clear," he wrote in 1906, "that the existing status of economic theory calls urgently for the restatement of economic concepts and for the revision of fundamental economic problems." After alluding to the impact of the evolutionary point of view on science in general and to the many changes in industrial organization and technique that had been effected during the preceding half-century, Hoxie went on to say that "the great body of generally accepted economic theory seems to have remained essentially unmodified by [this] recent progressive revolution in science and economy."[30]

Another early labor economist, Carlton H. Parker, who in 1914 was asked to investigate the riot among the migratory hop workers in California, later wrote that he found he "had no fundamentals which could be called good tools with which to begin an analysis of this riot."[31] Parker held that

our conventional economics today analyzes no phase of industrialism nor the wage relationship, nor citizenship in a pecuniary society, in a manner to offer a key to distressing and complex problems. . . . The confusion and metaphysical propensities of our economic theory, our neglect of the consequences of child labor, our lax interest in national vitality and health, the unusableness of our theories of labor unrest and of labor efficiency . . .—all this delinquency can be traced back to our refusal to see that economics was social economics, and that a full knowledge of man, his instincts, his power of habit acquisition, his psychological demands were an absolute prerequisite to clear and purposeful thinking on our industrial civilization.[32]

Enough has been said perhaps to suggest the necessity for qualification concerning Samuelson's assertion that labor economics (among other applied fields) offered the opportunity for an economist to "follow his empirical inclinations without cutting himself off from the body of economic theory," at least for the period with which we are here concerned. The early students of labor problems, before the era of "labor economics," nearly all rejected traditional economic theory, and many of their efforts were toward reforming that theory. During the 1920s, and to some extent during the 1930s, many labor economists simply ignored economic theory. Certainly, for more recent years, Samuelson's observations are not far wide of the mark. "One of the most impressive qualities" of the research in labor economics since World War II has been, George Hildebrand has noted, "the emergence of an informed theoretical empiricism, which frames hypotheses and then tests them with evidence."[33]

To be sure, some texts included a chapter on economic theory, but not very often. Indeed as late as 1945, Carroll R. Daugherty observed, "There is, in fact, no labor textbook which satisfactorily employs and integrates the tools of economic analysis in its discussions." "The need for analysis is evident in all discussions of relations between employers and unions," Daugherty wrote, "but the need is particularly acute with respect to discussions involving economic theory. . . . Every labor 'problem' exists in a frame of reference determined by economic as well as other forces. Every effort and every proposal to 'solve' a labor problem requires appraisal in economic terms and with the use of economic-analytical methods."[34]

Thus although labor problems were coming to be more closely associated with the economic process of industrial capitalism, rather than being thought of as temporary evils amenable to particular solutions, the integration of those problems with economic theory had been less fully accomplished. A large part of the reason inheres in the judgment of the early labor economists as to the insufficiency of economic theory for analyses of the modern economic process. Nor can these issues be considered apart from the relations between economic theorists and labor economists. Many labor economists, for example, have qualified the notion of the close working relations between themselves and the theorists. Edwin Witte has even suggested that the term *labor economist* was originally one of derision: "The study of unions as institutions was begun many years ago by the institutional economists who were called, derisively, 'labor economists' by many of their professional colleagues." In much the same vein, but in a more explanatory manner, Daugherty, himself a labor economist, has asserted:

The fact that "price economists" have looked down their noses at teachers of labor courses is almost entirely the fault of the latter. The ranks of labor teachers have contained too many sociologists, political scientists, and historians whose education, if any, in the use of the tools of economic analysis has been distressingly inadequate, and it is a feeble defense at best for such teachers to accuse the price economist of ivory-towerism and devotion to impractical theory. The same thing is true of some labor textbook writers.[35]

Daugherty's criticism was directed not to sociologists, political scientists, and historians as such, who were teaching within their own disciplines, but to labor economists who eschewed economic theory in favor of a more sociological, legal, political, or historical approach.

During this period, however, many students of labor began increasingly to identify with the economist's approach and to relate their studies to the continuing economic process more closely. Paradoxically at this time, according to Homan, "the whole subject of economic theory" was in "utter confusion."[36] Writing on contemporary economic thought in the late 1920s and focusing on the works and influence of J. B. Clark, Thorstein Veblen, Alfred Marshall, John A. Hobson, and Wesley C. Mitchell, Homan concluded: "Nothing can be more evident to anyone surveying the field of contemporary economic thought than that those economists who concern themselves with general theory hold widely divergent ideas of the purpose, scope, and method of economics. . . . Between the limits of an extreme individualistic and an extreme organismic theory of society lies a field for infinite diversity of view."[37]

Clearly a close relationship exists between the trends in economic theory in the direction of institutionalism that marked the 1920s and the quality of the emerging labor economics of the period. Perhaps nowhere is this better illustrated than in the inclusiveness of the early labor economics. Much more than in the past two or three decades, the labor economists of the interwar years were multiple social scientists.

THE INCLUSIVENESS OF LABOR ECONOMICS

"The study of labor problems," Gordon S. Watkins wrote in 1922, in the first edition of a work that was widely used for more than twenty years, "is fundamentally a part of the social science of Economics, but it is related definitely to Sociology, History, Politics, Law, Ethics, and Psychology."[38] Many institutionalists of the time would have gone even further to assert the necessity for economics as a whole drawing closer to these other social sciences.

Interestingly it was the economists who pursued their inquiries into these other fields rather than the other social sciences participating to any significant degree in the study of labor. Of course, labor study had been established as the province of the economist soon after the turn of the century. The reason seems quite natural since the term *labor* denotes an economic activity undertaken for economic gain. The inevitability of the dominance of the economic framework in labor studies was reinforced when both the ends and the means toward those ends that were espoused by organized labor in the United States were (unlike the situation in some European countries) predominantly economic. But these considerations cannot entirely explain why sociologists, in whose domain the study of labor problems had largely been during the 1880s and 1890s, did so little with labor studies during the first three decades of the twentieth century. It has been suggested that sociologists have sought to improve their standing as scientists by theorizing about social processes rather than perpetuating a more mundane concern with solving social problems.[39] Certainly the emergence of a specialized field of social work as distinct from sociology lends credence to this view. But during the early 1920s, the study of many social problems—crime, delinquency, and poverty, among others—was very much a part of sociology.

Of considerable significance in explaining why the study of labor was so exclusively the province of economists seems to be the orientation and the abilities of the labor economists themselves. Ely, Commons, Hoxie, Millis, Perlman, and others were equally at home in economics and in other social sciences to varying degrees. Thus the study of labor after the turn of the century was broadly conceived. The economics of many of the early students of labor included as well large amounts of history, law, ethics, psychology, and sociology. In fact, Commons's *Institutional Economics* was initially conceived of as sociology.[40]

A large part of the explanation why sociologists eschewed labor study generally during the first three or four decades of the twentieth century may well be that the sociological aspects of labor study were being well covered by the labor economists. One sociologist has re-

marked, "Some of the best sociological studies of industrial life were
made by non-sociologists."[41] Few social psychologists or sociologists,
one supposes, were any better equipped to apply their disciplines to
labor study than was the labor economist Selig Perlman. Indeed a
leading sociological journal has reminded American sociologists that
they "have at their disposal the Wisconsin studies which constitute a
valuable foundation in the historical sociology of American Industrial
Relations. Particularly relevant . . . is Selig Perlman's emphasis on the
social psychology of 'job-scarcity consciousness.' "[42]

Selig Perlman's *Theory of the Labor Movement* was generally taught as
labor economics, but his work bore little relation to the economist's
traditional method or approach. It was eminently in the tradition of
Commons's dictum to his students to "go out and find out what is on
the worker's mind."[43] Perlman found that what was very much on the
workers' minds was the scarcity of job opportunities:

"Scarcity groups" regularly endeavor to "own" as groups the limited opportunities at their disposal. Thus no issue relating to the conditions upon which
they will permit an individual to connect with an opportunity can escape becoming strongly tinged by this fundamental aspiration to "own" all the opportunities extant. It would be erroneous to try to account for an industrial
struggle solely by the specific demands which are its proximate causes: wages,
hours, freedom from discriminatory discharge, etc., while leaving out this
group "hunger" for controlling the job opportunities to the point of
"ownership." . . . behind each strike there always lurks the struggle for the
control of the jobs.[44]

Nor were essentially sociological studies the only ones in which the
labor economists made important contributions outside the field of
economics. A somewhat similar situation developed with respect to
labor history. Ely's *Labor Movement in America* was essentially a history
of organized labor in the United States up to 1886, and his intention
from the outset was to follow up that work with one on a larger scale.
It was to complete that larger work that he brought Commons to Wisconsin in 1904. The result was the four-volume *History of Labor in the
United States.*[45] From the time of Ely's work to the present day, the
dominance of economists in the field of labor history has been a
familiar phenomenon. Mark Perlman says that it was probably Ely's
standing as a leading professional economist that "explains why the
history of American unionism became associated initially with economics rather than political science or history," although this does not
explain the later primacy of the economists in this field.[46] Perlman's
view to some extent is supported and amplified by Irving Bernstein,
who asserts that the labor economists preempted the field of labor
history, citing especially the influence of Commons.[47]

Walter Galenson, on the other hand, writing in the 1950s, believed that the historians had abandoned the field of labor history to the economists. The result, he said, was that "the historians have rendered a disservice to the cause of scholarship, particularly since the economists themselves have been more and more disposed to look down on 'mere history' as an unworthy mental discipline."[48] But the special reasons for the predominance of economists among labor historians are of less relevance here than is the reality of their long predominance to the point at issue: the breadth of the domain of labor economics.

The quality of the labor economics of the interwar years can be determined by examining certain issues relating to labor history. Galenson points to two main currents in American labor history. The first is that associated with Commons, which is "characterized by a fairly straightforward, narrative approach. There is typically little conscious effort to apply the tools and concepts of economic and sociological theory to the data. The Commons school was very much in the tradition of continental social history." The second, identified with George E. Barnett and Jacob H. Hollander of Johns Hopkins, tried to explain what Commons and his associates had documented: "Their approach was primarily that of economic history; they looked upon the trade union as a peculiar economic institution, operating within certain economic constraints, and their concern was with the reciprocal relationships of institution and environment. They had no interest in the chronology, and very little in the politics, of unionism." This classification is, as Galenson admits, overly simplified—Commons, in some of his articles, applied analysis fully as much as did the Johns Hopkins group and some labor historians associated with neither the Wisconsin nor the Johns Hopkins groups—but basically most early work belonged to one category or the other.[49]

Galenson was not alone in describing the Wisconsin approach as that of social history in contrast to the economic history of the Johns Hopkins studies. Mark Perlman, also, after pointing out that Hollander and Barnett were "both rigorous students of traditional economic theory," has said that Commons fundamentally "applied the methods of the social historian to problems of political administration."[50] Philip Taft dissented from these views but admitted that the economics of the labor movement was not well integrated in the early volumes of the Commons *History.*[51]

One reason why there was little conscious effort to apply the tools and concepts of economic theory to the data in the Commons *History* is that Commons was one of the most trenchant critics of that theory. The Johns Hopkins group, while seeking to improve economic theory by increased use of inductive verification of hypotheses, was nevertheless much closer to the orthodox approach than were Ely or Commons. Hollander, for example, who held that trade unionism was the most significant labor problem of the day, also held that "the *crux* of trade unionism is the determination of a natural law of wages, and, no less significant, the determination of a practicable method of ascertaining it." He urged a "closer parallelism in method of investigation between Political Economy and Physical Science."[52] Hollander was in no sense suggesting a return to the a priori dogmatism of some nineteenth-century economists who had drawn comparisons between the finality of the laws of economics and laws of physical science. He did urge, however, that the economist try to sharpen his tools of analysis by extensive collection and classification of data and by the use of these data as tests of hypotheses.

The Johns Hopkins studies have been described as topical rather than historical and have been presented as complementary to, rather than competitive with, the Wisconsin approach. Mark Perlman quotes David A. McCabe, a student of Barnett and Hollander, as explaining that the reason for the two focuses was to avoid duplicating work. He believed that "there was an understanding . . . between Commons and the Hopkins pair (Hollander and Barnett) on this general division of labor."[53] There was, however, a much greater division than one of labor between the Wisconsin and Johns Hopkins approaches. Hollander was critical of the Continental influence, which weighed heavily in the outlook of Ely and, through him, Commons:

On the one hand, we have permitted the Comptian [*sic*] influence and the "extreme Historismus" of the German school to justify economic microscopics; and, on the other hand, dismayed by the vast area, the extensive activities, and the scattered data subject to economic inquiry, and poorly equipped both in requisite resources and opportunities, we have refrained from attempting comprehensive induction.

In consequence, economic investigation in the United States, although pursued with unexampled activity, has been almost exclusively historical or institutional, on the one hand, and local or intensive on the other. Of extensive economic investigation, economic induction in the proper sense of the term, little has been attempted and less achieved.[54]

Nor was the Johns Hopkins group as reform oriented as the Wisconsin school. "The purpose of the political economist," Hollander wrote, "is to investigate, not to advocate."[55] On the whole, then, the Johns Hopkins approach to labor study might well be described as an attempt at economic science in contrast to the political economy of the Wisconsin school.

In the face of these considerations, let us return now to the question, Whence the dominance of the labor economists in the field of labor history? We are at once faced with a dilemma if we accept as the reason that which is sometimes put forward by historians: they have not had the requisite training in economic analysis. Bornet, for example, has said of historians that they "have been overawed by the needless complexity of the articles and books issued by their colleagues in economics. Potential students of labor history who venture into economics department seminars struggle valiantly with the literature of labor theory."[56] But as Galenson has replied, the difficulty facing history students is easily exaggerated: "Historians venturing into labor seminars cannot expect, without any preliminary training, to comprehend the vocabulary of economics. However, the extent of the preliminary proficiency required is not great, certainly no more than can be acquired by an outside field in economics on the part of the history Ph.D. candidate. The economic sophistication of trade unionists with little formal education would tend to support this view."[57]

Of even greater relevance is that such explanations as that offered by Bornet for the relative inactivity of historians in labor history seem applicable only to the Johns Hopkins type of labor history, clearly not the dominant trend in this country during this period. If the Wisconsin tradition was in fact in the tradition of Continental social history, with relatively little integration of economic analysis, then the reticence of historians to enter labor seminars is all the more perplexing. Commons did not dominate the field of labor history by virtue of his abilities as an economist (for he seldom integrated his economics with his history) but rather precisely because of his abilities as a historian. It was, indeed, this latter ability that attracted some of his students. Edwin Witte, for example, said that it was Commons the historian, not Commons the economist, with whom he originally wanted to study.[58]

The significance of the breadth of interests and abilities of John R. Commons relates to the generally accepted opinion that no other single figure so well represents the field of labor economics during the pre–World War I years. As Neil Chamberlain has remarked, Commons "is often regarded as the most eminent labor economist this country has produced."[59] Certainly the philosophy and approach of the Wisconsin school, characterized by an intense zeal for public service and social reform and coupled with both a critical attitude toward traditional economic theory and a disregard for the conventional boundaries between the social sciences, best describes the general temper of labor economics during the 1920s and 1930s. It is not simply that the University of Wisconsin was the leading center for labor studies; the temper of the Wisconsin approach attracted and was characteristic of many other leading students of labor.

172 THE INSTITUTIONALIST MOVEMENT

LABOR ECONOMICS AND INSTITUTIONALISM IN PERSPECTIVE

At the annual meeting of the American Economic Association in 1931, a round table conference was held on the much discussed topic of the day, "Institutional Economics." One of the participants was Richard T. Ely, almost eighty years old, who charged the discussants with "ignorance of the history of economic thought and especially of American economic thought." The essence of Ely's assertion was that the institutional economics of the 1920s was really nothing new. It began in 1885 and was enunciated in the Statement of Principles by the founders of the American Economic Association. Ely held that Veblen could not be regarded as the "founder of institutional economics in this country because in my judgment institutional economics as something distinctive goes back in this country to 1885." Commons, he pointed out, was "regarded and correctly regarded as an outstanding institutional economist. But Commons was an institutional economist way back in the nineties." As far as he himself was concerned, Ely concluded, "I want to say that I am an institutional economist or I am nothing."[60]

Whether in fact the institutionalist movement began in 1885 or whether that earlier movement was "pre-institutionalist" and "a rebellion of a very mild order," as Kenneth Boulding has characterized it, it is nonetheless interesting to note that both labor problems and labor economics emerged during periods of unrest and upheaval in the general field of economics.[61] The study of labor problems began as part of the general effort in the late nineteenth century by American economists trained in Germany to infuse new life and relevance into economics. Similarly the 1920s, the decade during which the transition from labor problems to labor economics was generally accomplished, was marked by the institutionalist movement in the United States. Regardless of where one places the roots of this movement (and the use of the term itself predates World War I), it was during the 1920s that institutionalism reached its peak as an effort to revamp economic theory.

Some economists, like Boulding, have thought of both of these efforts to infuse new vitality into economics as essentially negative movements of dissent from the mainstream of orthodoxy.[62] Others, like Allan Gruchy, disagree and argue that the efforts of the institutionalists must be seen as "a positive, creative movement which aims at broadening the nature and scope of economic science by pushing beyond basic theory to create a theory of our developing economic system."[63] There is, insofar as institutionalism related to the development of both economic theory and labor economics, some validity in each of these views.

Of the early institutionalists who are generally regarded primarily as labor economists, the two most original and influential were Hoxie and Commons. Their efforts were seriously directed toward restructuring economic theory and, toward that end, their labor studies played a part. Their efforts may be conceived of as positive attempts at improving economic theory. Many of their students, on the other hand, while sharing an interest in the study of labor, did not push on with this work in the larger field of theory. For these, institutionalism meant a rejection of economic theory in a more negative sense. Certainly many of the early studies of unions as institutions reflect the sociologist's approach; many of the historical studies, the historian's approach; and so on, all instead of the economist's approach, with its traditional focus on the efficiency of resource allocation. Perhaps a distinction ought to be made, as it seldom is, between the terms *institutional economist* and *institutionalist*. Many teachers of labor courses were evidently institutionalists in the more negative sense of not having mastered economic theory. These were the sociologists, political scientists, and historians who were yet, in all probability, members of economics departments—specifically, labor economists. But institutional economists in the positive sense of a Hoxie or a Commons had an unexcelled grasp of economic theory, despite their frequent and trenchant criticisms of it.

Economics is usually defined as the study of the organization through which scarce resources are allocated to satisfy man's material wants. But the organization through which this resource allocation takes place is typically dominated by the concept of the market. If economists discuss the role of legislative policies, trade unions, regulatory commissions, or a host of other institutional influences in their general analyses of the mixed economy of twentieth-century capitalism, at the heart of economic theory itself remains the market. Theorists, however, have been somewhat less than fully successful in "integrating labor into the market schema," and dissatisfaction with market analysis has been a long-standing and continuing criticism on the part of labor economists.[64] In labor matters, in the words of Richard Lester, market forces "are modified, restricted, and even replaced by social and other non-economic elements."[65]

This attitude toward the market was at the heart of the institutionalist controversy. The institutional economists, including the students of labor, discovered in their special studies serious limitations of an analytical framework in which the market alone was the regulating mechanism. They sought not to replace market analysis but to complement it by incorporating into economic theory other institutional controls as well. As Walter W. Stewart long ago expressed it,

The advantage of a clear recognition of the general problem by the economists working in the special fields is that as their work develops their results will come to constitute a coherent body of theory, organized around the central problem of control. In the work now being done in banking and in taxation, in problems of labor and of valuation, there is implied a body of principles which will make good its claim to be economic theory. The detailed analysis of the market, already made by value theorists, will find its place in such a body of theory, but instead of being studied in logical isolation the market will play its role along with the other agencies of control.

Perhaps this attitude towards the market as simply one of the institutions requiring analysis is the determining characteristic of institutional theory . . . [which] regards as the fundamental data for analysis such underlying institutions as ownership, inheritance, the standards of consumption, and the development of technology. These phenomena have not been overlooked by the value theorist, but they have been put into a separate compartment called "dynamics"; and have finally been left unincorporated. These rejected facts are regarded as fundamental by an economic theory of the institutional type.[66]

That the results of those institutional economists who were working in the applied fields have not fulfilled the expressed hopes for a coherent body of theory is commonly agreed upon. But what is relevant here is the search for that body of principles that would "make good its claim to be economic theory." Commons opened his *Legal Foundations of Capitalism* in 1924 by saying, "The aim of this volume is to work out an evolutionary and behavioristic, or rather volitional, theory of value."[67] That effort began, he added, thirty-five years earlier as a student of Ely at Johns Hopkins University. From 1890 on, then, Commons must have been formulating his theoretical ideas. Yet as Neil Chamberlain has remarked, Commons's extensive writings up to 1924 "showed relatively little interest in economic theory": "On the whole his attention and writing were absorbed in specific reform programs and particular institutions. What was not then apparent was that all the specific experience and direct observation, the personal involvement and the case study, were simply ingredients which, over the years, would be molded and shaped in the reflective processes of the mind into concepts of general applicability, designed to reduce the welter of casual and transient experience into a more orderly and comprehensible pattern."[68]

Few graduate teachers, from all accounts, have so inspired their students as did Commons. Yet his students failed generally to share his interest in developing the theoretical aspects of his new economics. Gruchy has analyzed some of the possible reasons for this. Commons, he said, "was too prone to have his graduate students work on highly specialized aspects of economic activity rather than upon the broad theoretical foundations of economics. He was more successful in stimulating his students' interest in labor and other specialized problems than in enticing them into the more intangible realms of philosophical and scientific thought which are of great importance to those who are concerned with the nature and significance of economic science."[69] Even so astute and eminent a disciple of Commons as Edwin E. Witte, speaking of his own student days, has said: "I vaguely recall that even then he was beginning to formulate his theoretical economic ideas. They were lost upon me. I confess that I have had the same difficulty in following Commons's terminology and some of his reasoning which so many students of his later theoretical writings have experienced. But new to economics as I was, I grasped something of Commons's philosophy of economics in action, which seems to me to be central in institutional economics."[70]

Commons himself said that many of his students told him that they did not know what he was driving at and that his theories were so personal that "perhaps nobody could understand them."[71] If, however, Commons failed to excite his students' interests to the point of their sharing in his efforts to revamp economic theory, he did nonetheless encourage them successfully not only toward public service but also toward accepting the current theory with no small degree of caution.

Commons, a critic and reformer of economic theory no less than historian, sociologist, and applied economist, passed on to his students his intense interest in labor and other social problems and his doubts about economic theory, but not his interest in reforming that theory. When Joseph Dorfman says that "Commons was fortunate in having a large number of first rate students who clarified his ideas and extended his influence," he is referring to labor studies, social legislation, and the administrative and regulatory functions of government.[72] Economic theory, in the hands of many of Commons's disciples in the field of labor, simply went by default.

A somewhat similar situation developed in the case of Hoxie. Hoxie's "interest in general economics was too. keen," as Walton Hamilton pointed out, "to allow of his losing himself in one of its isolated fields, wherein, solaced by descriptive labor, he would soon have found himself beyond the point where the problems of theory would have bothered him."[73] From his earliest contacts with economics, Hoxie had been an avid critic, as well as avid student, of economic theory; he believed that it was irrelevant to and inadequate for an analysis of modern industrial society. The wage problem was only one of several modern problems with which the theory could not come to grips. "But, since the theories were convicted of irrelevancy when applied to the affairs of everyday life, why not reverse the process and make an analysis of the practical problem the point of departure in economic work?"[74]

In trade unionism Hoxie found the means—the particular problem—that would be used in implementing his goal, the economic analysis of industrial society. He believed that trade unionism should be studied because it affects "practically every social pie that is baking. If we are to study unionism, we shall study, not a narrow slice of reality, but society as a whole from one particular aspect or with some particular problem or series of problems in mind."[75] Thus through unionism, Hoxie could pursue the economist's analysis of industrial capitalism:

> In the more general "labor problem" [Hoxie] found the "economic factors" which are the ultimate recipients of income in theoretical discussion, replaced by creatures of flesh and blood struggling in their several ways for shares of the world's goods. In the more particular problems of trade unionism he found involved in this conflict, not only the laws of value underlying "the distributive process," but practically the whole scheme of our social conventions. And, as he watched the struggle proceed, he saw that the world of ideas was an inseparable part of it. Accordingly, it was in trade unionism that he attempted to study developing society.[76]

Most of Hoxie's students, however, shared, but did not understand the reasons for, his interest in the study of trade unionism. Very often, they shared Hoxie's aversion to traditional economic theory without seeming to understand the more positive theoretical function of trade unionism in Hoxie's scheme.

Thus both Commons and Hoxie, although themselves positive contributors in the effort aimed at broadening the scope and nature of economic theory, failed to interest their students along these lines, and many of the latter became dissenters in a more negative sense—so far as economic theory is concerned (although in other ways, they were activists who frequently made invaluable contributions). Had Commons been more successful in integrating his analytical ideas with his labor studies or in encouraging his students to seek meaningful alternatives for the orthodox theoretical framework to accompany their efforts in labor economics, or had Hoxie lived and been successful in perpetuating through his students his viewpoint (which was always that of the economist) and his method (which was always analytical), then the interwar period might have witnessed greater integration of the theoretical and empirical literature. As it was, the integration of labor economics and economic theory did not occur to any significant extent until the post–World War II period.

ECONOMICS AND THE STUDY OF LABOR: THE MODERN SYNTHESIS

8

In 1948, Edwin E. Witte, a distinguished labor economist of the Wisconsin school and later president of the American Economic Association, reviewed a book, *Insights into Labor Issues*.[1] The contributors included a number of relatively young labor economists, most of whom had received their doctoral degrees after 1940, and the book was intended to be representative of the type and quality of research then being undertaken in labor economics. Witte concluded:

> Whatever may be their shortcomings, these essays clearly establish that this younger group of labor economists has much to contribute to a better understanding of labor-management relations and the development of more intelligent policies in this field. Combining, as they do, the ability to use economic analysis with awareness of reality, they have great advantages over both the labor economists who are regarded by the profession as being weak in theory and the pure theorists who develop their theories without reference to the facts.[2]

What Witte discovered in this book—the integration of economic analysis with labor studies to a more pronounced extent than had been the case in the preceding decades—has become the distinguishing characteristic of labor economics in more recent years. It is this, more than any other single feature, that distinguishes contemporary labor economics from the pre–World War II period.

SOME PREWAR PRECURSORS

Despite the generally valid view of labor economics in the 1920s and 1930s as to some extent antitheoretical and as standing somewhat apart from its parent discipline, some roots of the postwar unification of labor and general economics can be found in the prewar period. One of these is in the work of A. C. Pigou, successor to Alfred Marshall's chair at Cambridge. Pigou's work promoted a more systematic integration of economic principles and labor problems. His *Wealth and Welfare*, first published in 1912 and later retitled *The Economics of Welfare*, was described by Schumpeter as "the greatest venture in labor economics ever undertaken by a man who was primarily a theorist."[3]

Pigou's interest in bringing economic analysis to the study of labor problems was evident as early as 1905, when, still in his twenties, he emphasized in his *Principles and Methods of Industrial Peace* that in studying the problem and formulating policy for industrial peace between employers and employees, "concrete economic analysis" was "the instrument of knowledge by which the leading part must be played. For, in order to determine the merits of any scheme of industrial policy, we need to discover the sequence of effects to which it is likely to lead." The book was also very much in the tradition of institutional labor economics and was richly informed with historical and empirical detail. Its focus was primarily on the operation and improvement of arbitration and mediation procedures and drew heavily on the investigations of such institutionalist labor economists as Sidney and Beatrice Webb, John R. Commons, and others, as well as on the results of governmental investigation in the United Kingdom, the United States, and elsewhere. Among its conclusions were those that "unions ought to be recognized, if only with a view to converting them to moderation," and that voluntary means be relied upon to the maximum extent possible in industrial disputes, but that coercive intervention by the state might at times be required in handling industrial strife in "certain specially important industries."[4]

In *The Economics of Welfare*, Pigou integrated his interest in labor problems into a more comprehensive treatment of economics. His focus was both macroeconomic and microeconomic, addressed to the question of the determinants of the size of the national dividend (the gross national product) as well as to questions of allocative efficiency. The book was influential in the development of modern welfare economics, as well as the field of public finance, the economics of externalities, and other topics. The labor economics part dealt extensively with a wide variety of labor-related topics, including industrial peace, wages, hours of labor, methods of remuneration, occupational and geographical distribution of labor, and labor mobility.

Pigou had a keen interest in the quality of labor and dismissed the arguments of the leading biological scientists of his time that heredity and not environment would determine the quality of future generations. In arguing for governmentally supported programs to improve the quality of life, Pigou insisted that "the environment of one generation *can* produce a lasting result, because it can affect the environment of future generations. Environments, in short, as well as people, have children. Though education and so forth cannot influence new births in the physical world, they can influence them in the world of ideas." Pigou placed much emphasis on the value of education and training in enhancing the productivity of labor. The world of ideas was the real source of economic well-being, and capital itself was "tradition or social memory."[5] His emphasis on qualitative improvements in the work force and his rejection of the concept of capital as limited to physical goods only puts him in the ranks of the forerunners of the human capital school of modern labor economics.

A second major contributor to the prewar effort to unify labor economics with economic theory was another English economist, J. R. Hicks, whose *Theory of Wages* (1932) opened with the declaration that "the theory of the determination of wages in a free market is simply a special case of the general theory of value."[6] But, Hicks emphasized, it was a special case because "the historical fact which dominates the wage history of the present century . . . is the growth of Trade Union power and the development of State Regulation of wages," a fact with which earlier theorists of wages such as J. B. Clark and Alfred Marshall had not had to contend.[7] Nonetheless, Hicks argued, while modifying "very considerably the range of problems with which we have to deal," the existence of government regulation and of labor union power did not justify any attempt "to change the whole structure of our theory":

> The same forces which determine wages in a free market are still present under regulation; they only work rather differently. It is therefore best for us to begin in the traditional manner with the determination of wages under competition; though at a later stage we must examine regulation in more detail than the traditional theories do. By proceeding in this way, we secure the great advantage of being able to build directly upon familiar doctrines; and we naturally start with a consideration of that principle which was regarded by the economists of Marshall's generation as the basis of their theory of wages—the principle of Marginal Productivity. The validity and the importance of this principle we shall see no reason to question.[8]

Hicks's approach was an effort to incorporate the labor union into the analytical apparatus of neoclassical economics and, especially, its marginal productivity theory of labor demand, and to preserve the basic structure of neoclassical theory for labor economics. The analytical core of his contribution was his treatment of industrial disputes in terms of the costs of disagreement, as perceived by both employers and employees. As the demand and supply analysis of traditional theory is based on schedules that relate quantities to prices, so Hicks's theory of industrial disputes, as he termed it, sought to relate the length of strikes to wage rates. From the premise that a demand by a labor union for higher wages (or a resistance to lower wages) offers an employer the alternative of conceding to the union demand, and probably thereby lowering his profits for at least a considerable period, or resisting the union demand, and enduring the loss from the work stoppage that would probably occur, Hicks concluded that the employer in such a situation "is less well off than he would have been if his men had not combined, but one alternative will generally bring him less loss than the other. If resistance appears less costly than concession, he will resist; if concession seems cheaper, he will meet the Union's claims."[9]

Hicks's theory of industrial disputes, in the tradition of economic theory, was an equilibrium model based on expected or assumed behavioral responses on the part of both parties to the disputes.

> First of all, it is obvious that the higher is the wage demanded, the greater will be the cost of concession; and therefore the more likely [the employer] is to

resist. On the other hand, the longer he expects the threatened strike to last, the more likely he is to give way. . . . We can then construct a schedule of wages and lengths of strike . . . [and] express it graphically by an "employer's concession curve." . . . The curve cannot rise higher than some fixed level since there evidently is some wage beyond which no Trade Union can compel an employer to go.[10]

Just as the expected length of a threatened strike influenced the wage an employer would be willing to pay to avoid it, so too would the wage offered affect the length of time the strikers might be willing to stay out. In this case, "we can draw up a schedule, a 'resistance schedule,' giving the length of time they would be willing to stand out rather than allow their remuneration to fall below the corresponding wage. This again can be translated into a 'resistance curve.' "[11] Hicks's graphical exposition showed how the employer's concession curve and the union's resistance curve intersected at some point and explained why the wage corresponding to that point was the highest that the union could expect to get.

Like Pigou, Hicks had a strong interest in actual industrial relations problems, and his *Theory of Wages* included many qualifications, exceptions, and institutional or historical illustrations to counterbalance the "other things equal" assumptions and approach that he employed in his theoretical analysis. On balance, however, his approach was in the neoclassical tradition, and his efforts to adapt the neoclassical method of analysis to industrial disputes in which the relevant quantity is the expected length of a strike represent major contributions to the subsequent integration of labor study and theoretical economics.

Hicks's model of the collective bargaining process has not gone unchallenged, but the criticisms, while pointing out deficiencies in Hicks's model, do not detract from the pioneering importance of his work.[12] As Allan Cartter has noted, "*The Theory of Wages* has stood the test of time surprising well. Hicks recognized the problem of bargaining in a realistic manner, and his discussion is one of the few prewar attempts to bring realism into the theoretical analysis of wage determination under collective bargaining."[13]

A third contributor whose work during the 1930s anticipated and promoted the integration of economic theory and of rather sophisticated quantitative techniques with the specialized study of labor was Paul H. Douglas. His *Theory of Wages* (1934) was an almost perfect complement to Hicks's book. Hicks had begun his analysis with the theory of marginal productivity, but his approach was largely in the neoclassical deductive tradition and relied very little on data except for occasional illustrations. Douglas's study, in contrast, was a major statistical effort to test the marginal productivity theory. It was his view that "the inductive, statistical, and quasi-mathematical method must be used if we are ever to make economics a truly fruitful and progressive science." He believed that the neoclassical school provided an important theoretical base, but that was "only a beginning; for in order to make the analysis precise, to forecast, and to detect interactions in economic society it is plainly necessary to determine the slopes of the demand and supply curves of the various commodities."[14]

Douglas did his graduate study at Columbia University, where he had been influenced by Wesley Mitchell and Henry L. Moore, who pioneered in the application of data and quantitative techniques to economic problems. He was especially impressed with the increasing quantification of what came, after Keynes, to be known as microeconomics. Douglas saw merit in both the theoretical traditions of neoclassical economics, as well as in the historical, institutional, and inductive approach that had marked American labor economics since the work of Richard T. Ely. But what was needed was a blend of the two. Despite the theoretical appeal of the received theory, he argued, "We need to know whether the assumed curves of diminishing incremental productivity are merely imaginative myths or whether they are real, and if the latter what their slopes are. We need to know more about the supply functions of the factors of production and whether the actual processes of distribution furnish any degree of corroboration to the inductive tendencies discovered."[15]

Douglas began by reviewing the historical development of the theory of production and the problem of distribution, emphasizing its interdependent character. He also emphasized the societal character of the theory he was explaining and testing:

Wages, according to the productivity theory, are fixed at a margin which runs through society as a whole. The relative productivity of the workers of any given plant has but comparatively little influence on this general margin. Thus if the productivity of the major industries were to increase so that the laborers in these industries were each to turn out more products with greater value than before, then wages for farmhands in New England would also rise (as they have) even though no increase in their relative productivity has taken place. More workers would leave the farms for industry, the margin of cultivation would recede, and the farmers would have to pay more for the laborers whom they retained. This process would go on until an equalized marginal product in terms of value was established in both lines of industry.[16]

Douglas's *Theory of Wages* contained a comprehensive review and analysis of the underlying postulates and assumptions of the marginal productivity theory. Some of the assumptions, he pointed out, such as those concerning knowledge by businessmen of relative productivities of labor and capital, and mobility of capital, were "largely valid but not wholly so." Others—the assumptions concerning competition between laborers for work, competition between employers for laborers, and mobility of labor—were "primarily valid but with a strong opposing tendency." Still others—the assumptions that all capital and labor is employed, that laborers know their productivity, and that the bargaining powers of labor and capital are equal—were "partially true but on the whole not true." In short, "None are completely true and none are completely false."[17]

Douglas's balanced judgments concerning both the validity and the limitations of the assumptions underlying neoclassical wage theory undoubtedly help to explain the wide appeal of his book to both theorists and institutionalists and its significance in the development of labor economics. Proponents of protective labor legislation and labor unions could take heart from his finding that "the assumptions which depart most from reality are those which ascribe more power to the workers than they actually possess" and that "up until the summer of 1933 the forces which operated against labor's receiving its marginal product were stronger than those which tend to prevent capital from securing its margin." It followed that "an increased activity by the state in behalf of labor, or further unionization on the part of the wage-earners themselves, would have helped to redress this balance." Economists in the neoclassical tradition might tend to agree with his qualification that labor legislation and unionization "might indeed conceivably become so strong as to turn the scales the other way." Moreover, he concluded, despite the limitations on the validity of the assumptions underlying the marginal productivity theory, "the assumptions do represent real tendencies which in the aggregate are probably more powerful than those of a conflicting nature."[18]

Douglas also undertook to measure statistically the growth of capital and labor in the United States economy between 1899 and 1922 and then to measure the relative contributions of each to production during the period. He concluded that the increase in fixed capital had occurred at a rate of 6 percent per year compounded, or double that estimated for Western Europe.[19] The percentage increase in fixed capital over the twenty-three year period was 331 percent, while the labor force increased only 61 percent over the same time. Product had increased by 140 percent. Given these data, "The task remained of finding the probable quantitative influence of labor and capital upon production." With the help of a mathematician, Charles W. Cobb, a theoretical production curve was developed and fitted to the actual production data over time. The measurement of marginal productivities resulted in the finding that 75 percent of the manufacturing productivity in the American economy was due to labor and 25 percent to capital. Data from Massachusetts and New South Wales reflected remarkable uniformity with the experience of the United States.

Douglas's finding that 75 percent of the manufacturing product in the United States was attributable to labor was remarkably consistent with the conclusion of the National Bureau of Economic Research that "wages and salaries formed on the average 74 percent of the total value added by manufacture during these years. This is certainly as close an agreement as could be expected," he asserted, "and indicates that in practice labor tended to receive during this period approximately that share which our equation of production attributed to them." That finding, however, was qualified by the observation that "the results for the period, 1923–1929, when the share of capital increased greatly would probably have been different from this." Also, he cautioned, "we should not conclude because of the substantial uniformity of the production equation in the United States, Massachusetts, and New South Wales, that it will be the same for all times and countries."[20]

Douglas's work was not accepted altogether without criticism, and in a 1957 reprint he generously acknowledged the validity of some of that criticism. Reviewing the original book in 1935, Don D. Lescohier, a member of the Wisconsin school and a former student of Commons and Perlman, reported that he had "laid down *The Theory of Wages* convinced that Professor Douglas relies too much upon the truth of assumptions and estimated probabilities which he incorporates as raw materials into his analysis; and that the reader must watch carefully lest he accept conclusions based in part upon foundations that are questionable." Similar caveats would be offered during the following decades for the field of economics in general by those somewhat skeptical of the emerging marriage of economic theory and quantitative techniques. Despite his qualifications, however, Lescohier felt that "the work is an important contribution to economic theory" and that "it deserves the careful study of professional economists." His closing words applied not only to Douglas's work but increasingly to the work of all economists in the field of labor: "It will be little understood by those lacking rigorous training in economics and statistics."[21] Writing in the late 1940s, Schumpeter described the *Theory of Wages* as "one of the boldest ventures in econometrics ever undertaken."[22]

THE POSTWAR ENVIRONMENT: WAGES AND UNIONISM

The study of labor in the United States in the years following World War II was influenced by a number of factors that distinguish the period from the prewar era. First, sustained prosperity, despite many predictions to the contrary, marked the early postwar years and, with but short cyclical lapses, carried into the 1950s and 1960s. Labor shared importantly in this prosperity. Average hourly earnings in manufacturing, which had stood at $0.437 per hour in October 1932, had risen to $1.227 per hour by June 1947.[23] This increase was accompanied by an increase in the availability of wage data, with the activities of the Bureau of Labor Statistics and other data-collecting agencies significantly expanded. Second was the emergence of the new, or the Keynesian, field of macroeconomics, in which the questions of wage levels, movements, and policies figured importantly in the larger question of the determination of the overall level of prices, employment, and output. Third, the period was marked by an expansion in union membership following such pro-labor legislation of the 1930s as the Norris LaGuardia Act and the National Labor Relations Act. From less than four million members in 1932, organized labor had increased its ranks to fourteen million members by 1945. By the 1940s, such basic industries as automobiles, rubber, steel, petroleum products, textiles, and a host of others had come to be industries in which both the level and structure of wages were importantly influenced by collective bargaining. The price of labor, concomitantly, was increasingly coming to be viewed less as a market price than as an administered price, the result of the conscious decisions of a few individuals sitting around the bargaining table. As such, it shared certain characteristics of other imperfectly competitive prices, interest in which had recently been stimulated by the work of E. H. Chamberlin and Joan Robinson.[24] Not surprisingly, the study of wages, and especially of the wage policies of labor unions, occupied a central place in the research of labor economists in the early postwar years.

The synthesis of labor economics and general economic theory, like most other developments in the history of social science, emerged not suddenly but gradually and, perhaps, even only partially, for there remain today important dissenting voices. The study of labor problems in the United States began during the nineteenth century partly in response to a dissatisfaction by a number of economists interested in the problems of an industrializing society with the nature and approach of economic analysis. And even when the labor problems approach gave way during the interwar period to what Joseph Dorfman has called the new specialty of labor economics, which was somewhat closer to the mainstream of its parent discipline than the earlier study of labor problems had been, it was still a multidisciplinary variety of economics grounded largely in the rejection of neoclassical theory and closely allied with the institutionalist movement. In view of the long history of dissatisfaction with orthodox economic theory on the part of labor economists and despite various efforts during the 1930s to inject more economic analysis into the study of labor, it is hardly surprising that theoretical and methodological controversy should have persisted into the postwar period.

An example is a series of articles on the relevance of marginalism that appeared in the *American Economic Review* in 1946 and 1947. The marginal productivity theory teaches that there is a direct relationship between the wage level and the employment offered by the individual firm, the role of which, as Marshall put it, is to act as "the medium through which the principle of substitution so adjusts the employment of each agent that, in its marginal application, its cost is proportionate to the additional net product resulting from its use."[25] Accordingly a change in wage costs should lead to a change in the amount of labor hired by the firm. But Richard A. Lester, on the basis of interviews with executives and a questionnaire on wage-employment relationships submitted to a number of business firms, reported in 1946 that most of those questioned considered the demand for their product more important than wages in determining their employment levels. Lester also called attention to "the technical difficulties involved in any attempt to discover the marginal product of an added unit of labor in large-scale industry and to impute to that unit of labor its value-contribution to a joint, multi-processed product." He cited other difficulties with the theory and concluded that "much of the economic reasoning on company employment adjustments to increases or decreases in wage rates is invalid, and a new theory of wage-employment relationships for the individual firm must be developed."[26]

Six months later, Fritz Machlup replied. All too often, he asserted, criticism of marginal analysis is "due to a failure to understand it, to faulty research techniques, or to mistaken interpretations of 'findings.' " Lester, according to Machlup, was guilty on all counts: "The questions in Professor Lester's research project on employment did not even approach" the necessary standards for sound empirical research, and "he received only 56 usable replies from 430 manufacturers whom he had asked to fill out his questionnaires." Moreover Lester's "fact-finding and theorizing on substitution between labor and capital and on other adjustments of the firm to changes in wage rates" were "marred by inconsistencies and misunderstandings." As for the alleged difficulty of calculating a worker's marginal product, it was not greater than that faced by the driver of an automobile making a routine decision to pass a truck proceeding at a slower speed in front of him. The driver had to take into account such factors as the truck's speed, the distance between the car and the truck, and the speed with which the car in the other direction is coming. Clearly, Machlup admitted, the driver will not actually measure or calculate the variables involved in a numerical way, but he would size up the situation. "And a 'theory of overtaking' would have to include all these elements (and perhaps others besides) and would have to state how changes in any of the factors were likely to affect the decisions or actions of the driver." Machlup dismissed Lester's points concerning the difficulty of calculating with exact magnitudes the variables that the marginalist theory believed were significant. Those difficulties, he held, "show merely that the explanation of an action must often include steps of reasoning which the acting individual himself does not *consciously* perform (because the action has become routine) and which perhaps he would never be *able* to perform in scientific exactness (because such exactness is not necessary in everyday life). To call, on these grounds, the theory 'invalid,' 'unrealistic' or 'inapplicable' is to reveal failure to understand the basic methodological constitution of most social sciences." In contrast to Lester, Machlup concluded that "the marginal theory of business conduct of the firm has not been shaken, discredited, or disproved."[27]

A somewhat similar criticism of Lester's work, and another strong defense of the marginalist approach, came from George J. Stigler. But twenty years later, in his presidential address to the American Economic Association, Professor Machlup suggested that the controversy had perhaps "ended in a draw." Marginalism, he said, "has continued to dominate the teaching of microeconomics, perhaps though with occasional reservations and references to current attempts at greater realism. But look at the journals and monographs and you find that research on alternative approaches to the theory of the firm is regularly reported with the implication that a superior theory may eventually replace marginalism." Any replacement of the marginalist approach, Machlup added, was likely to be limited to cases where firms are few and not under effective competitive pressures. "The marginalist solution of price determination under conditions of heavy competition is not contested."[28] Nor has the accuracy of that observation yet been seriously contested.

Another line of inquiry in the early postwar years focused on the adequacy of traditional wage theory not because of the difficulty of measuring its variables but because of the increasingly apparent influence of labor unions in wage determination. Hicks's *Theory of Wages* represented an attempt to incorporate the labor union into the analytical framework of the neoclassical theory of wages. It was Hicks's position that although union bargaining power could affect wages by raising them above market levels, the principle of marginal productivity still controlled the volume of employment. He noted, however, that "the effects on employment of artificially high wages may easily be slow in making their appearance." But a number of other labor economists by the late 1940s were troubled by the belief that "the marginal productivity doctrine had swallowed collective bargaining without a second glance at its indigestible contents, with the result that reasoning about the effects of *wage increases* on the one hand, and of *union rules* on the other hand, went on in more or less separate compartments with little cross-fertilization from one to the other." Belfer and Bloom, in a 1948 analysis, "Unionism and the Marginal Productivity Theory," examined the effects of union rules and regulations on the wage-employment decisions of the unionized firm. They found—in union restrictions on entrepreneurial substitution of factors of production, in the effects of seniority provisions, in such restrictions on dismissals as severance wages and guaranteed annual wages, and in several dimensions of the nature of union wage pressure—that the firm's employment decision was often not, despite Hicks's conclusion, bounded by the principle of marginal productivity: "In the traditional theory, the approximate equality of marginal revenue product and wage would leave no room for absorption of wage increase except through reduction in output and employment. But because unionism has more than a wage dimension, because it alters the nature of industrial organization and control, unions can raise wages without producing unemployment."[29] "The existence of a margin of uncertainty" that unionism introduces into the bargaining situation and the firm's wage and employment policies, does not mean, Belfer and Bloom cautioned, "that unions have discovered an inexhaustible pool which they can drain to the advantage of union labor. It is a margin of uncertainty, not an indefinitely extendible upper limit."

Indeed, union leaders have a grave responsibility, for, since the impersonal working of the marginal productivity principle can no longer be depended upon to operate in its traditional fashion, the duty devolves upon union leaders to pursue a wage policy designed to maximize employment opportunities. . . . The great difficulty, however, is that even those union leaders who recognize the need for a wage policy designed to maximize production are often compelled to follow a wage policy based on less desirable economic considerations because of the political exigencies incidental to union leadership.[30]

The character of the wage policies pursued by unions was dealt with in greater detail by John T. Dunlop and Arthur M. Ross, whose differing views dominated the subject during the late 1940s and early 1950s. Dunlop's *Wage Determination under Trade Unions* (1944) opened with the observation that the time was ripe for the incorporation of the union more fully into the analytical schema of economics, by treating it as an organization somewhat analogous to the business firm. The subject of unionism, he argued, "cannot be left any longer merely to institutional and historical methods." He continued: "Just as the process of product-price formation has been illuminated by theoretical analysis of discrimination, small numbers, price leadership, and flexible plant, so organized labor markets represent a field of important theoretical enquiry. A systematic knowledge of the wage-fixing features of collective bargaining is indispensable if this analytical work is to be more than gymnastics."[31]

Dunlop's position was that since "the trade union is clearly a decision-making unit," which, like other organizations dealt with in economic theory, could reasonably be assumed to be trying "to maximize (minimize) something," one could usefully construct an economic model of the trade union as a market enterprise. Although this approach was "strewn with pitfalls," including the "fallacy of misplaced concreteness which would treat the model as the real world," it would nonetheless "abstract no further from the richness and complexity of behavior than does the ordinary analysis of the enterprise." Moreover, he emphasized, "economic models in terms of the variables of economic theory can only be one approximation," and "wider analytical models than economic theory must be constructed for successful explanation of even market-oriented behavior" on the part of labor unions.[32]

Dunlop's trade union model consisted of the traditional demand function for labor and, in place of the traditional supply function, which he claimed "loses almost all relevance" under conditions of trade unionism, a "wage-membership function," which showed "the total amount of labor that will be attached to the labor organization at each wage rate." Given the union's objective, Dunlop showed how standard techniques of economic analysis could be used to determine the wage rate that the union would prefer. As possible union maximization objectives, he considered the following: "the largest wage bill, the largest labor income including public unemployment compensation or out-of-work benefits, the maximum collective rents over the minimum price required to induce attachment to the union." Of these, he believed that "probably the most generalized assumption respecting actual aims of trade unions would be the maximization of the wage bill."[33]

Wage Determination under Trade Unions contained several chapters on other topics, including cyclical variations in wages, labor's share of national income, and labor costs, bargaining power, and trade union interest in related product markets, in which Dunlop advanced hypotheses, presented data, and offered suggestions for further research. His emphasis throughout was on economic reasoning, although he frequently pointed to the need to refine, modify, or expand existing theory. Nonetheless his approach troubled some. In a generally favorable treatment in the *American Economic Review,* Lloyd

G. Reynolds characterized Dunlop's work as "one of the most significant studies of wages which has appeared in recent years." It was, he said, "rich in intriguing research suggestions and will prove highly stimulating to investigators of wage phenomena." However, Reynolds believed that Dunlop's economic model had limited usefulness in the study of labor unions. In particular, "the assumption that effort is being bent toward maximizing some value quantity, which requires a considerable leap of faith even in the study of business managements, is still less plausible when one is dealing with union officers."[34]

Arthur Ross's *Trade Union Wage Policy*, which appeared in 1948 (although most of its chapters had earlier been published separately as articles in economics journals), represented a stronger criticism of Dunlop's approach. Ross contended that not only was the wage policy of unions "not to be found in the mechanical application of any maximization principle," but that a purely or even primarily economic approach to the subject was incorrect because the union is not primarily an economic organization but "a political instrumentality not governed by the pecuniary calculus conventionally attributed to business enterprise." Although the union was necessarily concerned with economic matters, among other things, they were not its raison d'être in a sense comparable to that of a business firm. The union, Ross emphasized, was "a political agency operating in an economic environment."[35]

Ross did not deny that the business firm and labor union had some common characteristics, among them a stated purpose and a desire to maximize, respectively, profits or economic welfare. But, he said, the union's formal purpose is vaguer: " 'Economic welfare' is a congeries of discrete phenomena—wages, with a dollar dimension; hours of work, with a time dimension; and physical working conditions, economic security, protection against managerial abuse, and various rights of self-determination, with no dimension at all. Therefore, the union leader has considerably more discretion in interpreting the formal purpose."[36]

The union leader's discretion, while perhaps less well defined in terms of formal purpose, was nonetheless circumscribed by several threats to his organization's—and his own—survival. The traditional apathy of American workers toward unions, actual or potential hostility on the part of employers, threatened encroachments by other labor unions, the power of government to enact repressive labor legislation—all of these threatened the leadership position of the union leader. The leader's personal insecurity thus makes him particularly sensitive to the demands and expectations of its members, whose judgments about their own well-being are influenced by "orbits of coercive comparison" with those around them. Comparisons are important to the worker, in that they "establish the dividing line between a square deal and a raw deal. He knows that he cannot earn what he would like to have, but he wants what is coming to him. In a highly competitive society, it is an affront to his dignity and a threat to his prestige when he receives less than other workers with whom he can legitimately be compared."[37]

Ultimately, Ross asserted, the structure of wages had less to do with economics than with social, political, and moral forces:

There are forces in society and in the economy making for uniformity in the wage structure, but they are not merely the forces of supply and demand. Ideas of equity and justice have long permeated industrial society, but the growth of organization has endowed them with compelling force. They provide the substance of equitable comparison, and they govern the administration of consolidated bargaining structures. . . . A sixty-day strike over two cents an hour may be irrational in the economic lexicon, but viewed as political behavior it may have all the logic of survival.[38]

Ross was not alone in emphasizing the political character of labor unions. Charles E. Lindblom, Peter F. Drucker, and others took a similar point of departure for the analyses of labor-management relations. Their work was complemented by that of a number of major analysts—Neil W. Chamberlain, Richard A. Lester, Florence Peterson, Joseph Shister, and others—who focused on the goals, methods, and operations of labor organizations.[39] Dunlop himself, in the 1950 preface to his reprinted work, applauded these developments: "The systematic study of the decision-making process affecting wage rates in labor unions as well as managements is certainly to be encouraged," and "it is not to be denied that the institutions of the collective bargaining process have some independent effect on wage rates." But generally, in his view, emphasis on political wage setting was applicable to newer unions and represented "a preoccupation with the very short run to the exclusion of other factors. . . . There is no denying that wage determination under collective bargaining is different from wage fixing under non-union conditions. But the difference is not as great on the record to date as has been assumed. Most of the same wage making forces operate through the institutions of collective bargaining. The critical question is how much difference do unions make?"[40]

In subsequent years, that question—how much difference do unions make?—became a central concern of labor economists, largely as a result of the influence of H. Gregg Lewis and the Labor Workshop at the University of Chicago. The question itself was not new; it was related to John Stuart Mill's recantation in 1869 of the wages fund theory, and Alfred Marshall devoted lengthy passages to the topic.

What was new was the growing body of data available to researchers, as well as their increasingly sophisticated statistical and econometric techniques. During the late 1950s and early 1960s, a number of studies analyzed the impact of unionism on wages in a wide variety of individual industries, following earlier economy-wide studies.[41] These later ones used a variety of analytical techniques and dealt with varying time periods. Partly for these reasons, their conclusions were "as varied as the methodology adopted. To the casual observer, the postwar studies on the impact of unionism are frequently conflicting, and the composite findings are inconclusive."[42]

The situation changed with the appearance in 1963 of H. Gregg Lewis's *Unionism and Relative Wages in the United States*. In this book, Lewis undertook both a review—which often included substantial reworking, in order to increase their comparability—of the earlier studies, many of which were in fact written as doctoral dissertations under his direction, as well as an extensive independent investigation of the impact of unionism on percentage, or relative, wage differentials among laboring groups. He sought to provide quantitative answers to specific questions: "By how much has unionism increased the average wage of union labor relative to the average wage of all labor? . . . To what extent has unionism affected, in different proportions, the average wages of different industries? . . . How variable were the effects of unionism on relative wages from one date to another during the last forty years? . . . How much higher or lower is the relative inequality in average wages among industries than it would be in the absence of relative wage effects of unionism?"[43]

Lewis's findings confirmed the belief of many labor economists that unionism's power to raise or maintain the wages of its members relative to the nonunion sector is stronger in periods of depression than in periods of full employment and inflation. The peak impact of unionism during the preceding forty years, he found, came in 1932–1933, at the bottom of the Great Depression. "At the peak, the effect of unionism on the average wage of union workers relative to the average wage of nonunion workers may have been above 25 percent. In the ensuing inflation the relative wage effect declined sharply to a level between 10 percent and 20 percent . . . by the end of the 1930s." The decline in the wage impact of unionism continued "until about 1947 or 1948, near the peak of the inflation immediately following World War II," falling at the trough to "close to zero—under 5 percent." In the first postwar decade, unionism once again made a difference. Lewis estimated that "the average union/nonunion relative wage was approximately 10 to 15 percent higher than it would have been in the absence of unionism." Moreover "the average wage of union workers was about 7 to 11 percent higher relative to the average wage of all workers, both union and nonunion, than it would have been in the absence of unionism. Similarly, the average wage of nonunion workers was about 3 to 4 percent lower relative to the average wage of all workers than in the absence of unionism."[44]

Lewis's greatest influence was probably in the redirection of labor economics toward analytical and quantitative work. During his years at the University of Chicago, he played a major role in the development of what Albert Rees has recently termed analytical as distinguished from institutional labor economics: "the application of economic theory and econometrics to problems of the formation of human capital, the allocation of time between market and nonmarket activities, the allocation of labor among alternative uses, and the compensation of labor." Like John R. Commons before him, Lewis attracted a large number of talented young economists to the study of labor, but with different results. Today, "the analytical approach is predominant in most of the leading departments of economics. . . . The overwhelming majority of analytical labor economists have been his colleagues, his students, or the students of his students."[45] The analytical approach to the study of labor is also becoming increasingly characteristic of schools of business and industrial relations, although an interdisciplinary rather than a strictly economic approach is also characteristic of the work in those institutions.

LABOR AS HUMAN CAPITAL

The modern synthesis of labor studies with economic theory is perhaps nowhere better illustrated than in the literature on human capital, which began to emerge during the late 1950s and early 1960s and which has grown rapidly since. The concept itself was not altogether new to economics, for the recognition of human resources as the wealth of nations was a common theme in mercantilist literature, and a number of economists—Sir William Petty, Adam Smith, Nassau Senior, A. C. Pigou, and others—all dealt in one way or another with the importance of the quality of the nation's human resources. The maiden issue of the British Economic Association's *Economic Journal* in 1891 carried an article by J. S. Nicholson, "The Living Capital of the United Kingdom," in which the author estimated that Britain's living capital—"that is to say, the capital fixed and embodied in the people as distinguished from the lands, houses, machinery, and the like" was "about five times the value of the dead" capital embodied in such fixed assets. As B. F. Kiker has shown, "The concept of human capital was somewhat prominent in economic thinking until Marshall discarded the notion as 'unrealistic.' "[46] The modern work on human capital, however, bears little resemblance to its intellectual antecedents except perhaps in terms of its most fundamental conceptualizations, for it represents a much more theoretically rigorous and quantitatively oriented approach. Its founding fathers can fairly be identified as Jacob Mincer, Theodore W. Schultz, and Gary S. Becker.

Mincer's approach was from the standpoint of personal income inequalities. As he noted in 1958 in the first modern treatment of the human capital theme, economists had long shown interest in the question of the causes of inequality in personal incomes, but only in recent years had the field been characterized by empirical research, often in connection with studies of the consumption function, interest in which had been greatly stimulated by the work of Keynes. Mincer's contribution helped to redirect economic analysis toward the production function through the construction of a model in which both interoccupational and intraoccupational earnings differentials could be explained on the basis of investment in human capital "in which the process of investment is subject to free choice":

The choice refers to training differing primarily in the length of time it requires. Since the time spent in training constitutes a postponement of earnings to a later age, the assumption of rational choice means an equalization of present values of life earnings at the time the choice is made. . . . Interoccupational differentials are therefore a function of differences in training. . . . Intraoccupational differences arise when the concept of investment in human capital is extended to include experience on the job.[47]

Two years later, investment in human capital was given greater prominence when Theodore W. Schultz made it the topic of his presidential address to the American Economic Association. Writing at a time when the problems and processes of economic growth and development were coming to be uppermost in the minds of both economists and economic policy makers, Schultz's emphasis was on the contributions made to those processes by the human factor in production. Looking back to the unexpectedly rapid postwar recovery in Europe, he recalled that he and other economists had "overestimated the prospective retarding effects" of the wartime losses of physical capital. They had failed to pay sufficient attention to human capital, whose growth, he said, "may well be the most distinctive feature of the economic system."[48]

Schultz drew attention to five major forms of investment in human capital: health facilities and services; on-the-job training by business firms; formal elementary, secondary, and higher education; adult study programs; and migration to adjust to changing employment opportunities. "The exciting work under way," he believed, "is on the return to education." A few years later, that topic was given its most thorough and rigorous treatment up to that time by Gary S. Becker, whose 1964 volume summarized and extended his earlier work and which, as Mark Blaug has noted, "has ever since served as the *locus classicus* of the subject." [49]

Becker's original aim had been to estimate the money rate of return to college and high-school education in the United States and, in order to put the estimates "in the proper context, a brief formulation of the theory of investment in human capital was undertaken." But more was needed, he found: "There had been few, if any, attempts to treat the process of investing in people from a general viewpoint or to work out a broad set of empirical implications. I began then to prepare a general analysis of investment in human capital." [50]

Becker began by constructing a mathematical model of on-the-job training and extending it to schooling and the acquisition of other forms of knowledge. On-the-job training was further divided into general training (that which is useful to firms other than the one providing it) and specific training (that which is more useful to the firm providing it). Becker's analysis showed that for general training, "the wages of trainees would not equal their marginal product but would be less by the total cost of training," since trainees would be willing to pay for training that would enhance their marginal products to other employers in the future. This is, as Blaug has noted, a somewhat "startling prediction," since it contradicts "the older Marshallian view that a competitive market mechanism fails to provide employers with adequate incentives to offer optimum levels of in-service training," but it is generally consistent with the actual behavior of employers, who seldom pay directly for the schooling of their employees. [51]

Becker's empirical analysis focused on the private and social rates of return from college education. For urban native white males graduating in 1939, the private rate was calculated at "slightly over 14.5 percent," and for those graduating in 1949, the figure was "close to 13 percent." The social rate of return was found to be slightly below the private rate, and somewhat lower rates were found for college dropouts, nonwhites, women, and rural persons. Also gains from college education were found to vary substantially within groups: "A large dispersion makes it difficult for any individual to anticipate his gain from education, a difficulty that is compounded by a payoff period of some twenty to twenty-five years." As Becker noted, this poses real problems from the standpoint of strictly rational individual calculation, anticipating a point made by some critics of human capital theory. So great is the variation in the gain from college within a given category, Becker reported, "that an individual can be only loosely guided by the gain of his cohort, and has to place considerable weight on his own situation and hope for the best." Moreover the long payoff period for college education "provides an economic justification for flexible or 'liberal' education since most of the benefits would be received when the economic environment was greatly different from that prevailing at the time of entry into the labor force."[52]

The early work of Mincer, Schultz, and Becker has since given rise to a vast outpouring of theoretical and empirical work. A 1976 survey of the literature of human capital referred to more than one hundred studies, and yet was not altogether inclusive of recent work done on the topic.[53] While some of this work supports, extends, and refines the human capital theory of labor supply, some of it has led to findings inconsistent with the predictions of human capital theory and has been critical of its assumptions and approach. One early critic was Neil W. Chamberlain who in 1967 took issue with the concept of education as investment. It threatened, he believed, to "put education in the position of having to *defend* its value in the form of a rate of pecuniary return." Moreover, "some values come with a moral content that preclude—or should preclude—our putting them on the same scale with groceries, to see where the marginal trade-off lies, or to measure the value of one in terms of the other." A different sort of criticism has come from Ivar Berg, who, while not challenging the education-earnings correlation, has noted that the relationship between education and productivity is vague at best and that to "argue that well-educated people will automatically boost efficiency, improve organization and so on may be to misunderstand in a fundamental way the nature of American education, which functions to an important, indeed depressing, extent as a licensing agency."[54] Berg's own research indicates that a substantial number of American workers are in jobs that in fact require and utilize less education than they have.

The licensing or screening function of education was noted by Albert Rees in an early review of Becker's work as a possible explanation for the apparent "increasing returns" that Becker had attributed to the third, fourth, and later years of college. "Perhaps a clue to the puzzle," Rees suggested, "lies in employer discrimination in favor of high school and college graduates over high school and college drop-outs."[55]

A similar but perhaps somewhat stronger criticism of the traditional concept of increasing returns to human capital from the final years of schooling has come from Lester C. Thurow, who argues that "the American labor market is characterized less by wage competition than by *job* competition. That is to say, instead of people looking for jobs, there are jobs looking for people—for 'suitable' people." "In a labor market based on job competition," he concluded, "the function of education is not to confer skill and therefore increased productivity and higher wages on the worker; it is rather to certify his 'trainability' and to confer upon him a certain status by virtue of this certification. Jobs and higher incomes are then distributed on the basis of this certified status."[56]

Thurow's colleague, Michael J. Piore, is another critic who sees "the enterprise of human capital and the endeavor of labor economics as fundamentally distinct. The one is an applied field concerned with the solution of particular problems; the other is applied theory." Piore notes that "at least in that broad band of industries and occupations over which . . . [various manpower] programs have operated, training and education are not essentially economic processes." And John T. Dunlop, criticizing the extent to which "human capital activities have imperialistically sought to take over all of labor economics," has offered his "considered judgment . . . that virtually all of this enormous outpouring [of research on human capital] is irrelevant to private and public policy making and to the allocations of public and private funds for training and education." The criticism of Samuel Bowles and Herbert Gintis has a Marxian flavor: "The theory of human capital formally excludes the relevance of class and class conflict to the explication of labor market phenomena . . . [but] the social relations of the educational process itself can only be accounted for through an explicit class analysis." Human capital theory "provides, in short, a good ideology for the defense of the status quo."[57]

Despite these and other criticisms, the human capital theory seems to have successfully resisted efforts to discredit or replace it, although the emerging theory of signaling may overtake it in the coming years.[58] The apparent appeal of human capital theory lies largely in its ability to integrate labor economics not only with the economics of health, education, and other social services but also with general economic and capital theory, through a theory of labor supply based on rational investment behavior by the future-oriented individual or household. Despite the validity of much of the criticism of the human capital approach to the study of labor, its essential insights can hardly be denied. Individuals and households do sacrifice present consumption in favor of the returns to education, whether because of the traditional values and advantages associated with it or because of such screening or licensing advantages as it may confer. Indeed the human capital theory of labor supply has led to new insights into demand theory and the nature of the household, as in the recent reformulation by R. T. Michael and Gary S. Becker, which "transforms the family from a passive maximizer of the utility from market purchases into an active maximizer also engaged in extensive production and investment activities. . . . In the traditional theory, households maximize a utility function of the goods and services bought in the marketplace, whereas in the reformulation they maximize a utility function of objects of choice called commodities, that they produce with market goods, their own time, their skills, training and other human capital, and other inputs."[59]

Through the new insights into the economic process that their theory has provided, through its success in generating testable hypotheses and replicable research, and through its ability to integrate labor economics with economics in general on the basis of a common grounding in neoclassical theory, the human capital theorists have significantly transformed the economist's study of labor. This was perhaps implicit in a prediction made in 1965 by Albert Rees in his review of Becker's book: "Although this work is very different from much of the traditional work of labor economics, it will have an important place in the literature of the field for many years to come." Surveying that field more than a decade later, Glen G. Cain confirmed its transformation. Despite challenges from various quarters, "the neoclassical theorists dominate the profession today," he reported, "even within labor economics where . . . they were not dominant" until the fairly recent past.[60]

INDUSTRIAL RELATIONS AND THE INTERDISCIPLINARY HERITAGE

The rapid growth and development of industrial relations following World War II as a multidisciplinary field inclusive of many of the social sciences has complemented and perhaps to some extent facilitated the shift away from the interdisciplinary approach that has generally characterized the study of labor within university departments of economics in recent years. The study of industrial relations was itself hardly a new phenomenon in the postwar period, dating back at least to 1897, when Sidney and Beatrice Webb published their classic *Industrial Democracy*. By the early 1930s—partly as a result of the gains of organized labor, partly as a result of protective labor legislation, and partly as a result of changing managerial perceptions and procedures—Leo Wolman reported that "in every important industrial country, attempts more or less advanced have been made to apply the procedures of democratic government to the conduct of human relations in industry."[61] One of the roots of industrial relations was in the labor relations component of labor economics, which had replaced the study of labor problems as specific evils to be remedied by appropriate labor union action and governmental policies. Once labor relations came to be conceptualized as ongoing, inevitable, and, indeed, a quite normal aspect of the employment relationship in an industrial society, the field became less narrowly the province of reform-minded economists than had earlier been the case and of greater interest to other social scientists, as well as to students of business management.

The extension of interest in labor problems to such fields as psychology and sociology is nowhere better illustrated than in the literature on human relations that grew rapidly in the early postwar years. Its genesis was in the studies undertaken by Elton Mayo and his colleagues from the Harvard Business School at the Hawthorne Works of the Western Electric Company during the late 1920s and early 1930s. The substantive result of Mayo's work was to show the importance of social and organizational factors for the morale and productivity of workers. But from the standpoint of the development of social and behavioral science, more was involved. The story of the work at Hawthorne is one "of broadening interests as the researchers involved sought to find more satisfactory explanations of employee behavior. It is a story of academic flexibility as the researchers shifted from psychological to sociological analysis of human relations. It is a story above all of a group of insightful men from many different disciplines who, through a melding of many ideals, tried to develop a useful science of human and organizational behavior."[62]

Reflecting both the labor problems heritage of institutional labor economics, with its heavy emphasis on the role of the labor union and collective bargaining, as well as governmental labor policy, and the human relations heritage of Mayo and his colleagues and successors, with its emphasis on social, psychological, and organizational factors, the field of industrial relations grew rapidly in the postwar years. Before World War II, only a few universities—Princeton, Yale, Stanford, Michigan, the Massachusetts Institute of Technology, and the California Institute of Technology—had established separate industrial relations sections or departments. But as Milton Derber has pointed out, the situation changed rapidly during the middle and later forties.

Starting in 1944 at Cornell University, there was a sudden movement toward the development of industrial and labor relations centers or institutes to stimulate and conduct teaching and research on a broad interdisciplinary basis. Among the most prominent centers established, in addition to the School of Industrial and Labor Relations at Cornell, were those at California (1945), Chicago (1945), Minnesota (1945), Illinois (1946), and Wisconsin (1947). By 1965, with the addition of the University of Massachusetts, some forty universities in the United States and Canada had joined the procession. . . . Despite variations in organizational structure and function, almost all of these institutions sponsor faculty and graduate student research. . . . Research in the field, however, is not limited to the . . . centers. Some of the most distinguished contributors come from the social science departments and business schools of universities without formal centers, such as Harvard, Columbia, and Pennsylvania.[63]

The growth of interest in industrial relations was also evidenced in the emergence of new scholarly journals devoted to research in the field, such as the *Industrial and Labor Relations Review*, which first appeared in 1947, and, some years later, *Industrial Relations*. On October 25, 1947, a meeting held at the Columbia University Men's Faculty Club in New York City brought together a number of the leading contributors to the field. The result was a new organization, the American Association for Labor Research. At its first formal meeting in December of that year, the name was changed to the Industrial Relations Research Association because it was felt that "the term 'industrial relations' is rapidly gaining acceptance as the all-inclusive term to denote the entire field, including industrial sociology and psychology, social security, and labor legislation."[64] Through its meetings and publications, the IRRA has done much to sponsor research in the field.

The field of industrial relations has become heir to much that was formerly a part of labor economics, including labor history; collective bargaining; union organization, structure, and government; social security; forms and levels of compensation; hours of work; labor legislation, and other topics. It has also led to the development of such newer fields as personnel administration and organization behavior and development.

Conceived of in broad terms, the field of industrial relations might be considered to be inclusive of labor economics but it also includes labor government, labor history, labor law, labor sociology, and much more. A similar sort of comprehensive interdisciplinary tradition has characterized the work in manpower economics pioneered by E. Wight Bakke, Eli Ginzberg, Frederick H. Harbison, Richard A. Lester, Charles A. Myers, and others, and carried on over the past several decades by such institutions as the Conservation of Human Resources program at Columbia University, where the research staff includes not only labor economists but also labor sociologists, labor lawyers, political scientists, and other specialists in industrial relations. The existence of programs in industrial relations and manpower means that students of labor who distrust the simple psychology of assumed behavior based on constrained maximization, which is at the heart of economic theory no less now than in the past, simply eschew that approach in favor of one of the other social sciences. But those students are no longer called labor economists, with the connotation that designation carried a generation or two ago. The development of industrial relations as a larger, separate, interdisciplinary field has destroyed the validity of Carlton Parker's observation, made some years ago, that "economics officially holds the analysis of labor problems," while at the same time facilitating the work of scholars who continue to favor a somewhat broader approach to the study of labor than that offered by contemporary economics.[65] Clearly the difference between labor economics and industrial relations is less one of subject matter than of methodological approach. This was recognized and emphasized some years ago by Lloyd G. Reynolds, who, in a survey of labor economics, also considered the emerging literature on human relations. Reynolds noted that in human relations,

the problems range over the whole field of labor and industrial relations, including such things as the motivation of the individual worker (and, for that matter, the business manager and the trade union official); the relation between the behavior of these people in the plant and outside the plant; the social structure of the factory—the formal and informal lines of communication, hierarchy of authority, organization of work groups, and so on; worker response to various structures of incentives and to various personal and social situations, as indicated by output, absenteeism, turnover, and the like; and the possible ways of integrating the various groups in this enterprise into a more harmonious work team.

This subject matter, as Reynolds pointed out, "is identical with that used by economists and other students of labor questions. The phrase *human relations in industry* connotes not a separate subject specialty but a different point of view and method of approach."[66] We are reminded that "economics, as Keynes once said, is not so much a body of settled doctrine as a mode of approach."[67]

THE QUALITY OF MODERN LABOR ECONOMICS

Jacob Viner once defined economics as what economists do, and by that token, labor economics ought to be describable as what labor economists do. The wisdom of Viner's observation is in its implicit recognition that economics is not defined once and for all at a point in time—except perhaps in the most general terms—but that what economists do, both in terms of the kinds of problems they seek to analyze, as well as the analytical techniques they bring to bear on those problems, change and develop over time. Thus economics, like all of science, represents an evolutionary development. Any attempt to summarize or synthesize the current state of the field must be done in the recognition that the result is a small part of the long-term development of social thought.

Perhaps the most fundamental point to be made about the current state of labor economics is that at no other time in the history of the field has it been more closely aligned with its parent discipline. The study of labor by economists is generally characterized by the same analytical approach that their colleagues are bringing to bear upon problems in other subdivisions of the field: the formulation of hypotheses based generally on observations consistent with economic theory and empirically tested with econometric techniques applied to such data as are available. Moreover the problems analyzed by labor economists extend over a field conceived of in much broader terms than was true of an earlier era, when, for example, the study of unionism was the dominant item on the research and teaching agenda of labor economists. Edward H. Chamberlin's charge, made in the 1950s, that "the typical university course in 'Labor Problems' is a course in trade unionism with little, if any attention paid to the unorganized sector," could not be made today.[68] To the question posed in the 1960s and referred to earlier—"Are labor courses obsolete?"—the answer is that they are not but that the kind of courses taught in the 1940s and 1950s, which focused almost exclusively on organized labor and which paid little attention to labor markets, were rapidly becoming outdated. Indeed, a renewed interest in the workings of labor markets—a topic long neglected by the institutionalist labor economists—has been a distinguishing characteristic of research in the field in the 1960s and 1970s.[69] This was evident as early as 1962 when the report of the Conference on Labor Economics of the Universities-National Bureau Committee for Economic Research was published. Presented as a "sample of current research on problems in labor economics," the papers presented at the conference were intended to be "not narrowly limited to a particular problem area or set of areas within the labor field, and the subjects treated in the papers therefore, . . . [were meant to be] diverse."[70] Yet what was common to most of the papers was an emphasis on market structure and operations that, a decade or two earlier, would hardly have been typical of research in labor economics. Of the eight papers presented, three dealt with aspects of market organization or structure; two focused on relative wage differentials among groups within the labor force; one was an analysis of white-collar labor markets; and one was an analysis of the relationships between various measures of income and the labor force participation rates of married women. Since that report was issued, the interest of economists in the operations and efficiency of labor markets has been sustained and increased, as is illustrated in the recent and current emphasis on such topics as the return to investment in human capital, wage levels and movement, wage differentials, unemployment, minimum wages, discrimination, income maintenance, antipoverty programs, dual labor markets and other forms of market segmentation, labor market signaling, and so forth.

Part of the relatively new interest shown by labor economists in the workings of labor markets is undoubtedly due to the findings of H. G. Lewis and others that wage levels were affected less by labor unions than had earlier been thought, that therefore "part of the economic power attributed to American unionism is more illusory than it is real," and that "the traditional view of the role of market forces in the determination of the levels of wages and employment appears to be as appropriate today as it was" in the preunion era.[71] But more is involved. The approach taken by economists to the study of unionism has also changed. The sorts of questions raised in the Ross-Dunlop debate on the nature, goals, and methods of unions have not recently been as central a part of the research done in labor economics as was true two or three decades ago. One result, as Daniel J. B. Mitchell has noted, is that "the lack of an adequate model of union wage policy behavior is still a major problem."[72] The earlier interest on the part of economists in the behavior of unions seems to have been largely replaced in recent years by their interest in its economic effects. As George E. Johnson, in a survey of the economic analysis of trade unionism has concluded, "While little progress has been made in modeling the behavior of trade unions—their objectives and the role of the bargaining process—there has been a great deal of sound empirical work on the economic effects of unionism."[73]

The integration of the study of labor into mainstream economics is further illustrated by the fact that much of what can reasonably be called labor economics may be the work of people who do not consider themselves to be labor economists, such as Kenneth Arrow's work on discrimination.[74] In meetings of the Allied Social Sciences, one is as likely to find papers in labor economics being presented at the sessions of the Econometrics Society as at those of the American Economic Association or the Industrial Relations Research Association. Jacob Mincer's 1958 work on personal income differentials would probably not have been considered by many at the time to be work in labor economics as that term was then understood, yet it was influential in transforming the field. A similar situation exists today: "The work of Martin Feldstein on unemployment insurance and of [Joseph] Pechman, [Henry] Aaron, and [Michael] Taussig on social security, and of Harold Watts and Robert Lampmann among others on the negative income tax could have major policy implications in the years ahead. Not all of these researchers would think of themselves as labor economists, yet in fact they are."[75]

The current trend toward greater integration on the part of labor economists with their parent discipline has had its dissenters; indeed we have examined and noted the validity of a number of their criticisms. And the kind of economics being utilized in current labor studies is not seen as satisfactory by all. On the contrary, a significant number of young economists who are among the most active researchers in the field, the group whose work Glen G. Cain has analyzed under the heading segmented labor market theorists and which includes Samuel Bowles, Peter B. Doeringer, Michael J. Piore, A. Michael Spence, Lester C. Thurow, and others, have expressed dissatisfaction with the adequacy of neoclassical theory for the analysis of problems in labor economics and have made numerous suggestions for and contributions to its improvement.[76] This dissatisfaction to some extent is consistent with what has been happening within the parent discipline itself, where a number of distinguished economists—including John Kenneth Galbraith, Oscar Morgenstern, Wassily Leontief, and Robert A. Gordon—have expressed serious reservations in recent years concerning the adequacy of current economic theory and analysis.

Much of the criticism of modern labor economics, as well as of its parent discipline, is grounded in the assumptions and approach of neoclassical competitive theory and is reminiscent of such earlier periods as the 1870s and 1880s, when Richard T. Ely and others led American labor economics toward a more historical and institutional approach, as well as of the 1920s and 1930s, when John R. Commons, Wesley Mitchell, Thorstein Veblen, and others took the lead in a similar movement. Despite numerous differences due to changed conditions, both of the times and of the field of economics, many of the current critics of neoclassical labor market economics are trying to bring a similar sort of institutional realism to research in labor to that which their forebears sought in earlier periods. The many critics of human capital studies, for example, who argue that the role of education cannot adequately be viewed within the narrow terms and framework of neoclassical investment theory but must be analyzed in terms of the wider implications of its role and function as a social institution, or those who argue for the need for more realistic analysis of such social problems as poverty and income inequality, worker alienation, and job discrimination are eminently in the tradition of the earlier institutionalists.

Labor economics, as well as the larger field of economics itself, may be influenced by the critics of its current position, and the field may see in the coming years something of a return to the historical and institutional considerations that were its hallmarks in the past. "Because of the development of human capital theory," as George E. Johnson has observed, "we now have a much more satisfactory theory of income distribution, but the analysis of the effects of various institutional rigidities, unionism being one of the major ones, is not well developed." Following a suggestion made earlier by Daniel S. Hamermesh, he points out that "it might be optimal for some of the resources presently devoted to the refinement of the new labor economics to be reallocated to a consideration of some of the problems considered by the old labor economics."[77]

A number of labor economists would undoubtedly agree. In the judgment of Albert Rees, "The academic quest for rigor and for quantification in labor economics has perhaps gone too far, at the expense of a proper grounding in history and institutions." "But," he adds, "the pendulum will not, nor should it, swing back to the pure institutionalism of Commons or Perlman. The best labor economists of the next generation will understand both institutions and econometrics, and have the ability to blend them skillfully." [78] A decade or two from now, we shall know whether this represents an accurate prediction. But for many now, it surely represents "a consummation devoutly to be wish'd."

NOTES

INTRODUCTION

1. John R. Commons, *Myself* (New York: Macmillan, 1934), p. 131.

2. Joan Robinson, *The Economics of Imperfect Competition* (London: Macmillan, 1954), p. 1.

3. The reason, according to Schumpeter, was that in economics "the filiation of ideas has met with more inhibitions . . . than it has in almost all others. . . . Methods of fact finding and analysis that are and were considered standard or wrong on principle by some of us do prevail and have prevailed widely with others. . . . In addition, much more than in physics have results been lost on the way or remained in abeyance for centuries." Joseph A. Schumpeter, *History of Economic Analysis* (New York: Oxford University Press, 1954), p. 6.

4. Adam Smith, *The Wealth of Nations* (New York: Modern Library, 1937), p. 30.

5. John Stuart Mill, *Essays on Some Unsettled Questions of Political Economy,* London School of Economics and Political Science Series of Reprints of Scarce Works, No. 7 (London, 1948), p. 94.

6. Philip W. Buck, *The Politics of Mercantilism* (New York: Henry Holt, 1942), p. 44.

7. Lewis H. Hancy, *History of Economic Thought* (New York: Macmillan, 1913), pp. 16–17.

8. J. Douglas Brown, "University Research in Industrial Relations," *Proceedings of the Industrial Relations Research Association* (1952), p. 2.

9. Edwin E. Witte, "The University and Labor Education," *Industrial and Labor Relations Review* 1 (October 1947): 6.

10. Philip Taft, "A Rereading of Selig Perlman's *A Theory of the Labor Movement,*" *Industrial and Labor Relations Review* 4 (October 1950): 70.

11. Joseph Dorfman, *The Economic Mind in American Civilization* (New York: Viking, 1959), 5:515.

12. Lloyd G. Reynolds, "Economics of Labor," in *A Survey of Contemporary Economics,* ed. Howard S. Ellis (Homewood, Ill.: Richard D. Irwin, 1948), 1:255.

13. Richard A. Lester, "Labor Policy in a Changing World," *Industrial Relations,* 2 (October 1962): 47.

14. See, for example, Neil W. Chamberlain, "Some Second Thoughts on the Concept of Human Capital," *Proceedings of the Industrial Relations Research Association* (1967), pp. 1–13.

15. Clark Kerr, John T. Dunlop, Frederick Harbison, and Charles A. Myers, *Industrialism and Industrial Man* (Cambridge, Mass.: Harvard University Press, 1960), p. 4.

16. Robert L. Aronson, *Research and Writing in Industrial Relations—Are They Intellectually Respectable?* Reprint Series No. 124 (Ithaca, N.Y.: New York State School of Industrial and Labor Relations). *No. 124*, 1962.

17. George Strauss, "Labor and the Academicians," *Proceedings of the Industrial Relations Research Association* (1963), pp. 239–240.

18. *Industrial Relations* 4 (October 1964).

19. Jacob Viner, quoted in Kenneth E. Boulding, *Economic Analysis,* rev. ed. (New York: Harper, 1948), p. 3.

CHAPTER 1

1. E. H. Phelps Brown, *The Economics of Labor* (New Haven: Yale University Press, 1962), p. 3.

2. Edgar S. Furniss, *The Position of the Laborer in a System of Nationalism* (New York: Kelly and Millman, 1957), p. 157.

3. R. H. Tawney, *Religion and the Rise of Capitalism* (New York: Mentor, 1958), p. 20.

4. Eric Roll, *A History of Economic Thought,* 3d ed. (Englewood Cliffs, N.J.: Prentice-Hall, 1956), p. 44.

5. Frank H. Knight, *On the History and Method of Economics* (Chicago: University of Chicago Press, 1956), p. 5.

6. Robert F. Hoxie, "Sociology and the Other Social Sciences," *American Journal of Sociology* 12 (1906–1907): 746.

7. Lloyd G. Reynolds, *The Structure of Labor Markets* (New York: Harper and Brothers, 1951), p. 1.

8. Allyn A. Young, "Some Limitations of the Value Concept," *Quarterly Journal of Economics* 25 (1911): 424.

9. Joan Robinson, "Euler's Theorem and the Problem of Distribution," *Economic Journal* 44 (1934): 408.

10. This position has not gone unchallenged. E. H. Chamberlin, for example, wrote: "With respect to entrepreneurs, the argument [that entrepreneurship is a unique and indivisible factor of production to which productivity analysis does not apply] no longer stands if we drop the assumption that varying entrepreneurs and varying firms are one and the same thing, and recognize that, in modern economic society, 'entrepreneurship' seems to be as highly divisible and capable of being redistributed as any factor." Edward H. Chamberlin, *The Theory of Monopolistic Competition,* 7th ed. (Cambridge: Harvard University Press, 1956), p. 218.

11. Frank H. Knight, "Profit," in *Encyclopaedia of the Social Sciences* (New York: Macmillan, 1934), 12:482.

12. Frank H. Knight, *Risk, Uncertainty, and Profit,* London School Reprints of Scarce Works, No. 16 (London, 1933).

13. Joseph A. Schumpeter, *The Theory of Economic Development,* trans. Redvers Opie (Cambridge: Harvard University Press, 1934).

14. John Stuart Mill, *Principles of Political Economy with Some of Their Applications to Social Philosophy* (London: Longmans, Green, Reeder and Dyer, 1869), p. 145.

NOTES TO PP. 11–15

15. Frank H. Knight, "The Ricardian Theory of Production and Distribution," *Canadian Journal of Economics and Political Science* 1 (1935): 22. Knight holds that classical distribution theory was not conceived of as a problem in competitive pricing and quotes from a letter of Ricardo to McCulloch to that effect. Ibid., p. 6.

16. Adam Smith, *The Wealth of Nations* (New York: Modern Library, 1937), p. 13.

17. Melvin M. Knight, *Economic History of Europe to the End of the Middle Ages* (Boston: Houghton Mifflin, 1926), p. 87.

18. Bede Jarrett, *Medieval Socialism* (London: T. C. and E. C. Jack, n.d.), p. 18.

19. Sir Alexander Gray, *The Development of Economic Doctrine* (New York: John Wiley, 1965), p. 29.

20. Ibid., p. 30.

21. Tawney, *Religion*, pp. 19–20.

22. "There are diversities of natures among us which are adapted to different occupations" says Plato. "Thus then all things are produced more plentifully and easily and of a better quality when one man does one thing which is natural to him . . . and leaves other things." Plato, *The Republic*, trans. B. Jowett (Boston: Jefferson Press, 1871), bk. 2, vol. 2, pp. 191–192.

23. Emil Lederer, "Labor," in *Encyclopaedia of the Social Sciences*, 8:618.

24. Rodolfo Mondolfo, "The Greek Attitude to Manual Labour," *Past and Present*, no. 6 (November 1954): 1–5.

25. P. Boissonade, *Life and Work in Medieval Europe* (London: Kegan Paul, Trench, Trubner and Co., 1937), p. 65.

26. This medieval attitude toward labor perhaps needs clarification in view of the Weberian thesis concerning the spirit of capitalism. The latter is, in the words of Talcott Parsons, "correlated with a particular attitude toward labor. . . . Labor is not looked upon as a necessary evil, whether because of its traditional origin in the curse of Adam or for any other reason. It is carried out with the same sense of positive ethical obligation, as a field for directly realizing the highest ethical aims of man; the capitalistic attitude toward labor is what Veblen calls the spirit of 'workmanship.' One of its most conspicuous symptoms is the *ethical* feeling against early retirement from active work. A man who does not 'produce' as long as he has strength and health, no matter how well he can afford to retire, is somehow neglecting his ethical responsibilities." What was new to the spirit of capitalism was the end to which labor was directed—acquisition—rather than the emphasis on labor itself. Physical labor occupied a position of centrality in Western monasticism. But it was labor for ascetic, as distinguished from (individual) acquisitive ends. See Talcott Parsons, *The Structure of Social Action* (Glencoe, Ill.: Free Press, 1949), pp. 515–518. Traces of appreciation for an ascetic conception of work can be found in Alfred Marshall: "Man ought to work in order to live; his life, physical, moral, and mental, should be strengthened and made full by his work. . . . Work, in its best sense, the healthy energetic exercise of faculties is the aim of life, is life itself." Alfred Marshall, "The Future of the Working Classes," in

A. C. Pigou, ed., *Memorials of Alfred Marshall* (London: Macmillan, 1925), pp. 108, 115. Here Marshall is much closer to the medieval mind than to classical economics, which drew a sharp line between labor and enjoyment, with the worker setting the disutility of work against the utility of consumption or leisure.

27. George O'Brien, *An Essay on Medieval Economic Teaching* (London: Longmans, Green, and Co., 1920), p. 137.

28. 2 Thessalonians 3:10.

29. Aristotle, *The Politics*, in *Early Economic Thought*, ed. Arthur Eli Monroe (Cambridge: Harvard University Press, 1930), pp. 5–6.

30. John U. Nef, *Cultural Foundations of Industrial Civilization* (Cambridge: At the Press, 1958), pp. 40–41.

31. Bede Jarrett, *S. Antonino and Medieval Economics* (London: Manresa Press, 1914), pp. 71–72.

32. Saint Antonino, *Summa Moralis*, vol. 2, I, 12, i. p. 192 (Verona, 1740), in ibid., p. 71.

33. See Saint Thomas Aquinas, *Quaestiones Quodlibetales, Quodlibetum* 7um, *Quaestio* 7, art. xvii, *ad corpus*, in Bernard W. Dempsey, "Just Price in a Functional Economy," *American Economic Review* 25 (September 1935): 478–479.

34. Saint Thomas Aquinas, *Summa Theologiae*, 1a 2ae, question 81, article 1 (New York: Blackfriers and McGraw-Hill, 1965), 26:9.

35. Gray, *Development*, p. 35.

36. Aristotle, *The Politics*, p. 7.

37. Matthew 7:12; Luke 6:31.

38. W. J. Ashley, *An Introduction to English Economic History and Theory* (London: Longmans, Green and Co., 1903), pt. II, p. 394.

39. Joannis Duns Scoti, *Opera Omnia* (Paris, 1894), vol. 18, *Quaestiones* in *Quartum Librim Sententiarum*, dist. XV, *quaestio* 2a, n. 14, in Dempsey, "Just Price," pp. 482–483.

40. Ibid.

41. As Schumpeter has pointed out, "There is no logical relation between mere emphasis upon the necessity, moral or economic, of remunerating *labor* (no matter whether we translate the Latin word by the English 'labor' or by 'activity' or 'effort' or 'trouble') and what is technically known as the labor theory of value." Joseph A. Schumpeter, *History of Economic Analysis* (New York: Oxford University Press, 1954), p. 91.

42. Ibid., p. 101.

43. Ibid.

44. Saint Thomas Aquinas, *Summa Contra Gentiles*, iii, 131, in O'Brien, *Essay*, pp. 78–79.

45. Matthew 25:34–46.

46. Smith, *Wealth of Nations*, p. 12.

47. Brian Tierney, *Medieval Poor Law: A Sketch of Canonical Theory and Its Application in England* (Berkeley: University of California Press, 1959), p. 64.

48. E. M. Leonard, *The Early History of English Poor Relief* (Cambridge: At the Press, 1900), p. 18.

49. Ashley, *Introduction*, pt. 2, pp. 316, 317, 330, 331, 338, 339, 340.

50. Tierney, *Medieval Poor Law*, p. 48.

51. Ibid., p. 63.

52. Ibid., p. 110.

53. Ibid., p. 111.

54. Florence Mishnun, "Statutes of Labourers," in *Encyclopaedia of the Social Sciences*, 9:6.

55. G. M. Trevelyan, *English Social History* (New York: Longmans, Green and Co., 1942), p. 11.

56. This was not altogether a change from medieval attitudes. "The canonists had quite consistently held that able-bodied beggars were to be denied alms in order that they should not be encouraged in idleness." Tierney, *Medieval Poor Law*, p. 130. But the problem of poverty for the canonists was not part of a general labor policy, intimately related to the level of wages and unemployment. Nor was there any general canonical legislation on vagrancy.

57. Michael T. Wermel, *The Evolution of the Classical Wage Theory* (New York: Columbia University Press, 1939), p. 149. "Politically, the British working class was defined by the Parliamentary Reform Act of 1832, which refused them the vote; economically, by the Poor Law Reform Act of 1834, which excluded them from relief and distinguished them from the pauper." Karl Polanyi, *The Great Transformation* (New York: Rinehart and Co., 1944), p. 168.

58. Furniss, *Position of the Laborer*, p. 159. "Contrast . . . the permission given by statute to employers of labor to enter into trade combinations . . . with the prohibition of such freedom among the laborers." Ibid., n. 1.

59. Harold J. Laski, *The Rise of European Liberalism* (London: George Allen and Unwin, 1959), p. 147. Thus Davenant: "For the profit of trade is not the advantage the merchant makes at home, but what the whole nation gets clear and nett, upon the balance in exchange with other countries of its commodities and manufactures." Charles Davenant, *An Essay upon Ways and Means* (1695), in *The Political and Commercial Works of . . . Charles Davenant, LL.D.* (London, 1771), 1:16.

60. "Thus time was regarded as the enemy of humanity. Horace's verse, *Damnosa quid non imminuit dies?* 'time depreciates the value of the world,' expressed the pessimistic axiom accepted in most systems of ancient thought." J. B. Bury, *The Idea of Progress* (New York: Dover Publications, 1955), pp. 11–12.

61. Ibid., p. 66.

62. Eli F. Heckscher, *Mercantilism* (London: George Allen and Unwin, 1935), 2:25–26.

63. Smith, *Wealth of Nations*, p. 625.

64. Furniss, *Position of the Laborer,* p. 7.

65. Smith, *Wealth of Nations,* p. 625.

66. There were exceptions. Brewster, Coke, and others acknowledged the macroeconomic effects of consumption in maintaining employment and trade. See T. E. Gregory, "The Economics of Employment in England, 1660–1713,"*Economica,* no. 1 (January 1921): 38.

67. Furniss, *Position of the Laborer,* p. 8.

68. Schumpeter, *History,* p. 271.

69. Roll, *History,* p. 66.

70. Smith, *Wealth of Nations,* p. 706.

71. E. A. J. Johnson, *Predecessors of Adam Smith* (New York: Prentice-Hall, 1937), p. 240.

72. M. Beer, *An Inquiry into Physiocracy* (London: George Allen and Unwin, 1939), p. 120; David Hume, *Political Discourses,* 2d ed. (Edinburgh, 1752), p. 50; Sir William Petty, "A Treatise of Taxes and Contributions," in *The Economic Writings of Sir William Petty,* ed. Charles Henry Hull (New York: Augustus M. Kelley, 1963), 1:68.

73. Petty, "Treatise," pp. 22, 34; Charles Davenant, *Discourses on the Publick Revenues and on the Trade of England* (London, 1698), pt. 2, dis. 3, p. 195; Daniel Defoe, *Giving Alms No Charity* (London, 1704), p. 10.

74. Heckscher, *Mercantilism,* 2:57, 76, 101ff.

75. Roger North, *A Discourse of the Poor* (London, 1753), p. 78; Daniel Defoe, *The Compleat English Tradesman* (London, 1726), 2: pt. 2, p. 118.

76. Gregory, *Economics of Employment,* p. 40.

77. E. Lipson, *The Economic History of England* (London: A & C Black, 1931), 3:416, 469, 470.

78. North, *Discourse,* pp. 14–17.

79. Lipson, *Economic History,* p. 471.

80. *Grand Concern of England Explained* (London, 1673), p. 60.

81. Davenant, *Political and Commercial Works,* p. 100.

82. Roger Coke, *A Detection of the Court and State of England During the Last Four Reigns and the Interregnum,* 2d ed. (London, 1696), 2: appendix, p. 57.

83. *Grand Concern,* pp. 54–55.

84. Ibid., p. 61.

85. D. C. Coleman, "Labour in the English Economy of the Seventeenth Century," *Economic History Review,* 2d series, 8 (1956): 281; *Brittania Languens, or A Discourse of Trade,* in *Early English Tracts on Commerce,* ed. J. R. McCulloch (Cambridge: At the Press, 1954), p. 349.

86. John Cary, *An Essay on the State of England, Its Poor, and Its Taxes for Carrying on the Present War Against France* (Bristol, 1695), p. 144.

87. Gregory, *Economics of Employment,* p. 42.

88. Ibid., p. 43.

89. Petty, "Treatise," p. 274.

90. Roll, *History*, p. 106.

91. Furniss, *Position of the Laborer*, pp. 195–196.

92. Smith, *Wealth of Nations*, p. 81.

93. Bernard Mandeville, *Fable of the Bees: or, Private Vices, Publick Benefits* (Oxford: Clarendon, 1924), 1:287.

94. Thomas Mun, *England's Treasure by Forraign Trade* (Oxford: Basil Blackwell, 1949), pp. 72–73.

95. Daniel Defoe, *The True Born Englishman* in *Essays and Studies by Members of the English Association*, vol. 4, collected by C. H. Herford (Oxford: Clarendon, 1913), p. 123.

96. William D. Grampp, "The Liberal Elements in English Mercantilism," *Quarterly Journal of Economics* 66 (Nov. 1952): 497.

97. Mun, *England's Treasure*, p. 12.

98. A few writers did not consider high wages disadvantageous. For some representative views of those holding this minority opinion, see Gregory, *Economics of Employment*, p. 45.

99. A. W. Coats, "Changing Attitudes to Labour in the Mid-Eighteenth Century," *Economic History Review* 11 (1958): 46.

100. Defoe, *Compleat English Tradesman*, 1:318–319. See also Grampp, "Liberal Elements," p. 476.

101. Jacob Vanderlint, *Money Answers All Things* (London, 1734), p. 122.

102. Coleman, "Labour," p. 287.

103. Cary, *Essay*, p. 146.

104. George Blewitt, *An Enquiry Whether a General Practice of Virtue Tends to the Wealth or Poverty, Benefit or Disadvantage of a People* (London, 1725), p. 15.

105. Coats, "Changing Attitudes," p. 48.

CHAPTER 2

1. Morris A. Copeland, *Fact and Theory in Economics* (Ithaca, N.Y.: Cornell University Press, 1958), p. 326; George Unwin, *Studies in Economic History: The Collected Papers of George Unwin*, ed. R. H. Tawney (London: Macmillan, 1927), p. 18.

2. "Political oeconomy, considered as a branch of the science of a statesman or legislator, proposes two distinct objects: first, to provide a plentiful revenue or subsistence for the people . . . and secondly, to supply the state or commonwealth with a revenue sufficient for the public services." Adam Smith, *The Wealth of Nations* (New York: Modern Library, 1937), p. 397.

3. Joseph A. Schumpeter, *History of Economic Analysis* (New York: Oxford University Press, 1954), p. 268.

4. Smith, *Wealth of Nations*, p. 14.

5. Ibid., p. 70.

6. Ibid., p. 30. This view was not original with Smith, who, in fact, quoted in a footnote David Hume's remark that "everything in the world is purchased by labour." The same idea had also been expressed by Cantillon.

7. See Overton H. Taylor, *A History of Economic Thought* (New York: McGraw-Hill, 1960).

8. Smith, *Wealth of Nations,* pp. 344, 357.

9. Taylor, *History,* p. 80.

10. Edgar S. Furniss, *The Position of the Laborer in a System of Nationalism* (New York: Kelly and Millman, 1957), p. 27.

11. Jacob H. Hollander, "The Present State of the Theory of Distribution," *Publications of the American Economic Association,* 3d series, 7 (1906): 24.

12. Adam Smith, *Lectures of Justice, Police, Revenue and Arms,* delivered in the University of Glasgow and Reported by a Student in 1763, ed. Edwin Cannan (Oxford: Clarendon, 1896), p. xxxi.

13. Furniss, *Position of the Laborer,* p. 157.

14. Cannan, introduction to Smith, *Wealth of Nations,* p. xxviii, xxxix.

15. Smith, *Wealth of Nations,* pp. lvii, lviiii.

16. M. Beer, *An Inquiry into Physiocracy* (London: George Allen and Unwin, 1939), p. 120.

17. Smith, *Wealth of Nations,* p. 3.

18. Plato, *The Republic,* trans. B. Jowett (Boston: Jefferson Press, 1871), bk. 2, vol. 2, p. 191.

19. Schumpeter, *History,* p. 56.

20. Smith, *Wealth of Nations,* p. 16.

21. Ibid., p. 314.

22. Alexander Gray, *The Development of Economic Doctrine* (New York: John Wiley, 1965), p. 124.

23. E. A. J. Johnson, *Predecessors of Adam Smith* (New York: Prentice-Hall, 1937), p. 245.

24. Quoted in Edmund Whittaker, *A History of Economic Ideas* (New York: Longmans, Green and Company, 1940), pp. 368–369.

25. Leo Rogin, *The Meaning and Validity of Economic Theory* (New York: Harper and Brothers, 1956), p. 20.

26. James Bonar, *Philosophy and Political Economy* (New York: Macmillan, 1895), p. 139.

27. Smith, *Wealth of Nations,* pp. 638–639.

28. Ibid., p. 314.

29. Ibid., p. 315.

30. Ibid., p. 639.

31. Ibid., p. 344.

32. Ibid., p. 641.

33. Ibid., p. 13.

34. Ibid.

35. Ibid., p. 14.

36. Ibid., pp. 28, 29.

37. Ibid., p. 30.

38. Ibid., p. 31.

39. Ibid., p. 33.

40. Ibid., p. 30.

41. John Locke, "An Essay Concerning the True Original, Extent and End of Civil Government," V, 27, in *The English Philosophers from Bacon to Mill,* ed. Edwin A. Burtt (New York: Modern Library, 1939), pp. 413–414.

42. Smith, *Wealth of Nations,* pp. 122, 170.

43. Ibid., pp. 64, 65.

44. Ibid., pp. 48, 49.

45. Ibid., p. 49.

46. Ibid., p. 65.

47. J. R. Hicks, *The Theory of Wages* (London: Macmillan, 1935), p. 1.

48. As Polanyi has pointed out, "The relations of master, journeyman, and apprentice; the terms of the craft; the number of apprentices; the wages of the workers were all regulated by the custom and rule of the gild and the town. What the mercantile system did was merely to unify these conditions either through statute as in England, or through the 'nationalization' of the gilds as in France. . . . Mercantilism, with all its tendency towards commercialization, never attacked the safeguards which protected these two basic elements of production—labor and land—from becoming the objects of commerce. . . . That mercantilism, however emphatically it insisted on commercialization as a national policy, thought of markets in a way exactly contrary to market economy, is best shown by its vast extension of state intervention in industry. On this point, there was no difference between mercantilists and feudalists. . . . They disagreed only on the methods of regulation: gilds, towns and provinces appealed to the force of custom and tradition, while the new state favored statute and ordinance." Karl Polanyi, *The Great Transformation* (New York: Rinehart, 1944), p. 70. Speaking of the various labor proposals of English mercantilist writers, Edgar S. Furniss writes: "Whether stated in a tone of bitterness or giving evidence of a more compassionate attitude toward the lower orders, these projects all represented similar points of view in their authors. They treated of the laboring class as a group, to be handled in the mass by the state. . . . In all of this it is apparent that the rapidly spreading individualistic concept of society did not extend to the laboring class." Furniss, *Position of the Laborer,* p. 114.

214

49. Lloyd G. Reynolds, *The Structure of Labor Markets* (New York: Harper and Brothers, 1951), p. 2.

50. Gray, *Development,* p. 119.

51. Smith, *Wealth of Nations*, pp. 48, 64.

52. Schumpeter, *History,* pp. 268–269.

53. Smith, *Wealth of Nations,* p. 815.

54. *Reflections on the Formation and Distribution of Riches by Turgot 1770* (New York: Macmillan, 1898), p. 7.

55. *Reflections*, p. 8.

56. Smith, *Wealth of Nations,* pp. 67–68, 79–80.

57. Ibid., p. 69.

58. Ibid.

59. Ibid., p. 71.

60. Ibid., pp. 69, 74.

61. George J. Stigler, *Selections from the Wealth of Nations* (New York: Appleton-Century-Crofts, 1957), p. viii.

62. Smith, *Wealth of Nations,* p. 75.

63. Ibid., p. 66.

64. Ibid., pp. 66–67.

65. Ibid., p. 77.

66. David Hume, *Writings on Economics,* ed. Eugene Rotwein (Madison: University of Wisconsin Press, 1955), pp. 208–209.

67. Smith, *Wealth of Nations,* p. 99.

68. Ibid., pp. 99, 100, 114, 116.

69. Ibid., p. 118.

70. Ibid., pp. 81, 565–566.

71. Ibid., p. 81.

72. Ibid., pp. 78–79.

73. Smith, *Lectures,* pp. 255–258.

74. Smith, *Wealth of Nations,* pp. 734–735.

75. Ibid., p. 3.

76. From an early draft of the *Wealth of Nations,* quoted in E. G. West, "Adam Smith's Two Views on the Division of Labour," *Economica,* n.s. 31 (1964): 24.

77. Schumpeter, *History,* p. 187.

78. Smith, *Wealth of Nations,* pp. 8–9.

79. West, "Smith's Two Views," pp. 25–26, 30.

80. Nathan Rosenberg, "Adam Smith on the Division of Labour: Two Views or One?" *Economica,* n.s. 32 (1965): 134.

81. Smith, *Wealth of Nations,* pp. 735–736.

82. Rosenberg, "Adam Smith," pp. 136–137.

83. Smith, *Wealth of Nations,* p. 736.

84. Ibid., pp. 122–123.

85. Ibid., pp. 140, 141.

86. Ibid., pp. 67, 142, 249. Smith added the qualification that workers, "sometimes, too, without any provocation of this kind, combine of their own accord to raise the price of their labour."

87. Nathan Rosenberg, "Some Institutional Aspects of the *Wealth of Nations,*" *Journal of Political Economy* 68 (1960): 560–561, 567.

88. David Brion Davis, *The Problem of Slavery in Western Culture* (Ithaca: Cornell University Press, 1966), pp. 434, 438.

89. Quoted in ibid., p. 440.

90. Smith, *Wealth of Nations,* p. 365.

91. Ibid., p. 366.

92. Ibid., p. 369.

93. Ibid., p. 700.

94. Ibid., p. 392.

95. Jacob Viner, "Adam Smith and Laissez-Faire," *Journal of Political Economy* 35 (1927): 207.

96. This chapter draws heavily on my article "Adam Smith's Concept of Labor," *Journal of the History of Ideas* 34 (1973): 345–366.

CHAPTER 3

1. John Maynard Keynes, *The General Theory of Employment, Interest and Money* (New York: Harcourt Brace, 1936), p. 3.

2. Joseph A. Schumpeter, *History of Economic Analysis* (New York: Oxford University Press, 1954), pp. 474, 560, 568, 673.

3. Overton H. Taylor, *A History of Economic Thought* (New York: McGraw-Hill, 1960), p. 172.

4. David A. Ricardo, *Works and Correspondence,* ed. Piero Sraffa (Cambridge: At the Press, 1951), 1:5.

5. Ibid., 8:278–279.

6. According to James Bonar. See Wesley C. Mitchell, *Lecture Notes on Types of Economic Theory* (New York: Augustus M. Kelley, 1949), pp. 133–134.

7. Ricardo, *Works,* 1:12.

8. Ibid., p. 5.

9. Frank H. Knight, "The Ricardian Theory of Production and Distribution," *Canadian Journal of Economics and Political Science* 1 (1935): 22. Knight holds that classical distribution theory was in fact not conceived of as a problem in competitive pricing and quotes from a letter of Ricardo to McCulloch to that effect. Ibid., p. 6.

10. Thomas Sewall Adams and Helen L. Sumner, *Labor Problems: A Textbook* (New York: Macmillan, 1905), p. 5.

11. Schumpeter, *History,* pp. 473, 541, 618, 668.

12. Ricardo, *Works,* 1:93–94.

13. Michael T. Wermel, *The Evolution of the Classical Wage Theory* (New York: Columbia University Press, 1939), p. 154.

14. Wesley C. Mitchell, "The Prospects of Economics," in *The Trend of Economics,* ed. R. G. Tugwell (New York: Alfred A. Knopf, 1924), p. 12.

15. Adam Smith, *The Wealth of Nations* (New York: Modern Library, 1937), pp. 30, 47; Ricardo, *Works,* 1:13.

16. Ricardo, *Works,* 1:14.

17. Ibid.

18. Ibid., pp. 16–17.

19. Smith, *Wealth of Nations*, p. 47. Ricardo, *Works*, 1:22–23.

20. Ibid., pp. 24–25.

21. George J. Stigler, "Ricardo and the 93% Labor Theory of Value," *American Economic Review* 48 (June 1958: 357.

22. Ricardo, *Works,* 1:20, 30. Emphasis added.

23. Stigler, "Ricardo," p. 361.

24. Mark Blaug, *Economic Theory in Retrospect,* 3d ed. (Cambridge: At the Press, 1978), p. 141.

25. Ricardo, *Works,* 1:93.

26. Ibid., pp. 94–95, 265.

27. Ibid., p. 390.

28. Ibid., p. 100.

29. Blaug, *Economic Theory*, p. 141.

30. Ibid.

31. Schumpeter, *History,* p. 473.

32. Nassau Senior, *An Outline of the Science of Political Economy* (1836), pp. 2–3, quoted in T. W. Hutchinson, *"Positive" Economics and Policy Objectives* (Cambridge: Harvard University Press, 1964), pp. 30–31.

33. Hutchison, *"Positive" Economics,* p. 23.

34. Ibid., p. 26.

35. Ibid., p. 25.

36. H. Sidgwick, *Principles of Political Economy* (1883), p. 15n, quoted in ibid., p. 26.

37. John Stuart Mill, *Essays on Some Unsettled Questions of Political Economy* (London: London School of Economics and Political Science, 1948), pp. 123, 124. Mill quickly added that "unless it be altogether a useless science, practical rules must be capable of being founded upon it."

38. Ibid., pp. 137–139.

39. Ibid., pp. 144–145.

40. Ibid., p. 140.

41. Ibid., pp. 150, 151.

42. Ibid., p. 155.

43. Ricardo, *Works,* 1:12. See also John Stuart Mill, *Principles of Political Economy with Some of Their Applications to Social Philosophy* (New York: Augustus M. Kelley, 1961), bk. 3, chap. 1, p. 440.

44. Marion Bowley, *Nassau Senior and Classical Economics* (London: George Allen and Unwin, 1937), pp. 238, 286.

45. George J. Stigler, *Five Lectures on Economic Problems* (New York: Macmillan, 1950), p. 35.

46. Nassau W. Senior, *Four Introductory Lectures on Political Economy* (London: Longmans, Brown, Green, and Longmans, 1852).

47. S. G. Checkland, "Economic Opinion in England as Jevons Found It," *Manchester School of Economic and Social Studies* 19 (May 1951): 143, 151–152.

48. "In that state of society which is presupposed by the Political Economist, ... [distribution] is principally effected by Exchange. We may indeed conceive a state of human existence admitting of distribution without the intervention of exchanges. But such a situation of society, if it can be called society, neither deserves nor requires scientific investigation. Political economy considers men in that more advanced state." Nassau W. Senior, *Political Economy* (London: Richard Griffin and Company, 1858), p. 87.

49. Asa Briggs, "The Language of 'Class' in Early Nineteenth-Century England," in *Essays in Labour History,* ed. Asa Briggs and John Saville (London: Macmillan, 1960), p. 62ff.

50. Nassau W. Senior, *Three Lectures on the Rate of Wages* (London: John Murray, 1830), p. iii.

51. Ricardo, *Works,* 1:95.

52. James Mill, *Elements of Political Economy* (London: Baldwin Craddock and Jay, 1821), p. 28.

53. John Stuart Mill, *Principles of Political Economy,* bk. 2, chap. 11, sec. 1, pp. 343–344.

54. Senior, *Political Economy,* pp. 175–176.

55. See F. W. Taussig, *Wages and Capital* (New York: D. Appleton, 1896), pp. 98–99.

56. George J. Stigler, *Production and Distribution Theories* (New York: Macmillan, 1948), p. 3.

57. W. H. Hutt, *The Theory of Collective Bargaining* (London: P. S. King & Son, 1930), pp. 8–9.

58. N. Jha, *The Age of Marshall* (Ashoka, Rajpath, Patna: Novelty and Company, 1963), p. 13.

59. Francis A. Walker, *The Wages Question* (New York: Henry Holt, 1876), p. 387.

60. Hutt, *Theory,* p. 79.

61. R. V. Clements, "British Trade Unions and Popular Political Economy 1850–1870," *Economic History Review* 14 (1961): 95.

62. Alvin Hansen, *The American Economy* (New York: McGraw-Hill, 1957), p. 153.

63. Sidney and Beatrice Webb, *Industrial Democracy* (London: Longmans, Green and Company, 1897), 1:viii.

64. Leo Wolman, "Labor Policy and Economic History," *The Tasks of Economic History: A Supplement to the Journal of Economic History* (December 1945): 87.

65. R. H. Tawney, *The Webbs in Perspective* (London: Athlone Press, 1953), p. 9.

66. Lord Beveridge, "The London School of Economics and the University of London," in *The Webbs and Their Work,* ed. Margaret Cole (London: Frederick Muller, Ltd., 1949), pp. 41, 45.

67. Clair Wilcox, *Public Policies Toward Business,* rev. ed. (Homewood, Ill.: Richard D. Irwin, 1960), p. 522.

68. Eli Heckscher, *Mercantilism* (London: George Allen and Unwin, 1934), 2:329.

69. Frank A. Fetter, "Price Economics vs. Welfare Economics," *American Economic Review* 10 (September 1920): 482.

70. Lionel Robbins, *The Theory of Economic Policy* (London: Macmillan, 1952), p. 105.

71. Smith, *Wealth of Nations,* pp. 79, 142.

72. Cited by Robbins, *Theory,* p. 104.

73. Schumpeter, *History,* p. 546.

74. John Stuart Mill, "Thornton on Labour and Its Claims," *Fortnightly Review,* n.s. 5 (1869): 517, 690.

75. See F. Y. Edgeworth, *Mathematical Psychics* (London: E. Kegan Paul & Co., 1881), p. 43.

76. W. Stanley Jevons, *The State in Relation to Labour* (London: Macmillan, 1882), p. 155.

77. According to Ricardo, "The principle of gravitation is not more certain than the tendency of such laws to change wealth and power into misery and weakness; to call away the exertions of labour from every object, except that of providing mere subsistence; to confound all intellectual distinction; to busy the mind continually in supplying the body's wants; until at last all classes should be infected with the plague of universal poverty." Ricardo, *Works,* 1:108.

78. Smith, *Wealth of Nations,* p. 736.

79. Bowley, *Nassau Senior,* p. 268.

80. Alfred Marshall, *Principles of Economics*, 8th ed. (New York: Macmillan, 1953), pp. 717–718.

81. Senior, *Political Economy*, pp. 134–135.

82. Thomas R. Malthus, *An Essay on the Principle of Population* (Middlesex, England: Penguin, 1970), p. 186; J. R. McCulloch, *Treatises and Essays on Money, Exchange, Interest, the Letting of Land, Absenteeism, the History of Commerce, Manufactures, etc.* (Edinburgh: A & C Black, 1859), pp. 454–455; Mill, *Principles*, bk. 4, chap. 6, sec. 2, p. 751.

83. Neither did contemporary observers. Writing in 1842, only six years before Mill, Edwin Chadwick, who according to T. S. Ashton "surely knew as much as anyone else of the squalor and poverty of large numbers of town dwellers in the [eighteen] forties," came to strikingly different conclusions. "The fact is," Chadwick wrote, "that hitherto, in England, wages, or the means of obtaining the necessaries of life for the whole mass of the labouring community, have advanced, and the comforts within the reach of the labouring classes have increased with the late increase of population." Quoted in T. S. Ashton, "The Standard of Life of the Workers in England, 1790–1830," in *Capitalism and the Historians*, ed. F. A. Hayek (Chicago: University of Chicago Press, 1954), pp. 125–126.

84. A. J. Taylor, "Progress and Poverty in Britain, 1780–1850," in *Essays in Economic History*, ed. E. M. Carus-Wilson (New York: St. Martin's, 1962), 2:388.

85. E. J. Hobsbawm, *Labouring Men* (New York: Anchor Books, 1967), pp. 409, 410. The reference is to E. J. Hamilton, *American Treasure and the Price Revolution in Spain, 1501–1650* (Cambridge: Harvard University Press, 1934).

86. Smith, *Wealth of Nations*, pp. 66–67.

87. Doris G. Phillips, "The Wages Fund in Historical Context," *Journal of Economic Issues* (December 1967): 330.

88. Mill, *Principles*, bk. 4, chap. 7, sec. 1, p. 753.

89. Reinhard Bendix, *Work and Authority in Industry* (New York: John Wiley, 1956), p. 73.

90. Rev. Joseph Townsend, *A Dissertation on the Poor Laws by a Well-Wisher of Mankind* (1786), quoted in ibid., pp. 73–75. Edmund Burke, "Thoughts and Details on Scarcity" (1869), cited in ibid., pp. 75–79.

91. Thomas R. Malthus, *An Essay on the Principle of Population* (Homewood, Ill.: Richard D. Irwin, 1963), p. 274.

92. Bendix, *Work and Authority*, p. 99.

CHAPTER 4

1. Emil Kauder, "The Intellectual Sources of Karl Marx," *Kyklos* 21 (1968): 282.

2. John Stuart Mill, *Essays on Some Unsettled Questions of Political Economy*, London School of Economics and Political Science Series of Reprints of Scarce Works, No. 7 (London, 1948), p. 94.

3. Henry D. Aiken, *The Age of Ideology* (New York: Mentor, 1956), p. 72.

4. G. W. F. Hegel, *The Philosophy of History,* quoted in ibid., p. 83.

5. Karl Marx, *Capital* (Chicago: Charles H. Kerr, 1912), 1:25.

6. Erich Fromm, *Marx's Concept of Man* (New York: Frederick Ungar, 1966), p. 8.

7. Karl Marx, *Critique of Political Economy* (1859), quoted in Karl Marx and Friedrich Engels, *The Communist Manifesto,* ed. Samuel H. Beer (New York: Appleton-Century-Crofts, 1955), p. lx.

8. Ernest Mandel, *The Formation of the Economic Thought of Karl Marx, 1843 to Capital,* trans. Brian Pearce (New York: Monthly Review Press, 1971), pp. 11–12.

9. Adam Smith, *The Wealth of Nations* (New York: Modern Library, 1937), pp. 30, 48.

10. Adam Smith's assertion that profit levels "bear no proportion to the quantity, the hardship, or the ingenuity" of the manager's or entrepreneur's activity but are rather "regulated altogether by the value of the [capital] stock employed" is a good illustration of the relatively unimportant role he assigned the entrepreneur. Ibid., p. 48. Later he wrote: "People of the same trade seldom meet together, even for merriment and diversion, but the conversation ends in a conspiracy against the public, or in some contrivance to raise prices." p. 128.

11. Ibid., pp. 49, 65.

12. Karl Marx, *The Economic and Philosophic Manuscripts of 1844,* ed. Dirk J. Struik (New York: International Publishers, 1964), p. 70.

13. Smith, *Wealth of Nations,* p. 314; Marx, *Capital,* 1:59.

14. Joseph A. Schumpeter, *Capitalism, Socialism, and Democracy* (New York: Harper and Row, 1950), p. 22.

15. Mandel, *Formation,* p. 10; Joseph A. Schumpeter, *History of Economic Analysis* (New York: Oxford University Press, 1954), p. 387.

16. Friedrich Engels, *The Condition of the Working Class in England,* trans. and ed. W. O. Henderson and W. H. Chaloner (Stanford: Stanford University Press, 1968). See especially the editors' introduction, pp. ix–xxix, as well as their comments throughout the book.

17. Ibid., p. xv.

18. Schumpeter, *History of Economic Analysis,* p. 386.

19. Engels, *Condition,* pp. 97–98.

20. Marx, *Economic and Philosophic Manuscripts,* p. 5.

21. Aiken, *Age of Ideology,* pp. 93, 94.

22. Marx, *Economic and Philosophic Manuscripts,* p. 113.

23. Fromm, *Marx's Concept,* p. v.

24. Marx, *Economic and Philosophic Manuscripts,* p. 114.

25. Ibid., pp. 107, 115.

26. E. G. West, "The Political Economy of Alienation: Karl Marx and Adam Smith," *Oxford Economic Papers* 21 (March 1969): 4. See Marx, *Economic and Philosophic Manuscripts*, pp. 121, 150.

27. Ibid., p. 155.

28. Ibid., p. 156.

29. Ibid., pp. 107–108.

30. Ibid., pp. 110–111.

31. Ibid., p. 108.

32. Ibid., p. 113.

33. Ibid., pp. 108, 115.

34. Ibid., p. 114.

35. Quoted in ibid., p. 32.

36. See ibid., p. 116.

37. Ibid., pp. 116–117.

38. Ibid., p. 117.

39. Ibid., pp. 117, 118–119.

40. Marx, *Capital*, 1:708–709.

41. Daniel Bell, *The End of Ideology* (Glencoe, Ill.: Free Press, 1960), p. 344.

42. Marx, *Capital*, 1:190, 255.

43. Ibid., p. 215.

44. Ibid., p. 240.

45. Ibid., pp. 240–241.

46. Joan Robinson, *An Essay on Marxian Economics* (London: Macmillan, 1964), p. 6.

47. Marx, *Capital*, 1:241.

48. Joan Robinson, "Review of Paul Sweezy, ed., *Karl Marx and the Close of His System* by Eugen Von Böhm-Bawerk and Böhm-Bawerk's Criticism of Marx by Rudolf Hilferding," *Economic Journal* 60 (June 1950): 362; Paul A. Samuelson, "Understanding the Marxian Notion of Exploitation: A Summary of the So-Called Transformation Problem Between Marxian Value and Competitive Prices," *Journal of Economic Literature* 9 (June 1971): 418, subscribed to and emphasized this position.

49. Marx, *Capital*, 3:971.

50. Ibid., 1:239–240.

51. Thomas Sowell, "Marxian Value Reconsidered," *Economica*, n.s. 30 (August 1963): 297.

52. Marx, *Capital*, 1:195.

53. Ibid., pp. 216, 217.

54. A. C. Pigou, *The Economics of Welfare* (London: Macmillan, 1932); Joan Robinson, *The Economics of Imperfect Competition* (London: Macmillan, 1933).

55. Marx, *Capital*, 1:195, 216.

56. Ibid., pp. 216–217. Emphasis added.

57. Ibid., 3:286.

58. Ibid., 1:193.

59. Ibid., p. 625.

60. Ibid., pp. 254, 352.

61. Ibid., pp. 291–292.

62. Ibid., p. 345.

63. Ibid., pp. 396, 397–398, 431.

64. Ibid., pp. 431–432.

65. Ibid., p. 432.

66. Ibid., p. 444.

67. Marx and Engels, *Communist Manifesto*, p. 31.

68. Ibid., pp. 9–10.

69. Ibid., pp. 17–18.

70. Marx, *Capital*, 1:649.

71. Ibid., p. 836.

72. Ibid., pp. 836–837.

73. Marx and Engels, *Communist Manifesto*, pp. 31, 32.

74. Paul A. Samuelson, "Economists and the History of Ideas," *American Economic Review* 52 (March 1962): 12.

75. Schumpeter, *Capitalism*, pp. 5–8.

CHAPTER 5

1. John Stuart Mill, "Thornton on Labour and Its Claims," *Fortnightly Review*, n.s. 5 (1869): 505–518, 680–700. The wages fund doctrine had earlier been criticized "by, among others, Sir Edward West, Mountifort Longfield, Richard Jones, Francis D. Longe, and Cliffe Leslie." Scott Gordon, "The Wage-Fund Controversy: The Second Round," *History of Political Economy* 5 (Spring 1973): 15.

2. Gordon, "Wage-Fund Controversy," p. 16.

3. J. E. Cairnes, *Some Leading Principles of Political Economy Newly Expounded* (New York: Harper & Brothers, 1874); W. Stanley Jevons, *The Theory of Political Economy*, 4th ed. (London: Macmillan, 1911). The book first appeared in 1871. T. W. Hutchison, *A Review of Economic Doctrines, 1870–1929* (Oxford: Clarendon Press, 1953), pp. 22–23, is the analyst cited here.

4. Cairnes, *Some Leading Principles*, pp. 61, 67.

5. Ibid., p. 88ff.

6. Ibid., p. 149.

7. Ibid., p. 150.

8. Alfred Marshall, *Principles of Economics,* 8th ed. (New York: Macmillan, 1953), p. 825.

9. Cairnes, *Some Leading Principles,* pp. 174–175, 177–178.

10. Ibid., pp. 185–186.

11. Thornton, *On Labour,* quoted in ibid., p. 181.

12. Cairnes, *Some Leading Principles,* p. 185.

13. Ibid., p. 225.

14. Ibid., p. 168.

15. R. D. Collison Black, "W. S. Jevons and the Foundation of Modern Economics," *History of Political Economy* 4 (Fall 1972): 372. For a comprehensive treatment of the marginalist revolution in economic thought, see *History of Political Economy* 4 (Fall 1972).

16. Cairnes, *Some Leading Principles,* p. 168.

17. Ibid., p. 168.

18. Ibid., p. 169.

19. Mark Blaug, "The Classical Economists and the Factory Acts: A Reexamination," *Quarterly Journal of Economics* 72 (May 1958): 226.

20. Francis A. Walker, "The Wage Fund Theory," *North American Review* 120 (January 1875), pp. 101, 118.

21. Ibid., pp. 102, 108.

22. Ibid., p. 105.

23. Ibid., pp. 109–110, 113.

24. Ibid., pp. 113–114.

25. Ibid., pp. 107–108.

26. Gordon, "Wage-Fund Controversy," p. 26.

27. F. W. Taussig, "The Employer's Place in Distribution," *Quarterly Journal of Economics* 10 (1895): 67.

28. F. W. Taussig, *Wages and Capital* (New York: D. Appleton, 1896), pp. 122–123, 322.

29. Ibid., p. 322.

30. Gordon, "Wage-Fund Controversy," p. 29.

31. Thomas S. Kuhn, *The Structure of Scientific Revolutions* (Chicago: University of Chicago Press, 1962), p. 10.

32. Ibid., pp. 18–19.

33. Mark Blaug, "Was There a Marginal Revolution?" *History of Political Economy* 4 (Fall 1972): 269, 276.

34. George J. Stigler, "Does Economics Have a Useful Past?" *History of Political Economy* 1 (Fall 1969): 225.

35. Wesley C. Mitchell, "The Prospects of Economics," in *The Trend of Economics,* ed. R. G. Tugwell (New York: Alfred A. Knopf, 1924), p. 12.

36. Hutchison, *Review*, p. 15.

37. Blaug, "Was There a Marginal Revolution?" p. 277.

38. Frank H. Knight, "Marginal Utility Economics," *Encyclopedia of the Social Sciences* (New York: Macmillan, 1937), 5:360.

39. J. B. Clark, *The Philosophy of Wealth* (Boston: Ginn, 1894), preface.

40. Ibid., pp. 147–148, 203.

41. Ibid., pp. 68–69.

42. J. B. Clark, *The Distribution of Wealth* (New York: Macmillan, 1902), pp. v, vi.

43. Ibid., p. 3.

44. Ibid., pp. 101, 158–159.

45. Ibid., pp. 174–175.

46. Ibid., p. 175.

47. Ibid., p. 176.

48. Ibid., p. 177.

49. Ibid., pp. 7, 8.

50. Ibid., p. 9.

51. Paul T. Homan, *Contemporary Economic Thought* (New York: Harper, 1928), p. 195.

52. Marshall, *Principles of Economics*, pp. 514–515.

53. Ibid., pp. 348, 349.

54. Ibid., p. 532.

55. Ibid., p. 577.

56. Ibid.

57. Ibid., p. 42.

58. Ibid., p. 533. Marshall believed that the American sociologist F. H. Giddings had provided "a classification (of labor) more suited to our existing conditions" than that provided by Cairnes in his analysis of non-competing groups. Ibid., p. 218.

59. Ibid., p. 750. Marshall's early attitudes toward unions were more sympathetic than his later ones. In his *Economics of Industry*, written jointly with his wife Mary and published in 1879, there appeared a fairly extensive treatment of trade unions. In the *Principles*, published in 1890, there are few references to unions, reflecting a "gradual change in Marshall's attitude toward trade unions from a favorable and hopeful one in the 1870's to one of doubt and uncertainty in the 1880's and to a final position bordering on hostility." See Anastacios Petrides, "Alfred Marshall's Attitudes to and Economic Analysis of Trade Unions: A Case of Anomalies in a Competitive System," *History of Political Economy* 5 (Spring 1973).

60. Marshall, *Principles of Economics*, pp. 6, 9.

61. Homan, *Contemporary Economic Thought*, p. 204.

CHAPTER 6

1. Neil W. Chamberlain, "The Institutional Economics of John R. Commons," in Joseph Dorfman et al., *Institutional Economics* (Berkeley: University of California Press, 1963), p. 67.

2. Adam Smith, *The Wealth of Nations* (New York: Random House, 1937), p. 397.

3. Frank A. Fetter, "The Economists and the Public," *American Economic Review* 15 (March 1925): 13.

4. Quoted in Edward W. Bemis, "The Labor Question," *Independent,* December 31, 1885, p. 1705.

5. Joseph Dorfman, *The Economic Mind in American Civilization* (New York: Viking, 1949), 3:123.

6. Lewis H. Haney, *History of Economic Thought* (New York: Macmillan, 1913), p. 515; T. E. Cliffe Leslie, "Political Economy in the United States," *Fortnightly Review,* n.s. 28 (1880): 500; Richard T. Ely, *Ground under Our Feet* (New York: Macmillan, 1938), p. 125.

7. Francis Bowen, *Gleanings from a Literary Life, 1838–1880* (New York: Charles Scribner's Sons, 1880), p. 122.

8. Ibid., p. 123.

9. Charles F. Dunbar, "Economic Science in America, 1776—1876," *North American Review* 122 (January 1876): 140.

10. Arthur L. Perry, *Elements of Political Economy,* 5th ed. (New York: Charles Scribner and Company, 1869), pp. 140–141, 144, 146, 150.

11. Sidney Fine, *Laissez-Faire and the General Welfare State* (Ann Arbor: University of Michigan Press, 1956), p. 59.

12. Smith, *Wealth of Nations,* p. 66.

13. Perry, *Elements,* p. 136.

14. Fine, *Laissez-Faire,* pp. 59, 60.

15. Jacob H. Hollander, "Economic Investigation in the United States," *Yale Review* 12 (May 1903): 25.

16. Richard T. Ely, *The Labor Movement in America* (New York: Thomas Y. Crowell, 1886).

17. Philip Taft, "A Rereading of Selig Perlman's *A Theory of the Labor Movement,*" *Industrial and Labor Relations Review* 4 (October 1950): 70.

18. Mark Perlman, *Labor Union Theories in America* (Evanston, Ill.: Row Peterson, 1958), p. 55.

19. At least one prominent historian might disagree. Irving Bernstein holds that the labor economists "preempted" the field of labor history "at the end of the nineteenth century, and their influence—notably in the towering figure of John R. Commons—has since been supreme." Irving Bernstein, *The Lean Years: A History of the American Worker, 1920–1933* (Cambridge: Riverside Press, 1960), p. lx.

20. Carroll D. Wright, "The Relation of Political Êconomy to the Labor Question," (1882), reprinted in Wright, *Some Ethical Phases of the Labor Question* (Boston: American Unitarian Association, 1902), pp. 28–29, 32; Joseph Dorfman, "The Role of the German Historical School in American Economic Thought," *American Economic Review* 45 (May 1955): 22.

21. Joseph Dorfman, "Henry Carter Adams: Harmonizer of Liberty and Reform," in Henry Carter Adams, *Relation of the State to Industrial Action and Economics and Jurisprudence*, ed. Joseph Dorfman (New York: Columbia University Press, 1954), p. 33; Richmond Mayo Śmith, "American Labor Statistics," *Political Science Quarterly* 1 (March 1886): 45.

22. Wright, "Relation of Political Economy," pp. 55–56.

23. Simon N. Patten, "The Scope of Political Economy," *Yale Review* 2 (November 1893): 265–268.

24. Joseph A. Schumpeter, *History of Economic Analysis* (New York: Oxford University Press, 1954), p. 60.

25. *Annual Report of the President of Cornell University to the Board of Trustees* (Ithaca, N.Y., 1884–1885); Franklin B. Sanborn, "The Social Sciences, Their Growth and Future," *Journal of Social Science*, no. 21 (September 1886): 6.

26. Ibid., p. 8.

27. Perry, *Elements*, p. 37.

28. Ely, *Labor Movement in America*, p. 311.

29. Richard T. Ely, *Social Aspects of Christianity* (New York: Thomas Y. Crowell, 1889), pp. 127–128.

30. John R. Commons, *Social Reform and the Church* (New York: Thomas Y. Crowell, 1894), p. 22.

31. Ibid., pp. 46–47.

32. Lafayette G. Harter, Jr., *John R. Commons: His Assault on Laissez-Faire* (Corvallis: Oregon State University Press, 1962), p. 89.

33. John R. Commons, *Myself* (New York: Macmillan, 1934), p. 143.

34. Bemis, "Labor Question," p. 1706.

35. Thomas S. Adams and Helen L. Sumner, *Labor Problems: A Textbook* (New York: Macmillan, 1905), pp. 17, 173, 546.

36. Richard T. Ely, "Economic Theory and Labor Legislation," *Proceedings of the First Annual Meeting of the American Association for Labor Legislation* (Madison, Wis., 1908), p. 21.

37. The paper was Seager's first publication and was entitled "Economics at Berlin and Vienna." It appeared in the *Journal of Political Economy* in 1892. See Wesley C. Mitchell, "In Memory of Henry R. Seager," in Charles A. Gulick, Jr., ed., *Labor and Other Economic Essays by Henry R. Seager* (New York: Harper & Brothers, 1931), p. x.

38. Charles P. Neill, *Daniel Raymond: An Early Chapter in the History of Economic Theory in the United States,* Studies in Historical and Political Science, Ser. 15, No. 6 (Baltimore: Johns Hopkins University, 1897).

39. Richard V. Teggart, *Thorstein Veblen: A Chapter in American Economic Thought*, University of California Publications in Economics, vol. 11, no. 1 (Berkeley: University of California Press, 1932), pp. 5–6.

40. Richmond Mayo Smith, "Methods of Investigation in Political Economy," *Science*, July 23, 1886, p. 82.

41. C. H. Herford, *Germany in the Nineteenth Century* (London: Longmans, Green and Company, 1915), p. 37.

42. John Graham Brooks, "Labor Organizations: Their Political and Economic Service to Society," *Journal of Social Science*, no. 23 (November 1887): 68; Beatrice Webb, *Our Partnership*, ed. Barbara Drake and Margaret Cole (London: Longmans, Green and Company, 1948), p. 53.

43. Christopher Dawson, *The Crisis of Western Education* (New York: Sheed and Ward, 1961), p. 193.

44. Henry D. Aiken, *The Age of Ideology* (New York: Mentor, 1956), p. 79.

45. Richard T. Ely, "Cooperation in Literature and the State," in William E. Barns, ed., *The Labor Problem* (New York: Harper and Brothers, 1886), pp. 9, 10.

46. Ely, *Ground under Our Feet*, p. 136.

47. Ibid., p. 140.

48. Ibid., p. 44.

49. Ely, *Labor Movement in America*, p. v.

50. Ibid., p. v.

51. Ibid., pp. 295, 324.

52. Ibid., pp. 75–76, 78, 138.

53. According to Theodore Marburg. See his statement in E. Levasseur, *The American Workman*, trans. Thomas S. Adams and ed. Theodore Marburg (Baltimore: Johns Hopkins Press, 1900).

54. Ely, *Ground under Our Feet*, p. 178.

55. J. Laurence Laughlin, "Political Economy in the United States," *Journal of Political Economy* 1 (December 1892): 12–13.

56. W. H. Hutt, *The Theory of Collective Bargaining* (Glencoe, Ill.: Free Press, 1954), p. 32.

57. Dorfman, *Economic Mind in American Civilization*, 5:392.

58. Paul Brissenden, "Labor Economics," *American Economic Review* 16 (September 1926), 118, 119.

59. Edward H. Chamberlin, "The Monopoly Power of Labor," in *The Impact of the Union*, ed. David McCord Wright (New York: Kelley and Millman, 1956), p. 169.

60. John R. Commons, "Economists and Class Partnership," in *Labor and Administration* (New York: Macmillan, 1913), p. 58.

61. John T. Dunlop, "Research in Industrial Relations: Past and Present," in *Proceedings of the Industrial Relations Research Association* (1954), p. 94.

62. Perlman, *Labor Union Theories,* p. 51.

63. Laughlin, "Political Economy," p. 19.

64. The full report of the organization of the Association is contained in volume 1 of the *Publications of the American Economic Association* (1886).

65. Richard T. Ely, *The Past and Present of Political Economy,* Johns Hopkins University Studies in Historical and Political Science, vol. 2 (Baltimore: Johns Hopkins University, 1884), p. 31.

66. Mayo Smith, "American Labor Statistics," p. 83. The subsequent improvement upon this situation was largely the work of Wright. See James Leiby, *Carroll Wright and Labor Reform: The Origin of Labor Statistics* (Cambridge, Mass.: Harvard University Press, 1960).

67. Franklin H. Giddings, "The Natural Rate of Wages," *Political Science Quarterly* 2 (December 1887): 620.

68. Lloyd G. Reynolds, "The General Level of Wages," in *New Concepts of Wage Determination,* ed. George W. Taylor and Frank C. Pierson (New York: McGraw-Hill, 1957), p. 239.

69. Edward W. Bemis, "The Benefit Features of American Trades Unions," *Political Science Quarterly* 2 (June 1887): 290.

70. Edward W. Bemis, "The Coal-Miners' Strike," *Outlook,* May 12, 1894, pp. 822-823; Harry A. Millis, "Some Aspects of the Minimum Wage," *Journal of Political Economy* 22 (February 1914): 146.

71. Levasseur, *op. cit.,* pp. xix–xx.

72. Adams and Sumner, *Labor Problems,* p. 3.

73. This list of chapter titles is taken from a review by John Cummings in the *Quarterly Journal of Economics* 13 (October 1898): 85–100, and all do not appear in Adams's translation. Adams condensed Levasseur's two volumes into one and omitted many chapters.

74. L. L. Bernard, "The Social Sciences as Disciplines: The United States," *Encyclopaedia of the Social Sciences* (New York: Macmillan, 1930), 1:337. See also J. B. Parrish, "Rise of Economics as an Academic Discipline: the Formative Years to 1900," *Southern Economic Journal* 34 (July 1967): 1–16.

75. Bernard, "Social Sciences," p. 340.

76. *Annual Reports of the President and Treasurer of Harvard College, 1892–93* (Cambridge, Mass.: Harvard University Press, 1893).

77. *The President's Report, July 1898–July 1899* (Chicago: University of Chicago Press, 1899), p. 55.

78. *The President's Report, July 1892–July 1902* (Chicago: University of Chicago Press, 1903), pp. 31–38.

79. Mark Perlman does not mention this gift and seems instead to attribute the revived interest in labor study at Johns Hopkins to a visit there by E. Dana Durand: "At Johns Hopkins interest in trade unionism lagged for about a decade after Ely's departure. Except for some discussion of the Webbs' *Industrial Democracy,* in the late spring of 1898, when Jacob Hollander reviewed the

book for the Economic Seminary, there appears to have been no systematic examination of the trade union movement and its implications for labor until 1902, when E. Dana Durand, later professor at the University of Minnesota and tariff expert, addressed the Economics Seminary on 'Arbitration in the United States.' Durand was one of the two men in charge of labor research for the United States Industrial Commission. His visit and his intimate knowledge of unexplored aspects of the labor field possibly stimulated a latent interest. In any event, the following fall the Department of Political Economy adopted the subject of the methods and stratagems of unions as the primary area for specialized research." Perlman, *Labor Union Theories,* pp. 25–26. There seems little doubt, however, that it was the gift of fifteen hundred dollars, of which five hundred was "for the immediate purchase of additions to the University Library" in the field of labor, and one thousand dollars "for meeting the expenses incident to the inquiry in the academic year 1902–03," that made possible the actual conduct of the labor studies, whatever the latent interest or other forces involved. Durand's visit, in fact, may well have been the result rather than the cause of the revived interest in labor at Johns Hopkins. The gift that launched the project is mentioned prominently in the seminary descriptions in the next several *University Circulars,* e.g., April 1903 and July 1903.

80. Dorfman, "Department of Economics," pp. 172, 185.

81. *Annual Report of the President of Cornell University to the Board of Trustees* (Ithaca, N.Y., 1885–1886), p. 81.

82. *The University Records, Cornell University Register* (Ithaca, N.Y., Series 5, No. 2, 1904–1905).

83. David J. Saposs, "The Wisconsin Heritage and the Study of Labor— Words and Deeds of John R. Commons," *School for Workers Thirty-Fifth Anniversary Papers* (Madison: University of Wisconsin Press, 1960).

84. Commons, *Myself,* p. 131.

85. Henry R. Seager, review of Adams and Sumner, in *Political Science Quarterly* 20 (September 1905): 562–565.

86. This chapter draws heavily on my article, "Labor Problems and Labor Economics: the Roots of an Academic Discipline," *Labor History* 9 (Spring 1968).

CHAPTER 7

1. For a good statement of the meaning and significance of the institutionalist approach to economic analysis, see the introduction by Chandler Morse in Morris A. Copeland, *Fact and Theory and Economics: The Testament of an Institutionalist* (Ithaca, N.Y.: Cornell University Press, 1958), pp. v–xiv.

2. Thomas S. Adams and Helen L. Sumner, *Labor Problems: A Textbook* (New York: Macmillan, 1905), pp. 6, 14–15.

3. Ibid., pp. 14–15.

4. Frederic Meyers, *Economics of Labor Relations* (Chicago: Richard D. Irwin, 1951), pp. 2–3.

5. Henry R. Seager, review of Adams and Sumner in *Political Science Quarterly* 20 (September 1905): 562–565.

6. Adams and Sumner, *Labor Problems,* p. v.; Melvin W. Reder, "Wage Determination in Theory and Practice," in Neil W. Chamberlain, Frank C. Pierson, and Theresa Wolfson, eds., *A Decade of Industrial Relations* (New York: Harper and Brothers, 1958), p. 85.

7. Adams and Sumner, *Labor Problems,* p. 3.

8. Ibid., p. 24.

9. Ibid., pp. 241–242.

10. Joseph Dorfman, *The Economic Mind in American Civilization* (New York: Viking, 1959), 5:515.

11. Paul Brissenden, "Labor Economics," *American Economic Review* 16 (September 1926): 447.

12. Barbara Wootton, review of H. A. Silverman's *Economics of Social Problems, Economic Journal* 36 (1926): 275.

13. Richard A. Lester, *Economics of Labor* (New York: Macmillan, 1941), p. 157.

14. Solomon Blum, *Labor Economics* (New York: Henry Holt and Company, 1925), pp. 437, 438, 439.

15. Ibid., pp. 439, 449–450.

16. Paul H. Douglas, "Are There Laws of Production?" *American Economic Review* 38 (March 1948): 4–5.

17. Much of the literature produced during these years has been summarized by Milton Derber in his *Research in Labor Problems in the United States* (New York: Random House, 1967).

18. Willard E. Atkins and Harold D. Lasswell, *Labor Attitudes and Problems* (New York: Prentice-Hall, 1924), p. iv.

19. Dale Yoder, *Labor Economics and Labor Problems* (New York: McGraw-Hill, 1933), pp. 1, 13.

20. Orme W. Phelps, *Introduction to Labor Economics* (New York: McGraw-Hill, 1950), pp. 3–4.

21. Milton Derber, "Research in Union-Management Relations: Past and Future," *Proceedings of the Industrial Relations Research Association* (1956), p. 293.

22. Brissenden, "Labor Economics," pp. 445–446.

23. Paul A. Samuelson, "What Economists Know," in *The Human Meaning of the Social Sciences*, ed. Daniel Lerner (New York: Meridian Books, 1959), p. 194.

24. Dorfman, *Economic Mind,* pp. 591–592.

25. Eric Roll, *A History of Economic Thought,* 3d ed. (Englewood Cliffs, N.J.: Prentice-Hall, 1956), p. 371.

26. Ibid., p. 370.

27. Edgar S. Furniss, *The Position of the Laborer in a System of Nationalism* (New York: Kelly and Millman, 1957), p. 114.

28. Richard T. Ely, *The Past and Present of Political Economy,* Johns Hopkins University Studies in Historical and Political Science, vol. 2 (Baltimore: Johns Hopkins University, 1884), pp. 49–50; John R. Commons, "Institutional Economics," *American Economic Review* 21 (December 1931): 649; John R. Commons, *Myself* (New York: Macmillan, 1934), p. 62.

29. Lord Beveridge, "The London School of Economics and the University of London," in Margaret Cole, ed., *The Webbs and Their Work* (London: Frederick Muller, 1949), p. 41.

30. Paul J. McNulty, "Hoxie's Economics in Retrospect: The Making and Unmaking of a Veblenian," *History of Political Economy* 5 (Fall 1973): 449–484; Robert F. Hoxie, "The Demand and Supply Concepts," *Journal of Political Economy* 9 (June 1906), pp. 339–340, 342.

31. Cornelia S. Parker, *An American Idyll: The Life of Carlton H. Parker* (Boston: Atlantic Monthly Press, 1919), p. 111.

32. Carlton H. Parker, "Motives in Economic Life," *American Economic Review* 8 (March 1918): 213, 215.

33. George H. Hildebrand, "The Economic Effects of Unionism," in Chamberlain, Pierson, and Wolfson, *Decade*, pp. 138–139.

34. Carroll R. Daugherty, "The Field of Labor Economics," *American Economic Review* 35 (September 1945): 653, 655.

35. Edwin E. Witte, "Where We Are in Industrial Relations," *Proceedings of the Industrial Relations Research Association* (1948), p. 19; Daugherty, "Field," p. 653.

36. Paul T. Homan, *Contemporary Economic Thought* (New York: Harper, 1928), p. 175.

37. Ibid., pp. 439–440.

38. Gordon S. Watkins, *An Introduction to the Study of Labor Problems* (London: George G. Harrop, 1922), p. 5.

39. George Strauss, "Labor and the Academicians," *Proceedings of the Industrial Relations Research Association* (1963), p. 6.

40. Commons, *Myself,* pp. 43–44.

41. Robert Dubin, "Industrial Research and the Discipline of Sociology," *Proceedings of the Industrial Relations Research Association* (1958), p. 294.

42. Harold L. Sheppard, "The Treatment of Unionism in Managerial Sociology," *American Sociological Review* 14 (April 1949): 313.

43. Edwin E. Witte, "The University and Labor Education," *Industrial and Labor Relations Review* 1 (October 1947): 6.

44. Selig Perlman, *A Theory of the Labor Movement* (New York: Macmillan, 1928), pp. 242–243.

45. John R. Commons and Associates, *History of Labor in the United States* (New

York: Macmillan, 1918), 2 vols. Volumes three and four, by Don D. Lescohier, Elizabeth Brandeis, Selig Perlman, and Philip Taft, appeared in 1935.

46. Mark Perlman, *Labor Union Theories in America* (Evanston, Ill.: Row, Peterson and Company, 1958), p. 55.

47. Irving Bernstein, *The Lean Years: A History of the American Worker, 1920–1933* (Cambridge: Riverside Press, 1960), p. ix.

48. Walter Galenson, "Reflections on the Writing of Labor History," *Industrial and Labor Relations Review* 11 (October 1957): 90–91.

49. Ibid., pp. 86–87.

50. Mark Perlman, *Labor Union Theories,* pp. 26, 35.

51. Professor Taft commented on this in a letter to Professor Galenson, and is cited by the latter. See Galenson, "Reflections," p. 86.

52. Jacob H. Hollander, "The Political Economist and the Public," *North American Review* 180 (February 1905): 254, 260.

53. Mark Perlman, *Labor Union Theories,* p. 30.

54. Hollander, "Political Economist," p. 257.

55. Ibid.

56. Vaughn Davis Bornet, "The New Labor History: A Challenge for American Historians," *Historian* (Autumn 1955): 18, cited by Galenson, "Reflections," p. 91.

57. Galenson, "Reflections," p. 91.

58. Edwin E. Witte, "Institutional Economics as Seen by an Institutional Economist," *Southern Economic Journal* 21 (October 1954): 131. Emphasis added.

59. Neil W. Chamberlain, *Labor* (New York: McGraw-Hill, 1958), pp. 168–169.

60. Richard T. Ely, comments on "Institutional Economics," *American Economic Review* 22 (March 1932): 114, 115, 116.

61. Kenneth E. Boulding, "A New Look at Institutionalism," *American Economic Review* 47 (May 1957): 5.

62. Ibid., pp. 1–2.

63. Allan G. Gruchy, discussion of Boulding's "A New Look at Institutionalism," *American Economic Review* 47 (May 1947): 13.

64. Lloyd G. Reynolds, *The Structure of Labor Markets* (New York: Harper, 1951), p. 2.

65. Richard A. Lester, *Labor and Industrial Relations* (New York: Macmillan, 1951), p. 48.

66. Walter W. Stewart, "Economic Theory," Discussion, *American Economic Review* 9 (March 1919): 319–320.

67. John R. Commons, *Legal Foundations of Capitalism* (New York: Macmillan, 1924), p. viii.

68. Neil Chamberlain, "The Institutional Economics of John R. Commons," in *Institutional Economics,* ed. Joseph Dorfman et al. (Berkeley: University of California Press, 1963), pp. 68–69.

69. Allan G. Gruchy, *Modern Economic Thought* (New York: Prentice-Hall, 1947), p. 240.

70. Witte, "Institutional Economics," pp. 131–132.

71. John R. Commons, *Institutional Economics* (New York: Macmillan, 1934), p. 1.

72. Dorfman, *Economic Mind,* 4:395.

73. Walton F. Hamilton, "The Development of Hoxie's Economics," *Journal of Political Economy* 24 (1916): 864. See also McNulty, "Hoxie's Economics."

74. Hamilton, "Development," p. 869.

75. Robert F. Hoxie, *Trade Unionism in the United States* (New York: D. Appleton, 1928), pp. 3–6.

76. Hamilton, "Development," p. 876.

CHAPTER 8

1. Richard A. Lester and Joseph Shister, eds., *Insights into Labor Issues* (New York: Macmillan, 1948).

2. Edwin E. Witte, review of *Insights into Labor Issues* in *Journal of Political Economy* 56 (August 1948): 370.

3. Joseph A. Schumpeter, *History of Economic Analysis* (New York: Oxford University Press, 1954), p. 948.

4. A. C. Pigou, *Principles and Methods of Industrial Peace* (London: Macmillan, 1905), pp. 5, 107, 208.

5. A. C. Pigou, *The Economics of Welfare,* 4th ed. (London: Macmillan, 1946), pp. 113, 115.

6. J. R. Hicks, *The Theory of Wages* (London: Macmillan, 1935), pp. i, vi.

7. Ibid., p. vi.

8. Ibid., p. vi.

9. Ibid., p. 141.

10. Ibid., pp. 141–142.

11. Ibid., p. 142.

12. See J. Pen, "A General Theory of Bargaining," *American Economic Review* 42 (March 1952): 24–52, and G. L. S. Schackle, "The Nature of the Bargaining Process," in *The Theory of Wage Determination,* ed. John T. Dunlop (New York: St. Martin's, 1964), pp. 292–314.

13. Allan M. Cartter, *Theory of Wages and Employment* (Homewood, Ill.: Irwin, 1959), p. 129.

14. Paul H. Douglas, *The Theory of Wages* (New York: Augustus M. Kelley, 1964), p. xii.

15. Ibid.

16. Ibid., p. 45.

17. Ibid., pp. 93–94.

18. Ibid., p. 95.

19. Ibid., p. 123.

20. Ibid., pp. 123, 173–174, 203.

21. Don D. Lescohier, review of Douglas's *Theory of Wages, Quarterly Journal of Economics* 50 (June 1935): 277.

22. Schumpeter, *History,* p. 941.

23. Lloyd G. Reynolds, "Economics of Labor," in *A Survey of Contemporary Economics* (Homewood, Ill.: Irwin, 1948), 1:256.

24. Edward H. Chamberlin, *The Theory of Monopolistic Competition* (Cambridge, Mass.: Harvard University Press, 1933); Joan Robinson, *The Economics of Imperfect Competition* (London: Macmillan, 1933).

25. Alfred Marshall, *Principles of Economics,* 8th ed. (New York: Macmillan, 1953), p. 515.

26. Richard A. Lester, "Shortcomings of Marginal Analysis for Wage-Employment Problems," *American Economic Review* 36 (March 1946): 71, 75.

27. Fritz Machlup, "Marginal Analysis and Empirical Research," *American Economic Review* 36 (September 1946): 534–535, 548, 552, 553.

28. George J. Stigler, "Professor Lester and the Marginalists," *American Economic Review* 27 (March 1947): 154–157; Fritz Machlup, "Theories of the Firm: Marginalist, Behavioral, Managerial," *American Economic Review* 57 (March 1967): 3–4.

29. Hicks, *Theory,* p. 181; Nathan Belfer and Gordon F. Bloom, "Unionism and the Marginal Productivity Theory," in Lester and Shister, *Insights into Labor Issues,* pp. 239, 265.

30. Belfer and Bloom, "Unionism," p. 266.

31. John T. Dunlop, *Wage Determination under Trade Unions* (New York: Augustus M. Kelley, 1950), p. 4.

32. Ibid., p. 5.

33. Ibid., pp. 33, 118, 119.

34. Lloyd G. Reynolds, review of Dunlop's *Wage Determination under Trade Unions, American Economic Review* 24 (September 1944): 639, 641.

35. Arthur M. Ross, *Trade Union Wage Policy* (Berkeley and Los Angeles: University of California Press, 1948), pp. 8, 74.

36. Ibid., p. 27.

37. Ibid., p. 51.

38. Ibid., p. 74.

39. Charles E. Lindblom, *Unions and Capitalism* (New Haven: Yale University Press, 1950); Peter F. Drucker, *The New Society* (New York: Harper, 1950);

Neil W. Chamberlain, *Collective Bargaining* (New York: McGraw-Hill, 1951); Richard A. Lester, *As Unions Mature: An Analysis of the Evolution of American Unionism* (Princeton: Princeton University Press, 1958); Florence Peterson, *American Labor Unions: What They Are and How They Work* (New York: Harper, 1945); Joseph Shister, "The Theory of Union Wage Rigidity," *Quarterly Journal of Economics* 57 (August 1943): 522–542, and "The Locus of Union Control in Collective Bargaining," *Quarterly Journal of Economics* 60 (August 1946): 513–545.

40. Dunlop, *Wage Determination*, pp. iii, iv.

41. Albert E. Rees, "Postwar Wage Determination in the Basic Steel Industry," *American Economic Review* 41 (June 1951): 389–404; Joseph Scherer, "The Union Impact on Wages: The Case of the Year-Round Hotel Industry," *Industrial and Labor Relations Review* 9 (January 1956): 213–224; Irvin Sobel, "Collective Bargaining and the Decentralization in the Rubber-Tire Industry," *Journal of Political Economy* 62 (February 1954): 12–25; Stephen Sobotka, "Union Influence on Wages: The Construction Industry," *Journal of Political Economy* 61 (April 1953): 127–143; Rush V. Greenslade, "The Economic Effects of Collective Bargaining in Bituminous Coal Mining" (Ph.D. diss., University of Chicago, 1952); John E. Maher, "Union, Nonunion Wage Differentials," *American Economic Review* 46 (June 1956): 336–352; Elton Rayack, "The Impact of Unionism on Wages in the Men's Clothing Industry, 1911–1956," *Labor Law Journal* 9 (September 1958): 674–688; Melvin Lurie, "The Effect of Unionization on Wages in the Transit Industry," *Journal of Political Economy* 69 (December 1961): 558–572; Leonard A. Rapping, "The Impact of Federal Subsidies and Maritime Unionism on the Relative Earnings of Seamen" (Ph.D. dissertation, University of Chicago, 1961); Arthur M. Ross, "The Influence of Unionism upon Earnings," *Quarterly Journal of Economics* 62 (February 1948): 263–286; Arthur M. Ross and William Goldner, "Forces Affecting the Interindustry Wage Structure," *Quarterly Journal of Economics* 64 (May 1950): 254–281; Harold M. Levinson, *Unionism, Wage Trends, and Income Distribution, 1914–1947*, Michigan Business Studies, vol. 10 (Ann Arbor: Bureau of Business Research, Graduate School of Business, University of Michigan, 1951).

42. Gerald G. Somers, review of H. G. Lewis's *Unionism and Relative Wages in the United States*, *American Economic Review* 54 (December 1964): 1182.

43. H. G. Lewis, *Unionism and Relative Wages in the United States* (Chicago: University of Chicago Press, 1963), p. 1.

44. Ibid., pp. 4, 5.

45. Albert Rees, "H. Gregg Lewis and the Development of Labor Economics," *Journal of Political Economy* 84 (August 1976): S-3.

46. J. S. Nicholson, "The Living Capital of the United Kingdom," *Economic Journal* 1 (1891): 96; B. F. Kiker, "The Historical Roots of the Concept of Human Capital," *Journal of Political Economy* 74 (October 1966): 481.

47. Jacob Mincer, "Investment in Human Capital and Personal Income Distribution," *Journal of Political Economy* 56 (August 1958): 301.

48. Theodore W. Schultz, "Investment in Human Capital," *American Economic Review* 51 (March 1961): 1.

49. Ibid., p. 2; Mark Blaug, "The Empirical Status of Human Capital Theory: A Slightly Jaundiced Survey," *Journal of Economic Literature* 14 (September 1976): 827.

50. Gary S. Becker, *Human Capital,* 2d ed. (New York: Columbia University Press, 1975), p. 15.

51. Ibid., p. 21; Blaug, "Empirical Status," p. 831.

52. Becker, *Human Capital*, pp. 155, 181–182, 233.

53. Blaug, "Empirical Status," pp. 827–855.

54. Neil W. Chamberlain, "Some Second Thoughts on the Concept of Human Capital," *Proceedings of the Twentieth Annual Winter Meeting,* Industrial Relations Research Association (Madison, 1968), pp. 6–7; Ivar Berg, *Education and Jobs: The Great Training Robbery* (Boston: Beacon Press, 1971), p. 104.

55. Albert Rees, review of Becker's *Human Capital, American Economic Review* 55 (September 1965): 959–960.

56. Lester C. Thurow, "Education and Economic Inequality," *Public Interest,* no. 28 (Summer 1972): 68.

57. Michael J. Piore, "The Importance of Human Capital Theory to Labor Economics—A Dissenting View," *Proceedings of the Twenty-sixth Annual Winter Meeting, Industrial Relations Research Association* (Madison, 1974), p. 253; John T. Dunlop, "Policy Decisions and Research in Economics and Industrial Relations," *Industrial and Labor Relations Review* 30 (April 1977): 278; Samuel Bowles and Herbert Gintis, "The Problem with Human Capital Theory—A Marxian Critique," *American Economic Review* 65 (May 1975): 75, 82.

58. This is the view of Blaug, "Empirical Status," p. 850, who defines signaling as "the theory of how teachers and students, employers and employees, and indeed all buyers and sellers select each other when their attributes matter but when information about these attributes is subject to uncertainty." For the leading work in this area, see Michael Spence, *Market Signaling* (Cambridge: Harvard University Press, 1974).

59. George J. Stigler and Gary S. Becker, "De Gustibus Non Est Disputandum," *American Economic Review* 67 (March 1977): 77. The reformulation is developed in Michael and Becker, "On the New Theory of Consumer Behavior," *Swedish Journal of Economics* 75 (December 1973): 378–396.

60. Rees, review of Becker, *Human Capital,* p. 960; Glen G. Cain, "The Challenge of Segmented Labor Market Theories to Orthodox Theory: A Survey," *Journal of Economic Literature* 14 (December 1976): 1216.

61. Leo Wolman, "Industrial Relations," *Encyclopaedia of the Social Sciences* (New York: Macmillan, 1932), 7:710.

62. F. J. Roethlisberger and W. J. Dickson, *Management and the Worker* (Cambridge: Harvard University Press, 1939); Burleigh B. Gardner and David G. Moore, *Human Relations in Industry,* 4th ed. (Homewood, Ill.: Irwin, 1964), pp. 12–13.

63. Milton Derber, *Research in Labor Problems in the United States* (New York: Random House, 1967), pp. 8–9.

64. *Proceedings of the First Annual Meeting, Industrial Relations Research Association* (Champagne, Ill.: 1949), pp. 239–241.

65. Cornelia S. Parker, *An American Idyll: The Life of Carlton H. Parker* (Boston: Atlantic Monthly Press, 1919), p. 112.

66. Lloyd G. Reynolds, "Labor Economics," p. 285.

67. Lord Robbins, *The Evolution of Modern Economic Theory* (Chicago: Aldine, 1970), p. 244.

68. Edward H. Chamberlin, "The Monopoly Power of Labor," in *The Impact of the Union,* ed. David McCord Wright (New York: Kelley and Millman, 1956), p. 169.

69. Paul J. McNulty, "Labor Market Analysis and the Development of Labor Economics," *Industrial and Labor Relations Review* 19 (July 1966): 538–548.

70. National Bureau of Economic Research, *Aspects of Labor Economics* (Princeton: Princeton University Press, 1962), p. xi.

71. George H. Hildebrand, "The Economic Effects of Unionism," in *A Decade of Industrial Relations Research,* ed. Neil W. Chamberlain, Frank C. Pierson, and Theresa Wolfson (New York: Harper, 1958), pp. 137–138; Allan M. Cartter, *Theory of Wages and Employment* (Homewood, Ill.: Irwin, 1959), p. 178.

72. Daniel J. B. Mitchell, "Union Wage Policies: The Ross-Dunlop Debate Reopened," *Industrial Relations* (February 1972): 46.

73. George E. Johnson, "Economic Analysis of Trade Unionism," *American Economic Review* 65 (May 1975): 27.

74. Kenneth Arrow, "Models of Job Discrimination" and "Some Mathematical Models of Race Discrimination in the Labor Market," in *Racial Discrimination in Economic Life*, ed. A. H. Pascal (Lexington, Mass.: D. C. Heath, Lexington Books, 1972), pp. 83–102, 187–204.

75. Albert Rees, Comment on "Policy Decisions and Research in Economics and Industrial Relations: An Exchange of Views," *Industrial and Labor Relations Review* 31 (October 1977): 4.

76. Cain, "Challenge," pp. 1215–1257.

77. Johnson, "Economic Analysis," p. 23.

78. Rees, Comment, p. 4.

INDEX

Aaron, Henry, 202
Adams, Henry Carter, 133, 149, 150, 226n
Adams, Herbert B., 133, 142
Adams, Thomas S., 137, 147, 148, 151, 153–156, 157, 158, 216n, 226n, 228n, 229n, 230n
Aiken, Henry D., 220n, 227n
Alienation, Marxian theory of, 95–100
Allied Social Sciences, 202
Altmeyer, Arthur J., 151
American Association for Labor Research, 199
American Economic Association, 139, 143, 156, 159, 172, 177, 186, 193, 202
American Economic Review, 143, 185, 188
American Social Science Association, 148
Andrews, Irene Osgood, 151
Andrews, John B., 151
Antonino, Saint, 16, 208n
Apprenticeship, laws of, 59, 60
Aquinas, Saint Thomas, 14, 15, 16, 19, 43, 208n
Aristotle, 14, 15, 16, 17, 43, 118, 208n
Aronson, Robert L., 205n
Ashley, William J., 20, 208n, 209n
Ashton, T. S., 219
Atkins, Willard E., 160, 230n
Automation, 153
Ayres, Clarence E., 153

Ball, John, 23
Bacon, Francis, 25
Bakke, E. Wight, 199
Bargaining theory, 155–156, 158, 159
Barnett, George E., 149, 158, 159, 169, 170
Bastiat, Frederic, 129
Becker, Gary S., 193–197, 236n
Beer, M., 32, 210n, 212n
Belfer, Nathan, 187, 234
Bell, Daniel, 100, 221n
Bendix, Reinhard, 89, 90, 219n
Bentham, Jeremy, 82, 83, 102, 103, 138
Berg, Ivar, 195, 236n
Berkeley, George, 33

Bernard, L. L., 228n
Bernreither, Josef M., 138
Bernstein, Irving, 168, 225n, 232n
Beveridge, Lord, 81, 231n, 218n
Black, R. D. Collison, 223n
Black Death, 22
Blaug, Mark, 69, 70, 115, 118, 194, 216n, 223n, 224n, 236n
Blewitt, George, 34, 211n
Bloom, Gordon F., 187, 234n
Blum, Solomon, 127, 142, 157, 158, 159, 230n
Bohm-Bawerk, Eugen, 117
Boissonade, P., 207n
Bonar, James, 44, 212n, 215n
Bornet, Vaughn Davis, 171, 232n
Boulding, Kenneth E., 172, 206n, 232n
Boulton, Matthew, 39
Bowen, Francis, 129, 130, 225n
Bowles, Samuel, 196, 203, 236n
Bowley, Marion, 217n, 218n
Brandeis, Elizabeth, 232n
Bray, John Francis, 91
Brentano, Lujo, 138
Briggs, Asa, 217n
Brissenden, Paul, 142, 162, 227n, 230n
British Economic Association, 192
Brooks, John Graham, 227n
Brown, J. Douglas, 3, 205n
Buccleugh, Duke of, 41
Buck, Philip W., 205n
Burke, Edmund, 89, 219n
Bureau of Labor Statistics, 184
Burtt, Edwin A., 213n
Bury, J. B., 25, 209n
Business firm
  as adjustor of capital and labor, 185
  as analogous to labor unions, 187–189
  as basis for exploitation in Marx's analysis, 102–104
  in classical economics, 114
  as investor in human capital, 193–194
  in neoclassical economics, 78–79, 114–117
Business unionism, 128

Cain, Glen G., 197, 202, 236n
Cairnes, John E., 43, 111–115, 144, 222n, 223n, 224n